Rats and Squealers

RATS AND SQUEALERS

by
GORDON KERR

Futura

A *Futura* Book

First published by Futura in 2008

ISBN: 978-0-7088-0494-0

Produced by Omnipress, Eastbourne

Printed in Great Britain

Futura
An imprint of
Little, Brown Book Group
100 Victoria Embankmenet
London EC4Y 0DY

Photo credits: Getty Images

CONTENTS

PART ONE: ANCIENT TREACHERY

PART TWO: MEDIEVAL AND
RENAISSANCE TRAITORS

PART THREE: MODERN TRAITORS AND SPIES

PART FOUR: FEMMES FATALES

PART FIVE: MAFIA MEN

PART SIX: INFORMERS

PART ONE

ANCIENT
TREACHERY

LUCIFER

From the beginning of time Christian mythology describes the continual fight between good and evil. Nothing depicts this better than Lucifer's foolish attempt to overcome the power of God by leading a revolution against him. He can be seen as the first traitor of all time as his desire for power dramatically led him to turn against his own creator. However, he was not created evil and the meaning of the name Lucifer actually holds positive connotations and can be directly translated as 'Star of the morning' and 'Light bearer'. For many years this meaning was misunderstood and was wrongly translated by the fourth century scholar St. Jerome as 'Day star, star of the dawn'. No one is really able to make assumptions about what actually happened when Lucifer rebelled against God in heaven, but we can only conclude that a betrayal so great would have been a real blow to his own creator. Some Christians think that by virtue of the evil displayed, Lucifer and Satan are one and the same being. They believe that if Lucifer functions as Satan then he is still able to influence people to behave wrongly, even today. Obviously there is no way of verifying any of these beliefs and they could be dismissed simply as made up stories with Satan a mere concept of evil, but not that he is necessarily a living being. Whether Lucifer was, or indeed still is, a true being can never really be proven, but if we are to believe the ideas of the Bible then he was the world's first traitor and sought to betray God in an incredible way.

THE APPOINTMENT OF JESUS

As with many biblical topics there is wide discussion about the status of Lucifer; was he one of the highest archangels or even as some claim, Christ's own brother? Lucifer, or Satan as many people will refer to him, was certainly held in great esteem by his creator. If he really was an archangel then he would have been one of only a select few whom God would trust and share confidences with. Lucifer's plans for rebellion are shrouded in much mystery and speculation but many believe that it was God's plan to appoint Jesus Christ as his equal which was really the starting point of his animosity and resentment towards his own creator. Jesus was effectively appointed as God's right hand man and he was also there to play the part of co-creator of the Earth and all that roamed it.

Naturally Lucifer was not happy with this transition. He had considered himself to be a creature of great intelligence and the appointment of Jesus felt like a kick in the backside for him. He did not immediately approach God but, instead, harboured increasingly bad feeling towards him and he let his resentment of Jesus grow until it became a parasite within him. The simple principle that Lucifer had failed to understand was humility.

As God was enquiring who would be willing to act as a saviour and redeemer for the world that he was about to create, he was faced with two strong candidates. Believing himself to be the strongest contender, Lucifer came to plead his case first. Instead of stressing any sort of respect and devotion towards his father and creator, he emphasised his own desire for power. As if this wasn't making God aware enough of Lucifer's greed and aspirations, he then went on to say that he would claim all the glory for his acts as redeemer as his own. The Bible tells how he wished to place his power and recognition above God's and brazenly asked to have a throne raised for him above the stars of God's creation. This ultimately shows the negative traits of greed, lust for power and covetousness which shaped his character to conspire towards an uprising against God.

Unlike Lucifer, Jesus had no intention of claiming God's glory as his own and humbly bowed down to him, offering himself as the saviour and redeemer of the Earth. Jesus was then bestowed the honour of the sovereign of heaven and was given equal standing to God. Lucifer gradually began to raise an army of other dissenting angels to fight against those loyal to Jesus, and proposed a radical reformation of the government of heaven.

THE WAR IN HEAVEN

Unwilling to accept the limitations set against him, Lucifer decided to fight. This decision was only the first form of betrayal as he also persisted in rallying a large number of disloyal angels to fight with him for his cause. The archangel exploited their feelings of dissatisfaction and manipulated them into rebelling against God. The angels, who had remained consistent in their devotion to their creator, begged and pleaded with Lucifer's growing army that they might reconsider their battle plans and return to the harmony which had once prevailed throughout God's kingdom. Some of these dissenting beings admitted their own poor judgement and were again admitted into God's close circle. The fate of the other angels was not so bright. After fixing their minds to side with Lucifer, God saw no other option than to bring his foes into battle.

As a continually just God, he made every effort to match the good and evil participants fairly. All that was ordered was that each angel mark himself clearly as to which side he was standing for; his own or Lucifer's. The rebellious angel stood firm to the last, ridiculing God's promise to throw all of the apostate beings out of heaven. Up to this point Lucifer had probably felt that he would rise triumphant from the battle, but he had not reckoned with the true extent of God's power. He was easily suppressed and the consequences were harsh both for himself and his followers. They were faced with expulsion from the kingdom. Lucifer, who was responsible for so much of the disorder in heaven was finally gone. His treacherous acts were so serious that the finely balanced harmony in heaven was disrupted and the remaining angels wept at the loss of their friends.

LUCIFER'S NEW ROLE

If the stories are to be believed, then Lucifer is still

present within our society today, sent to tempt people and lead them away from God. He is just as disloyal as he has always been. If Lucifer really is Satan, then he has been planning the destruction of the human race ever since his expulsion from heaven. Satan's first and possibly most notable intervention with humans came at the creation of Adam and Eve.

Satan was sent to tempt the pair to eat from the tree of knowledge of good and evil. In order to deceive them further he disguised himself as a snake and appealed to them to eat the delicious fruit. He gradually managed to persuade Eve to eat of the fruit and when he saw what she had done Adam chose to do the same. In effect, he encouraged them to commit the same crime as he had, betraying the will of God. This proved them to be traitors in the sense that they had failed to adhere to his commandments. Their punishment was fierce. When God found out what they had done he unclothed them and made them ashamed of their bodies, he made them endure hard labour and sent weeds and ferocious animals to stand in their way. Never again would they know perfection.

By tempting Adam and Eve, Lucifer again broke down the perfect harmony of their society through encouraging the betrayal of God.

DELILAH

The story of Samson and Delilah reflects one of many common themes in the Bible. Although he was a remarkably strong man, Samson proved to have the same weaknesses as the rest of the judges before him, one of which was lust.

The reign of the seven judges in Israel took place around 1380–1050 BC. Each of these followed a common cycle; the Israelites would sin by worshipping idols and false gods, God would place them under the auspices of a neighbouring nation, then they would repent of their sins and live in peace until each of the respective judges died. After the sixth judge had died Israel fell again and was this time entrusted to the hands of the Philistines for the next forty years.

As a Nazarite, Samson had never maintained a good relationship with these people, but after one failed marriage with a Philistine woman he found himself attracted to another named Delilah and continually sought ways to win her trust.

SAMSON'S EARLY LIFE

Samson was born as something of a miracle because his parents had been unable to have children for years. As God-fearing people they pleaded with their maker that they could have a child and were prophesied not only that they would have a son, but he would also in some measure be responsible for delivering morality back to Israel. All that God asked for in return was for their son to be a Nazarite, a position normally reserved for those later in life. This was quite a rigorous calling for one so young, and there were three strict rules that Samson would be made to live by. Firstly he was not allowed to come in contact with a dead body of any kind, he could not partake of wine or any form of strong drink, and finally he must grow his hair long and never cut it. So long as these three rules were observed, Samson would be blessed with great strength and he would always rise victorious in battle.

Samson was given immense power in his body but his mind was not averse to temptation. From his youth he became interested in young women and one day returned home and demanded that his parents set up a wedding for himself and a beautiful Philistine girl that he had caught sight of that same day. His parents did all they could to discourage their son from making such an unwise match. Aside from the impulsiveness of the decision, their main concern was that Samson would be breaking the law by intermarrying. The Israelites had been discouraged against doing so because of fears that a match would leave the couple unequally yoked. Samson was determined and insisted on marrying the girl that he desired.

ANGER WITH THE PHILISTINES

It was not long before Samson discovered that he had made the wrong decision. At his own wedding feast he was deceived by his new wife into eating some meat from a dead lion. This was no accident as she cunningly disguised the meat in honey and fed it to all the members of the Nazarite's family. Samson was disgusted by her betrayal and left her in a rage that same night. Still reeling from this disloyalty he returned to his home and sought to speak to his spouse. What he discovered was to set his mind on becoming an enemy of the Philistines for good.

His wife had been given to his own best man and was no longer obligated to him. Samson was now incensed that a woman who could not only deceive him into breaking one of his own covenants, would also take off with his own best man. He then used his enormous strength to bring a campaign of destruction against the Philistines, burning down all their grain and destroying their orchards. His campaign of hatred lasted many years and brought mass destruction upon their lands. Eventually it all became too much for them and the leaders tried to concoct a plan to bring an end to the destruction.

Knowing that Samson was in possession of super human strength but not always able to master his own infatuations, the Philistines were keen to exploit his more carnal desires in order to find the secret behind his strength, and so Delilah was introduced to Samson.

DELILAH MEETS SAMSON

Just as he had fallen so deeply for his ex-wife, Samson then fell into the same trap with beautiful Delilah. Unbeknown to him she had been offered a large sum of money in return for the secret of Samson's strength. Since Delilah had no reason to hold any loyalties to the man, the 1,000 pieces of silver would have been a rather compelling incentive. Naturally, although Samson had very strong feelings for Delilah, he had reservations about putting his trust in her completely. For months the pair would spend many hours of the day and night together, where Delilah would constantly question Samson about the secrets behind his strength. He refused to tell the truth and came up with three good lies to put her off her questioning.

In the first he told Delilah that his awesome strength could only be overcome by being bound with fresh bowstrings. When he went to sleep Delilah took advantage of this information, bound him with the bowstrings and summoned the guards to seize Samson. Unsurprisingly his strength was not broken and he easily overcame them. A disappointed Delilah then tried to manipulate him further. She used her womanly wiles to manipulate Samson by saying that he must not love her if he would never divulge his secret to her. He evaded her persuasion two more times, once where she bound him with new ropes and finally when he told her to weave seven locks of his hair into a web. After these two methods failed she was getting very frustrated. She insisted that he must show that he trusted her or she would leave him.

In desperation he eventually revealed his secret. Cutting the long hair that he had been commanded to keep from birth was the only thing that could break down his strength. This act could not take place in just any way, but his hair had to be cut with a razor. Again Delilah waited till nightfall to pounce on the enemy of the Philistines. As Samson was sleeping peacefully she cut his hair away from him and this time when he was seized by the guards he was not able to overcome them with his strength. Again the great man had been betrayed by a woman whom he trusted and this time he was not able to have his revenge on the treacherous Philistines.

Delilah's betrayal condemned a powerless Samson to a life of torture. The Philistines reaped their revenge upon the Nazarite for the many years of destruction that he had brought to their country. Once he had been captured by the guards his fate was cruel. His eyes were brutally gouged out and he was bound with bronze fetters whilst being made to push a millstone for the rest of his life.

Throughout his years Samson had been spurred into action by his great passions. It was his desire for women which ultimately led to his downfall and his uncontrollable rage that ravaged a whole nation. In terms of strength Delilah was no match for the powerful man, but to bring him down was easy. Just as Samson was easily motivated by his lust, Delilah fell prey to her own greed.

JUDAS ISCARIOT

Judas was perhaps one of the greatest traitors in history. You would be hard pressed to find anyone who had not heard the story of him trading in the life of his friend and teacher in exchange for thirty pieces of silver. His name is synonymous with evil and many people believe his fate to double-cross Jesus was mapped out from birth.

If tales are to be believed, then Judas' early life was something of a parallel to the Oedipus myth. His mother Cyborea was extremely distressed by a dream she had shortly after the birth of her son. In the dream it prophesied that he would murder his father, commit incest with his mother and ultimately sell his own God. They were living in a highly superstitious society, and as a result his mother became increasingly worried about the dream. His parents decided that the best course of action was to get rid of their son. It was with great sadness that they wrapped him in a blanket, put the baby into a chest and left him floating in the middle of the sea. That was the last time that Judas' parents saw their son, but it certainly wasn't the end of his life.

The chest was eventually picked up on a distant shore and Judas began his life far away from his birthplace, destined to live out his fate. Perhaps it was inevitable that he would betray the son of God by virtue of the fact that he was essentially abandoned at birth and left to fend for himself soon afterwards. We do not know if other parts of the dream turned out to be true as not much is actually recorded about the disciple's early life, but it was certainly not filled with the love of his parents or even a basic teaching in morality, which is possibly why he committed the acts he did. Before Judas came into contact with Jesus he had led a life of thieving and had even committed murder. When he finally met Jesus, people were referring to him as 'the saviour of mankind', and Judas decided that it was time for a change.

JESUS APPOINTS JUDAS AS A DISCIPLE

Whether or not Judas genuinely tried to amend his ways is debatable but even if this wasn't his main aim, he certainly made a personal sacrifice to follow Jesus. He gave up all of his worldly possessions and to do this he must have truly believed that Jesus was the Messiah. Clearly Jesus saw something he liked about Judas, or perhaps he knew that he was the only one weak enough to bring God's plan into fruition and hand him over to the Romans with the lure of money. Either way, he was appointed as a disciple and was at first even numbered among the twelve apostles.

Judas increasingly began to stand out from the other disciples, firstly, and most obviously, by the way in which he addressed Jesus. Whereas the others would speak to him respectfully as their Lord and master, Judas referred to him simply as his 'teacher'. It is questionable though how much he really learned from the humble man, as Jesus certainly would not have encouraged betrayal in any of his teachings. Despite proving to be a somewhat dubious character, Jesus gave Judas the responsibility for the treasury. Only he and Judas knew what should have been coming in and going out of the coffers, and a discrepancy started to emerge when the treacherous man took over the job. Judas fell into his old habits and began regularly stealing from the funds. Jesus was aware of these thefts but turned a blind eye, perhaps in the hope that Judas would mend his ways. Needless to say he did not, and was constantly motivated by his thirst for money to commit bad deeds.

THE LAST SUPPER

Jesus knew that he had been sent to Earth by God in order to die for the world's sins. He expected that the final betrayal in which he would be handed over to the Romans would come from one of those closest to him. The night before he was crucified, Christ drew all of his disciples close to him. This evening has been termed as 'The Last Supper' because it was Jesus' final chance to say goodbye to his greatest friends. Judas was also in attendance and had made a secret agreement with the Roman army to trade Jesus for thirty silver coins. He sat uneasily at the gathering, knowing what was to come and waiting for the ominous knock on the door that would signal the beginning of his great betrayal.

Before Jesus was ready to eat he called upon the devoted Mary Magdalene. She came to his feet and began to tenderly wash them with an expensive oil. When she had finished she gently used her own hair to wipe off the excess and wept silently at his feet. For Jesus this symbolised a ritual cleansing and held a profound biblical significance, but Judas stood back in disbelief. Such was his own greed that he had the gall to upbraid Jesus for supposedly wasting such a luxurious oil on the simple washing of his feet. As usual the corrupt man was motivated by money and could think of nothing else. The other disciples did not question the sacred rites performed that night but Judas had clearly learned nothing from these teachings. As Jesus broke up the bread and poured the wine he announced that he knew that there were traitors within his midst. Instead of accusing anyone in particular he asked them simply to sit with him and partake of the emblems of his body and blood, the bread and the wine. Aware of what he was about to do, Judas could not bear to drink the wine, knowing that it was because of his treachery that Jesus' blood would be shed.

The guards entered the room quickly and looked to Judas to give them the sign they had agreed on previously. He slowly made his way over to Jesus and kissed him on the cheek. The action which normally denotes love was used to hand over a man who had shown nothing but kindness to Judas and can surely be judged as one of the greatest and most unwarranted betrayals of all time.

JUDAS' GRIEF

Judas was not alone in his betrayal of Jesus; his fellow disciple Peter denied that he knew him three times, but this was barely comparable to handing their teacher over to the authorities. As Christ was being crucified the seriousness of his crime dawned on Judas. He knew that the pile of silver coins he had earned was not worth a man's life and in desperation he chose to end his own life.

The general consensus is that Judas hung himself, but there is also an account in Revelations of him hanging himself off a clifftop and crashing down to his death when the branch which was supporting him broke off. He chose to end his own life as a form of compensation for the one that he had traded in. Perhaps it was always fated for Judas to betray the son of God, though even after all he had been taught he continued to be motivated by greed and it was this flaw in his personality which ultimately led to his own death.

MARCUS JUNIUS BRUTUS CAEPIO

Marcus Junius Brutus Caepio, or the infamous Brutus as he is often known, was born into a noble Roman family in 85 BC. His early life was shrouded in tragedy as his politician father was killed by the great general Pompey in 78 BC. Luckily for Brutus, this tragedy actually benefited him. Not only was he adopted by his uncle Quintus Servilius Caepio, but he was also privileged with connections from his mother's side of the family. Brutus' interest in politics had sprung from the political sympathies of his other uncle, Marcus Porcius Cato, who acted as both a teacher and mentor to his young nephew. In his later life Brutus was also able to build a strong relationship with Caesar himself, by virtue of the fact that Caesar was having an affair with Brutus's mother. This relationship acted as a form of protection for Brutus throughout his military career, but unfortunately for Caesar, Brutus did not reciprocate this loyalty and was continually plotting against him.

One of Brutus's closest friends was Gaius Cassius Longinus, who was married to Brutus's half sister. Not as much is written about his early life but his entrance into politics came in 53 BC as he was made quaestor under Marcus Licinius Crassus. Cassius and Brutus remained firm friends up to the point of their deaths and they each had a large role to play in the violent demise of Julius Caesar in 44 BC.

At this time the city of Rome was in a state of political unrest as Caesar had removed all traces of the once effective democracy in order to take power as a dictatorial figure. There was much dissatisfaction among the senators of Rome, who refused to accept this radical change to the government and gradually began to plot Caesar's assassination. Brutus and Cassius acted as a constant reinforcement to the plotting and sought to reinstate the government as it had been before Caesar had seized power.

RIVALRY BETWEEN POMPEY AND CAESAR

The rivalries between the two generals laid the foundation for the bad feeling that ultimately led to

Caesar's downfall. In 59 BC, Brutus and a number of other soldiers were accused of attempting to assassinate Pompey, then Caesar's ally. He was once again fortunate enough to exploit his connection with Caesar who worked tirelessly to clear his name and absolve him from committing any crime. Presumably to be kept out of trouble, Brutus was posted to Cyprus for the next two years. He showed himself to be a man of no scruples as he offered a loan to the floundering town of Salamis and demanded an extortionate 48 per cent interest repayment rate from them! Needless to say, he was a very wealthy man when he returned to Rome in 57 BC.

Both Brutus and Cassius were able to display an impressive amount of military prowess throughout their early years in the armed forces and developed many skills that proved invaluable to their plotting of Caesar's murder. Cassius in particular showed his prowess as a leader at the Battle of Carrhae, where after being defeated he managed to preserve not just his own life but also the lives of 500 cavalrymen.

At this time the frictions between Caesar and Pompey were at their peak. Pompey was in control of Rome and Hispania, whilst Caesar had recently gained the territory of Gaul and with it a reputable army and lots of popularity. As a result of great military successes on both sides, the two men decided to wage civil war upon each other. Brutus's sympathies still did not lie with Caesar, and he and Cassius continued to side against him with politicians such as Cicero and Cato who wanted to restore a republic. Despite their obvious allegiances with his opponent, Caesar continued to support them. He even unwisely granted the pair clemency after they had backed Pompey up to his ultimate defeat in 49 BC.

Whether Caesar was trying to build a relationship of trust is one question that could be asked, but more likely he was just trying to buy their allegiance with exoneration from their previous sympathies as a token gift. The ruler then proceeded to try to bribe them with influential positions and persuade them that they were considered to be amongst his closest friends and advisors. The first to benefit from these honours was Brutus. As he was keenly working behind the scenes to try to stir up bad feeling about Caesar, he was also traitorously maintaining an amicable friendship with the man. He was appointed as governor for Cisipine Gaul and bestowed with great priviliges. He effectively became Caesar's right hand man and was trusted implicitly with his thoughts and plans. Cassius did not receive the same extent of privileges but was in turn promoted to the office of *Praetor peregrinus* and promised the governorship of the Syrian province in 43 BC.

Despite these improvements to their station, the men were still driven by their desire to destroy Caesar. They had been secretly gathering support for their cause against him for months and as he became more like a king and less like a member of a democracy, they gathered together and started to put their plan into action. After Caesar's clear and final revocation of democracy in 44 BC it became even easier to gather opponents to the newly enforced form of government.

THE ASSASSINATION OF JULIUS CAESAR

On the morning of 15 March 44 BC, Caesar was not feeling his usual self. Despite his inclinations to stay at home he was persuaded by devious Brutus that his duty was to attend and talk at the meeting which had been scheduled for that day. He reluctantly left his house and made his way to the assembly. The plan had been perfectly masterminded by Brutus and he was careful to behave as normal so that nothing out of the ordinary would be suspected.

Upon arrival, Caesar was greeted with a seer who presented him with a number of fearful and dangerous omens. In an effort to convey himself as fearless and totally in control, Caesar mocked the omens and ridiculed the seer's prophecy. As soon as he entered the assembly the plan came into action. One of the senators came towards him as if to ask a question and promptly used the opportunity to stab him violently in the neck. No time was wasted as he was pounced upon by the men and stabbed over twenty times. As Brutus lifted a knife to strike his own blow, Caesar is said to have uttered the immortal words *et tu, Brutus?* (even you, Brutus?). Clearly he felt most betrayed by one of the men that he had felt closest to and considered almost as a son. After all that he had done for Brutus, furthering his career and offering him protection, it was hard to think of him as one of his killers. Whether or not it was out of determination to believe that Brutus would eventually support him, Julius Caesar had made a poor judgement of character in Brutus.

OCTAVIAN'S RESISTANCE

Following his death, Caesar's legacy fell upon his great-nephew to continue. The boy Octavian had been adopted from boyhood as Caesar's son and stood to inherit three quarters of his large estate. As he was only young when his adoptive father died he could not be expected to make the important decisions that were needed for Rome and so the consul, Mark Anthony, stepped into the breach. Although he knew that some action would have to be taken against Caesar's murderers, Marc Anthony decided that the best course of action to take was to grant an amnesty to those who were implicated within the plot, but to insist on granting Julius Caesar posthumous deification. Brutus and Cassius both fled from Rome and began to assemble armies overseas. As soon as Octavian came to power, Brutus and Cassius began to combine their forces together. What ensued were the two battles of Philippi and eventual defeat of their forces in 426 BC. Brutus could not face defeat and he fled with four of his legions to the nearby hills and ended his life at his own hands. Things were not going much better for Cassius and he too was forced to admit defeat. Assuming that Brutus had suffered the same fate, he commanded his slave to slay him and his body was buried at Thasos.

After years of plotting against Caesar and his successor Octavian, the two men took their own lives. They had never been loyal to Caesar but were sure in their conviction that a republic needed to be restored in Rome. They were so convinced by this that they chose not just to end the life of a man who had bestowed great favours upon them, but also to end their own lives when they realised that there was no chance of restoring a republic in Rome.

SALOME

As with many biblical stories, the fate of the prophet John the Baptist was decided by someone heavily influenced by lust. The tale of Salome is not very different from those of other women who have tempted powerful leaders, take for example Delilah who has been referred to earlier in this book. Her motivation for betraying Samson was money, but in this instance it seems to have been Salome's desire to appease and obey the will of her mother that led to the gruesome death of Saint John the Baptist.

John the Baptist was a renowned preacher and a good friend of Jesus. He had invested years into learning and teaching the word of God and as a result he had mustered up a number of followers who were more than happy to support him and fight his cause. At this time the ruler of Galilee was Herod Antipas and it was the fifteenth year of the reign of the Roman Emperor, Tiberias Caesar. Herod had been appointed as a provincial governor of a subdivision of Palestine and was responsible for Galilee.

THE ANGER OF HERODIAS

It was at this time that Herod made a somewhat controversial decision. The ruler had recently chosen to marry the ex-wife of his half brother Philip, and with her came her exotic daughter Salome, also his niece. As a man of God, John the Baptist saw the king's union as being deeply immoral and took it upon himself to warn those around him of what was going on in Herod's palace. First of all, his new wife had broken the law by arranging the divorce herself and not waiting for her husband to divorce her. Herod had in fact also committed a crime against Jewish law by taking his brother's ex-wife for his own, and he was not pleased to hear his name slandered around the land. However, Herod did not act against him as he revered the holy man and often went to him for advice on a range of matters.

His wife Herodias on the other hand was not so passive. Enraged that her introduction as Herod's wife would be met with such bad feeling, she persisted in pleading with her husband to execute John the Baptist. She told lies about the prophet, spread malicious rumours and did everything within her power to have him killed. At first Herod stood firm and would not allow any action to be taken against the man he both respected and feared, but as his wife's pleas persisted he was forced to comply with her demands and unwillingly threw John into the fortress of Machaerus. Herod was already showing himself to be a very weak-willed man, which would explain a great deal of the reasons behind what happened next.

SALOME'S DANCE

Ever the manipulator and feeling exasperated about her husband's reticence to put John to death, Herodias enlisted the help of her daughter, Salome. The girl would have been in her teens and strictly under the orders of her mother. When Herodias finally came to a decision about how to ensure the demise of John the Baptist, she realised that the only way to do this was to put Salome up to the job. As an unmarried woman in society, Salome was not faced with any alternative but to betray John the Baptist through seducing her own stepfather, Herod.

The perfect opportunity arose when Herod sat down with his friends for a sumptuous feast to commemorate his birthday. Salome danced with remarkable grace and beauty and had the eyes of each of the men on her. None was more mesmerised than Herod, and he impulsively promised to fulfil any of her wishes. He was so taken with her that he even offered her half of his own kingdom! She paused for thought and went to confer with her mother. After a short period she returned and asked an utterly grue-some request; she demanded the head of John the Baptist to be served to her on a silver plate.

Herod was disgusted by the demand and angry that he had left himself so vulnerable. He knew that he could not go back on his word after promising the girl so much, so he reluctantly summoned the execu-tioner to deliver the gory reminder to Salome and the fellow banqueters. Her mother was thrilled to have finally accomplished her plan and considered John the Baptist a good example of how people who castigated her and her family would be punished.

There was much sadness in Galilee when news broke out that John the Baptist had been murdered, and his followers came in droves to pay their last respects. What happened next to Salome has not been recorded but the date of her death has been placed at around 62–71 AD. John was firm in his convictions that Herod and Herodias were committing a grave wrongdoing through their marriage. He believed that his teachings were advocating the right way of life and that it was only through heeding the words of Jesus that one could be truly happy. John the Baptist died because he was not willing to stay quiet about what he believed in. Unfortunately for him he was powerless to counter the manipulative wife of Herod and was forced to suffer death at her own request.

JUDITH

Rarely in Jewish history has any woman had so much success in liberating her people and restoring faith in their God. The gospel of Judith was the fourth book of the Old Testament Apocrypha, a group of books not included in the Bible because they were written in Greek instead of the original Hebrew. Judith was clearly a very intelligent and shrewd woman, who really knew how to use her restricted abilities to fulfil the needs of her people.

She originally acted as a traitor in order to convince the Assyrians that they could trust her and to gain control of the army by killing their chief commander. She was able to double-cross the highest authority in her enemy's land by making him desire her and pretending to have changed allegiances. Scholars have argued about the dates of the Israelites' success over the Assyrians but most agree that the action took place after the end of the Babylonian captivity in 538 BC.

THE WAR AGAINST ISRAEL

For many years there had been unrest in Israel as the nation had refused to join King Nebuchadnezzar's forces in battle against Media. The Israelites strongly resisted becoming involved in such an economically damaging war and long after other nations had given in to the King, they began to incur the wrath of Nebuchadnezzar's formidable general, Holofernes. This took its toll on the Israelites and they began to doubt their god, wondering why their nation in particular should repeatedly be forced to endure such difficulties.

Judith thought that it was time that something was done. She decided to gain the trust of the general behind these campaigns and act as though she was informing on her own people. Judith, however, was dedicated to her people and determined to find a way to free them from further arduous years of war. She was a pious and very beautiful widow who had no plans to compromise her own principles. She knew that God had promised to defend the Israelites as long as they were faithful to him, and that after many years of war with the Abyssinians they really doubted their Lord's presence.

The virtuous woman made her way over to the camp of Holofernes and gradually managed to sway him to speak to her. Naturally he was cautious and at first was not convinced by her story. She was very persistent though and her eloquence and beauty impressed him greatly. After fine food and a small amount of drink had been consumed he allowed her to stay overnight and encouraged her to stay in his own tent. She declined, but met him warmly the next morning. This routine was maintained over the next three days but brave Judith was never given the opportunity to murder the man who had caused so much harm to the Israelites. On the fourth day, Holofernes invited Judith to another night of feasting, though this one proved to be fateful to the fearsome general. After they had all dined, the wine flowed freely and no one was more intoxicated than Holofernes.

Upon his drunken return to the camp, he promptly fell into what would be his last ever sleep. Judith saw his slumber as being the perfect opportunity to kill the man who had weakened the spirits of her people and she went into his tent with murder in mind. As she entered his tent she grasped her knife firmly and steeled herself to the gruesome act that she was about to commit. She plunged the knife deeply into his neck and did not stop until his head came off in its entirety. Perhaps it was unnecessarily violent, but she needed it for the next part of her plan.

THE ISRAELITES DEFEAT ASSYRIA

Judith quickly attached the bloody head to the battlements of his camp and sped back home to the Israelites to tell them of the success of her plan. During the night Israelite forces gathered together and planned to take the Assyrian camp by surprise. They knew that without their military leader the Assyrians would not be able to beat them and this raised their spirits as they prepared for battle. Their opposition woke as usual the next day, and news spread fast that their commander had been slaughtered. They did not know what to do since they had always had such a strong leader and they decided that the best form of protection was to flee from their own land. The Israelites, on the other hand, had been rallying their army through the night and were prepared to meet the Assyrians in battle. The camp was easily overcome and the Israelites rose victorious from the battle.

Following their triumph, the rejoicing and feasting in Jerusalem lasted for a whole three months. The people were reconciled to the greatness of their god and proved that his promise had been fulfilled. As for Judith, she chose to dedicate the rest of her life to honourable widowhood. She did not remarry but was constantly seeking opportunities to share out her long deceased husband's wealth. Indeed, she can be seen as a virtuous and noble woman despite the horrific way in which she killed the Israelites' main enemy. She was constantly driven by her desire to bring an end to the years of wars against Israel and to restore peace to a ravaged nation.

ALCIBIADES

The strength of the Greek army was understandably essential to the smooth running of the ancient city of Athens. The city was involved in a very damaging war waged against Sparta from 431–404 BC. The Peloponnesian war primarily came about as a trade dispute between the two countries and quickly escalated into full-scale warfare. The war dragged on for years but did not stop even after the death in battle of the military leader Cleon in 422. This left a vacancy for a new leader and with his expertise and military ability Alcibiades was a natural candidate.

Like Brutus, Alcibiades was also given a great head start in life. His father was Clinias and Alcibiades was born into an aristocratic family that traced its origins back to the King of Salamis. Even after his father's sudden death in 447 BC he was well provided for. He was brought up by the famous general Pericles and was closely associated with Socrates whom he would often engage in intellectual debates. Their friendship went far beyond the realms of intellectual thought as they had both saved each other's lives in different battles. In short, the military leader was never at a loss for influential friends and these provided him with the support he needed to be successful in warfare.

At the age of thirty he entered into the world of politics and, on becoming a general in 420 BC, he revealed himself as an advocate for the extension of the Peloponnesian war. He refused to accept the 'Peace of Nicias', drawn up to bring an end to the fighting, and instead pushed Athens to become involved in an anti-Spartan alliance with the three city states of the Peloponnese. This alliance was defeated by the Spartans in 418 BC and Alcibiades quickly fell from favour. He won his popularity back soon after with a great victory in the chariot races at Olympia, with three of his chariots winning first, second and fourth place. It did not take much to gain popular favour again, but Alcibiades was careful to err on the side of caution.

MASTER OF DECEPTION

Having acted as the driving force behind the Sicilian Expedition of 415 BC, Alcibiades was somewhat complacent about the necessity of his role to the city of Athens. He had proved himself not only to be a valuable addition to their army, but furthermore had impressed the population with his skills as an orator. However, his great political aspirations hindered him from gaining a place within the hearts of the people, as he was known more for being ferociously ambitious than by his other merits. As a result of the suspicion around his motives, Alcibiades was arrested just as his ships were due to set sail on the Sicilian expedition. The charges levied against him were grave; he was accused of being involved in the 'Mutilation of the Hermae' where he allegedly parodied the sacred events of the Festival at Eleusis, and went on a destructive rampage, damaging many of the statues in the town. Whether or not these allegations were actually true has never been established but the military leader knew that he needed to have all the supporters he could get in order for him to escape the charges. He proposed that he be tried at that very moment as he knew this would give him an advantage, but instead he was told he would be summoned for at a later date. Greatly annoyed, he left for Sicily.

A short time later he was summoned from Sicily to stand trial, but learning that he had been condemned to death in his absence, he promptly fled to Argos. In the years that followed Alcibiades proved to be a traitor in every sense of the word and as a result was unable to settle in any one place. Firstly, he switched his allegiance and approached the Spartans, offering them military advice. He suggested that the Spartans add more military protection to the town of Decelea in Attica, which would offer them a strategic advantage over the Athenians. This was a good plan, but during his time with the Spartans he committed another form of treachery by seducing the king's own wife. To make matters worse, she then became pregnant and it was widely reputed that Alcibiades was the father of her baby. Naturally King Agis was furious, and as time went on his anger grew inside him. The commander continued to work with the Spartans and encouraged them to make various tactical alliances in order to defeat the Athenians. However, his position was no longer safe as he began to hear rumours of conspiracies to have him killed. Not sparing a second thought for the woman and child he had left behind, he promptly fled from Sparta and sought refuge at the court of their ally, Tissaphernes of Persia. Using his silver tongue he managed to persuade the ruler to reverse any policies made in favour of the Spartans, and requested to remain safely in Persia.

RECALLED BY ATHENS

Having taken advantage of the Persians hospitality for a little too long, Alcibiades sought ways to regain his standing with the Athenians. At this time there were two revolutions taking place in Athens. The first saw the overthrow of democracy, and the second caused the downfall of oligarchy. He made sure to root himself firmly on the side of democracy and was instrumental in reinstating it in Athens. Not long after this he was officially pardoned by the Athenians who recognised his invaluable abilities as a commander and desired him more as their ally than their enemy. He was kept at arm's length initially and stationed with a fleet in Samos, but then he was reinstated within his previous standing as a general. In 407 BC he was finally allowed to return to Athens and was promoted to commander-in-chief. This prestige only lasted as long as the army was successful and Alcibiades promptly fell from favour again when his subordinate Antiochus was defeated.

In 404 BC Athens finally buckled under the strain of war. Following their devastating defeat against Sparta they had no more use for a man of Alcibiades calibre and, feeling that he had out stayed his welcome, he left Athens. It seems that he still had enemies wherever he went and he was murdered on the way to the court of the Persian king Ataxerxes.

Alcibiades led a selfish existence, constantly looking out for his best interests and not caring about the impact that his decisions would have on others. Although his abilities stood out, most people knew that he could not be trusted and he was forced, until his abrupt demise, to move aimlessly from place to place for the whole of his life.

EPHIALTES OF TRACHIS

Throughout Greek history there have been numerous stories of people who have turned against their country and sought new allegiances with their enemies. The reasons for this were often centred around their own greed and fears that the Greek side would not defeat their opposition. For many it was simply easier to defect to the opposition where there was a chance for a reward, rather than admit almost certain defeat. This was the option that Ephialtes chose and his decision ultimately led to the demise of a Greek king and 300 of the bravest Spartan warriors.

In 480 BC, ancient Greece was waging an extended war with the Persians. Under their King Xerxes the Persian Empire was continually expanding. Their acquired lands stretched from Persia's western border at Troy to their Eastern border, known today as Russia. Xerxes had set his mind to conquering

Europe, and with it the mighty Greece. The sides were never evenly balanced and the ancient historian Herodotus even estimated the Persians' army to amount to millions. Whether this was an exaggerated claim is unknown but they certainly outnumbered the Greek force in their thousands. The Greeks and Spartans had been reduced to a smaller army as religious obligations forbade them from forming an army during the festival of Cameia. The celebrations were due to continue for days, so all that was available to fight was a small troop of 300 soldiers and their commander and King, Leonidas.

FIGHTING FOR TIME

The 300 men knew that they were facing certain death. In an effort to preserve their lives for a bit longer they tried to raise as many allies as possible. The Spartans were essentially trying to stall for time whilst more troops were being rallied at home. They knew that numerically the Persians could not be defeated, but were also aware that their own minimal amount of fighters were much more skilled than many of the opposition. Knowing that the Persians would not be able to use their numbers to their advantage, the spartans planned to give themselves more time by occupying the narrow mountain passage of Thermopylae.

Along the way they had picked up 6,000 Greek hoplites, specially skilled fighters who relied heavily upon their shields. For two whole days the small group managed to hold off the advances of the Persian troops. Many of their small force perished but their position remained secure in the gap between the Trachinian cliffs and the Malian Gulf. The Spartans were also helped by over 1,000 Phocians who came into battle in order to protect their homes and families. Shortly after this they returned home on mass, putting their families as the priority over that of a seemingly hopeless battle.

THE BATTLE OF THERMOPYLAE

What happened next was to cement the fate of the remaining warriors. There are a number of differing opinions about Ephialtes, the popular film *300* depicting him as a mutated figure, physically unable to serve with the numbered Spartans. If this were the case he may have been motivated by his anger, but it seems more likely that his desire for a reward was the reason behind his betrayal. Having fought tirelessly for two days, Ephialtes offered the Persians a way around the resilient Spartans. He revealed to them a secret trail which led over the mountains at the south of Thermopylae and joined the main road behind the Greek position. This simple act had massive repercussions and the small force realised that they were surrounded. In an effort to preserve as many lives as possible, King Leonidas dismissed the remaining hoplites and instructed the 300 soldiers for the last time.

In ancient culture the greatest honour that could be won was gained by fighting fearlessly to the death. The Spartans were determined to battle and protect their land until they could fight no more and the 300 brave men fought the oncoming surge of Persians with their greatest might. They were bombarded with missiles and suffered an ignominious death as their corpses were ripped apart and the body of the great king Leonidas was torn into pieces.

Expecting to earn a great reward for his communications with the Persians, Ephialtes waited patiently. The reward for his treachery came to nothing, however, as the Persians were forced to withdraw from Greece following their abominable defeat at Salamis in the same year. The Battle of Salamis was fought at sea and Athens, under the generalship of Themistokles, used their navy to defeat the much larger Persian army and forced Xerxes to retreat. This victory signalled the turning point of the campaign and led the way for many other Persian defeats. Essentially the Greeks triumphed by ensuring that without a functioning navy, Xerxes would not be able to provide supplies for his huge army.

The small band of soldiers who had bravely fought at the Battle of Thermopylae were never truly fated to rise victorious. For two whole days they managed to hold off the Persians and preserve the lives of as many of their company as possible. The only reason that they were not able to hold out longer was because they were cruelly betrayed by the actions of one greedy man who was seeking a reward for his deception.

SOCRATES

The city of Athens had suffered greatly under the crippling strains of the Peloponnesian war waged between Athens and Sparta from 431–404 BC. Throughout this period Athens suffered many defeats and found itself considerably weakened both financially and militarily as the fighting continued. During this twenty-seven-year time span the Athenian leaders were keen to preserve a democratic system of government in which to control the citizens themselves. After the calamitous temporary overhaul of democracy in 411 BC, the city endured a short, but disastrous, stretch of political disruption which Socrates was allegedly associated with. Socrates's actions would not be classed as treacherous within our own society, as the crimes that he supposedly committed were more to do with challenging the established opinions and beliefs of others, than detectable crimes against the city. The ultimate defeat of Athens came in 405 BC, and the city was forced to accept a new government under the 'Thirty Tyrants' as a condition of the Spartan peace treaty. Socrates made his philosophical opinions available to anyone who would listen with an open mind and consequently began teaching young men such as Critias and Alcibiades, who both had strong ties with the newly formed tyrannical regime. As a result of his affiliations, the philosopher's own political and religious views were brought into question and he was summoned by the Athenian court to be tried in 399 BC.

HIS TEACHINGS

Socrates has established himself firmly as one of the world's most powerful and memorable philosphers, not just in the ancient world but also acting as a starting point for many of our current Western ideas. Socrates had many different areas of philosophical interest but because the great thinker never put pen to paper himself, we are forced to rely upon the accounts of others in order to determine an idea of who he was and the ideas that he stood for. One of Socrates's most renowned students was Plato, who became an unofficial observer and documenter on the life and teachings of Socrates. As with much of the literature that covers Socrates's teachings, Plato describes him in a highly respected manner and portrays him, not solely as one of the greatest thinkers of our time, but more importantly as a flawed human being who was constantly striving to better himself and encourage others to do the same.

From the beginning of his life Socrates set an intellectual and theoretical standard which has been hard to match even thousands of years after his initial messages were put forward. Born in 470 BC, he stood out from the crowd from his youth by virtue of his approachable manner and easy ability to speak to all ages and audiences. He fitted naturally into his role of teacher and educator by making his message access-ible to everyone, and could often be found talking to large groups of people, whether in the bustling Athenian streets, the business districts or even in the gymnasium!

The main ideas and messages that Socrates stood for can be seen throughout many of Plato's works, especially the *Republic*, *Symposium* and *The Last Days of Socrates*. A common theme preoccupies these accounts, and Plato seems convinced that Socrates was focused on the idea of the most perfect life that a person could aspire to could be fulfilled solely through fine tuning goodness and virtue in their perfect balance. One of Socrates's most contentious musings, which was met with a great measure of hostility, was his apparent denunciation of any democratic form of government. Socrates would have been viewed by many as a traitor to the city, as his controversial opinions posed a direct challenge to the successful democracy which had led to the now fading Golden Age of Athens. It may be slightly un-justified to speak of Socrates as a plotter or traitor within our modern sense of the word, but his radical views against democracy and influence over his youngest students would certainly have posed a threat to those seeking to regain democracy around this time.

The opposition to Socrates arose not just from fears about his messages, but more importantly from a wide and somewhat unfounded belief that he was imposing controversial and damaging beliefs upon his largest and most impressionable audience, the young men of Athens. No fees were charged, but the 'student' or person who was conversing would be encouraged to challenge an established viewpoint and arrive at a completely different conclusion than had first been expressed. Throughout his life Socrates was deemed a real opponent to democracy, and he maintained his belief that a city governed by a single leader was the only acceptable form of government, even up to his eventual execution.

SOCRATES'S DOWNFALL

Eventually the philosopher's radical views and ideas had become too much for the city to bear any longer. The three men who decided to press charges against him were Meletus, Antyus and Lyco. They thought that it was in the best interests of the city for Socrates to be removed so that he could no longer be of influence to the people of Athens. Ironically, these men did not understand one of Socrates's strongest convictions, that every man must follow the law or the very structure of society would be undermined. Despite these convictions, Socrates was summoned to be tried in 399 BC on charges of corrupting the young, denying the gods of the city and introducing new gods. Whether any of these allegations were true, is really a matter of opinion, but it is hard to imagine that a man who clearly revered and understood the laws of the state would intentionally go out to corrupt impressionable minds. It seems to be more likely that Socrates acted as a scapegoat for those who had lost power during the Peloponnesian war and were afraid that the young men who were taught by Socrates might be encouraged to take over. Socrates's opponents also wanted to implicate him as a traitor by virtue of his earlier associations with the Thirty Tyrants, who ultimate destroyed the last reminders of a democratic government in Athens.

Unfortunately, it was Socrates's philosophical fervour which ultimately led to his death in 399 BC. Following a slightly misguided attempt to defend himself where he essentially insulted his audience by informing them of their own ignorance, the jury – consisting of 501 members – came back with a verdict. It was only by a margin of thirty votes that Socrates was found guilty, but it was enough. To make matters worse for the great philosopher, when given the opportunity to suggest another punishment for himself other than death, he proposed that he be heavily rewarded instead of punished, as he believed that he had only been doing good for the Athenians.

As Socrates spent his last days in prison he was given one last opportunity for escape. His closest friends concocted several potential breaks for escape, but Socrates was stubborn to the very end. Despite their persistent entreaties for him to leave, he stressed the importance of accepting his fate and abiding by the laws that had been set down. He accepted a graceful death surrounded by friends, as he committed suicide by drinking the poison hemlock.

There is no question about the fact that Socrates was a great and pioneering philosophical thinker. Whether he was a traitor to his city is hard for us to judge. We might ask how a man who held learning and abiding by his laws in such esteem, could be found guilty of treason, though it is clear that his allegiances with anti-democratic ways of governing were not welcome in fourth-century Athens. What really matters is the legacy of philosophical thought that Socrates has left as both a great thinker and, more importantly, as a real human being.

PART TWO

MEDIEVAL AND RENAISSANCE TRAITORS

SIR ROGER MORTIMER

Roger Mortimer led a somewhat solitary early life under the supervision of his formidable and aggressive uncle, Roger Mortimer of Chirk. As was the custom in the 14th century, he was married relatively young to Joan de Geneville, daughter of a neighbouring lord, in 1301. This union benefitted him greatly and as a result he acquired various estates including Ludlow Castle and an increased influence in Ireland. His privileges did not end here though, and he was also able to succeed to the Lordship of Trim.

Mortimer's happiness was short-lived, however, when his father, Lord Wigmore, was killed near Builth in 1304. Mortimer was only sixteen at the time and therefore was not entitled to inherit his father's legacy for another two years. As a consequence, he was placed by King Edward I under the guardianship of his father's close friend, Piers Gaveston. In 1306 Mortimer was knighted by Edward, and when he came of age this same year he also received his entire inheritance. From an early age the young Mortimer set himself out as being rather an ambitious man. He had aspirations to leadership and would stop at nothing to achieve these. He was not concerned about morality but instead was preoccupied with his own personal gain.

UNREST ABROAD

In 1308 Mortimer was sent to Ireland by Edward II, in order to assert his authority over the country. In Ireland he was met with stern opposition in the form of the de Lacys who were in support of Robert Bruce, the King of Scotland. During this time Mortimer was promoted to the role of Lord Lieutenant of Ireland by Edward II. This seems to have been what triggered the king's ultimate downfall as he fed the desire for power that Mortimer was constantly pursuing. A successful campaign in 1316 meant that Mortimer was able to drive Bruce to Carrickfergus and the de Lacys into Connaught. Following this he led an aggressive campaign of vengeance upon all who were found to be adherents to Bruce or the de Lacys.

The next couple of years were less exciting for Mortimer as he was involved primarily in baronial disputes on the Welsh border until 1318. Throughout this time Mortimer was not afraid to take power by force, a theme commonly associated with the man of many ambitions. However, Mortimer's power was limited over the next few years as he joined the growing opposition against the king and refused to obey his summons to appear before him in 1321. Refusing to obey the king was a treasonable act in itself, and when Mortimer was forced to surrender to the king in January 1322, he was lucky to be punished only by consignment to the Tower of London. As was to be expected from Mortimer, he did not stay in the tower for long. A mere two years later he managed to escape and fled to France.

QUEEN ISABELLA

In 1325 Edward II's fragile hold over the throne was pushed to its limits. In an effort to escape from her husband Isabella double-crossed him by pleading to Edward to allow her to go to France in order to use her influence with her brother, Charles IV, in favour of peace. Queen Isabella had other plans in store though, and at the French court she met with Roger Mortimer and became his mistress soon afterwards. Mortimer continued to resist returning to England for as long as the Despensers remained favoured in the country. The Despensers were a particularly prominent family throughout this period and had managed to continually win the favour of Edward II. By the 1320s they had the king's protection but were loathed by many for their greed and land grabbing tendencies. It is not hard to imagine then that Mortimer and the Queen of England could easily raise the support that they needed for a full blown invasion of England.

Upon their return to England in 1526, they were joined by Henry, Earl of Lancaster. The support for Queen Isabella was overwhelming, and people paraded in the street to offer help towards the imminent invasion. Edward II quickly sought an escape from the invading surge of people and fled to the west of England. He was captured and imprisoned and, to add insult to injury, he was forced to abdicate in favour of his son who was crowned Edward III in January 1327. This meant little to Mortimer who sought the throne for himself. He proved that he would go to every length to gain himself the title of the King of England, even though he was not actually married to Queen Isabella.

MORTIMER'S GREED

Shortly after Roger Mortimer had seized the throne

with Isabella's assistance, he began to become part of something rather more sinister. Later that year he was implicated in the suspicious murder of Edward II and his greed was increasing. He began to make enemies through his bullyish behaviour, claiming estates and profits upon himself. Although Edward III was the rightful heir to the throne, he did not seem able enough to assert himself against the formidable Mortimer and instead let him act as king in his place. By 1330 things were simply getting too much. Henry Lancaster implored Edward III to assert his independence and fight back against Mortimer's tyranny. Later that year a parliament was called and both Mortimer and Isabella were seized and charges were put against him of attempting to seize royal power. He was condemned without a trial and hanged in 1330.

Mortimer's life was relatively short but he was able to accomplish many of his evil ends. His ambitions of becoming equal to a king's status were gradually realised as he used force and cunning to achieve this. He clearly felt no sense of loyalty towards his wife and jumped at the opportunity of taking Queen Isabella as his mistress. Mortimer revealed himself as a ruthless calculator, and altogether, a man who should never have been trusted.

WAT TYLER AND JACK CADE

The methods used by the two men in this chapter to obtain reform, were strikingly similar. Wat Tyler was born in England in the early 14th century, but very little is known about the man with the exception of his fame as leader of the English Peasants' Revolt in 1381. Jack Cade was also something of a mystery man, and even his name is uncertain. Some of his followers referred to him as John Mortimer and even claimed that he was related to Richard, Duke of York. He suddenly popped up in history in the spring of 1450 as the leader of the Kentish protests.

What is clear, though, is that both men sought radical reform from the government and an end to the woes that had been plaguing England for some time. Tyler, whose name probably comes from having a family connection with the job of tiling, was a strong character who was not afraid to stand up for what he believed in. Along with much of the English population, he had felt greatly angered by the way in which the peasantry had been treated throughout recent years. England had tragically suffered a massive blow in the form of the plague of 1348–9. So great was this loss that nearly a third of the population of England had perished as a result of disease.

Naturally this had a knock-on effect upon the English economy, namely the loss of people who were able to fulfil skilled professions. Worst of all, those that could continue their professions had their wages held down. This ruling was made official when parliament passed the Statute of Labourers in 1351 and understandably was not greeted well by the peasantry. In addition to this, labourers were forced to face the wrath of many angry landlords who were attempting to slow down the mobility of labour by using their privileges as landowners. The final blow came in 1380 when parliament ordered an increase in poll tax in order to raise funds in the economically floundering country.

THE PEASANTS' REVOLT

In 1381 Wat Tyler decided to take action against parliament. He appointed himself as leader and set out to stir up a rebellion which would compel parliament to make an agreement with the rebels. This uprising was centred in the south east and frequently used Kent as a base. Fighting first broke out in Essex and swiftly moved on to the borders of Kent. Following the seizure of Canterbury the growing number of rebels and peasantry began an attack on London. After a failed attempt to interview Richard II, Tyler led the heaving mob into the city. As they entered the country's capital they seemed intent on destruction. First came the brutal murders of a number of Flemish merchants, then followed the obliteration of the palace of the king's uncle, John of Gaunt.

The violence seemed to act solely as a warning to the king that the mob would stop at nothing to get the reform that they desired. After another serious rampage in which the rebels took control of the Tower of London, killing both the Archbishop and the treasurer, King Richard II decided it was time to speak to Tyler. On 14 June 1381 the king met the surging mob at Mile End. Tyler issued a series of demands including an end to serfdom and feudal service and also laid down restrictions upon buying and selling. The king reluctantly agreed to these terms and sent the crowd on their way. Sensing that he was on to a winning formula, Tyler returned the next day to ask for a confiscation of all church property. As it happened, the king was not willing to acquiesce to this demand and instead he had the Mayor of London take on Tyler in a fight which eventually killed the rebel.

After Tyler's death the king, who was a mere fourteen years of age, was able to take control of the mob and suppress them until the Mayor returned with assistance. The rebellion was finally crushed by the militant bishop of Norwich, Henry le Despenser on 25 June 1381. Tyler had lost his life for nothing as the king swiftly went back on his promises to the people. No reform was realised and the peasantry were forced to live the same life of poverty that they had become accustomed to.

JACK CADE'S REBELLION

Jack Cade's Rebellion was an uprising against the policies of Henry VI. Cade was joined by an army of peasants and small landowners from Kent, who objected to forced labour, corrupt courts, the seizure of their land by nobles and ever increasing taxes. Led by Cade, who was an ex-soldier, the mob gathered in London, but their violent behaviour soon turned the Londoners against them.

Most of Cade's mob were forced to accept a pardon issued from the king and returned home without any further bloodshed. Cade, reluctantly, accepted the pardon as well, but was later killed by the Sheriff of Kent.

Although Cade's Rebellion has been compared to the Peasants' Revolt of 1381, this is an inaccurate comparison. Although Cade's uprising did attract a large number of peasants, the leaders of the rebellion were land and property owners who objected to the greed of the royal officials who were lining their own pockets at the expense of the crippling tax system. The rebels were also joined by men of the Church who joined them in their fight to try and end the poor government. They were not asking for a sweeping change, but rather the removal of just a handful of councillors, the return of their estates and improved methods of taxation.

PERKIN WARBECK

Tudor England was a rather unstable place to live following the victory of Henry VII at the Wars of the Roses. The warring families of Lancaster and York had been fighting for years and this came to a head at the Battle of Bosworth in 1485 when Henry VII, a Lancastrian, killed the Yorkist king Richard III. But the first few years of the new king's reign were not smooth sailing. Between the years 1486–99 Henry's authority was challenged by the 'pretenders'; various young men who claimed to be heirs to the throne of England. The first of these was Lambert Simnel but the most threatening to Henry was young Perkin Warbeck.

Warbeck was born in Flanders around 1474. He was never expected to amount to much as he was the son of a lowly burgess, Jehan de Werbecque, and his opportunities to network were severely restricted by his background. His father died in Perkin's early childhood and he was moved on to Antwerp by his cousin, where he established himself as a boy servant to no one of significance. Having been employed in the service of a Portuguese knight for a year, Warbeck left for Ireland and became the servant of a Breton silk merchant, Pierre John Meno.

It was in Cork that the young man's fortunes were to change when some nobles, who had seen him wearing the silk garments of his master, believed him to be royalty. Ireland welcomed the boy with open arms as they had historically been allied with the House of York and were constantly plotting against the new king.

TREACHERY FROM OVERSEAS

Athough Warbeck was clearly struggling to master the English language, he was never short of supporters. It seems that Warbeck was manipulated and forced into assuming the identity of Richard, Duke of York, one of the princes who had disappeared in the tower. The Earls of Kildare and Desmond were the instigators of this plot and were careful to create rumours of Richard's apparent reappearance throughout Ireland. Word spread overseas and Warbeck was soon summoned by Margaret, the Dowager Duchess of Burgundy, sister to Edward IV, who had been a great enemy of Henry VII for family reasons. Margaret welcomed the boy as her own nephew and at this point Henry knew that things were starting to get serious. The king broke off all trade links with Flanders in 1493, severing the lucrative cloth trade which was worth a great deal at that time.

Henry was faced with a frightening prospect; rulers from all around Europe were flocking to support the young man and there was nothing that Henry could really do. The King was surrounded. By 1493 the king of France, Charles VIII, James VI of Scotland and the Holy Roman Emperor, Maximilian, all numbered themselves amongst Perkin's supporters. The boy had become a mere pawn in the plans of individuals with much more power than he had ever possessed. It is unlikely that any of his supporters actually believed that Warbeck was the prince, but more realistically, that they were unhappy that Henry had become king.

Warbeck's first public appearance as Richard was at the funeral of Emperor Frederick III in 1493 and he was treated as the rightful king of England at this time. Naturally, Henry was worried. He did not know how long the support would last for Warbeck, and made many efforts to have him seized. As this was going on, the boy's flagging supporters had been meeting in secret to discuss whether there was more to gain by supporting him or from giving him up.

ADVANCES ON ENGLAND

In 1495 the pretender Warbeck mounted his first attack on England. He had gained strength from the backing of the Holy Roman Emperor and was provided with men and ships with which to mount his attack. After his initial defeat in Kent earlier that year he fled to Ireland to rally the support of the Earl of Desmond. Following more defeats on the Irish side, he sought sanctuary in Scotland and was so well received that a marriage was arranged for himself and Catherine Gordon, the daughter of the Earl of Huntley. He was also allocated a generous pension of £1,200 a year in order to fund each of his attacks on England.

Henry had formulated a plan. From the beginning of his rule he had set up an intricate spying network across England and mainland Europe and was informed that support for the imposter was rapidly decreasing. Parliament passed a number of acts of attainder in 1495 and Henry was determined to make an example of those who had betrayed him. The chamberlain, Sir William Stanley was implicated in the plot and he was executed with all his estates passing to the king. Sir Robert Clifford was working as a double agent for the king, and frequently informed him of those who were plotting to betray him. The king had shown that he took a very strict stance on traitors and signposted what Warbeck could expect having fought against him.

After a short period of inactivity he began his invasion again. This time it was hugely less impressive as he was flanked by only a couple of small vessels and his wife and children. Again Warbeck appeared to be slightly deluded about the support that he would greet him in England, but he strategically chose the site of the recently suppressed Cornish Rebellion to bring his boats into harbour. As he arrived at Land's End in Cornwall he was met by the country people who had recently been revolting against the excessive taxation that Henry VII had imposed. Their response was mixed, but Warbeck was able to march up to Exeter where he was met by the royal troops. Perkin Warbeck had never put himself forward as a particularly brave young man and this situation was no different. He rapidly deserted both his supporters and his family and hastily fled to Hampshire where he was forced to surrender.

Like all who were accused of conspiring against the

king at this time, Warbeck faced a frightening end. Initially he was forced to make confessions to the public admitting his own wrongdoings, and his punishment was made all the more horrific by the fact that he was a foreigner and could not be tried for treason. He was instead forced to endure the brutality of being hung, drawn and quartered, and his body was laid out in the streets as a source of both ridicule and warning to any others who might go against the monarch.

EDWARD PLANTAGENET

Born in 1475, Edward Plantagenet was not blessed with an easy life. His struggles started in his childhood as he was troubled by the consequences of his father's disloyalty to the king, his brother, Edward IV. In order to understand why Edward's life ran the course that it did, it is first necessary to examine the life of his father, George Plantagenet, Duke of Clarence. Born the younger son of Richard, Duke of York, George was never going to amount to as much as his elder brother, Edward. In 1461 when Edward was crowned king, George was appointed the Duke of Clarence and Lord Lieutenant of Ireland. With his father-in-law, Richard Neville, at his side, he continued to act in a disloyal manner towards the king through his support of the rebels in northern England. Consequently he was deprived of his title and was forced as many had done before him, to flee to France.

Clarence proved to be a treacherous man as he quickly seized Neville's numerous estates only days after his death. His behaviour was continually erratic and Edward found his rule as a monarch threatened, whilst his brother continued to behave unpredictably towards him. He was placed in prison under charges of slander and conspiracy to rebel and died shortly afterwards when he was mysteriously suffocated. As a result his lands were allocated elsewhere and he was posthumously charged with an act of attainder.

EDWARD'S CLAIM TO THE THRONE

Needless to say, Clarence's son did not have the opportunity of a stable upbringing. Luckily for Edward he retained his mother Isabel's high connections and, upon his father's death, was still permitted the title of Earl of Warwick. In 1478, the same year that his father was murdered, he was ordained with this title and his supporters stood at his side to reinforce his claim to the throne. An opening seemed to become more apparent in 1483 after the deposition of his cousin, Edward V. Unfortunately for the Earl of Warwick he was prevented from becoming king by the acts of attainder against his father. This seemed even more unjust because the act could easily have been reversed in parliament.

Worse luck was to come to the young boy later that year when King Richard III had him locked up. There is much dispute as to whether this was just in the self-interests of the king or if, as has widely been reported, his detention was the result of the mental retardation that Warwick was a victim of. Either way it is likely that following the death of Richard's son, he only granted Warwick the position of heir to the throne to please his ailing wife, Warwick's guardian Queen Anne. After her death, Richard promptly denied Warwick's claim to the throne and named his other nephew the Earl of Lincoln, John de la Pole, as heir in Warwick's place. Edward Plantagenet, arguably the rightful heir to the throne, was sent back to his dank prison in the Tower of London and left to be forgotten.

THE PRETENDERS

Throughout the middle ages every government was posed with numerous threats to its leadership. England was no different as rulers had continually been forced to counter the efforts of others to overthrow their crowns. After the Battle of Bosworth in 1485, a new problem arose. The Yorkist family, headed by King Richard III was finally fought off by the victorious Lancasters and upon Richard's death, England had a new king. King Henry VII succeeded to the throne later in this year and was determined to overcome all of his opponents.

The years directly following Henry's accession proved to be very challenging to the new king. Although he had endeavoured to protect himself from the threat that Warwick posed through keeping him imprisoned, he had not reckoned upon the threat that others would pose to him. Throughout these first years of his rule, Henry Tudor was compelled to head off various imposters. The first of these was Lambert Simnel who assumed the identity of the Earl of Warwick himself and was assisted by members of the nobility in an attempt to overthrow the king. Henry acted fast to suppress his opposition and was lucky enough to discover that Simnel appeared to be an innocent pawn in the ambitious designs of others. The young boy was installed as the king's own falconer and let off with a mere caution. Meanwhile the real Warwick was still being detained in the Tower of London, but was granted one glorious day of freedom to meet the king's own ends. The young man was paraded through the streets of London to prove that he was very real and that pretenders to the throne would not be tolerated. Warwick's excursion was short lived and he was sent back to the tower immediately.

Although Simnel had been an easy contender to deal with, Henry was soon faced with a far greater threat. As mentioned earlier, Perkin Warbeck's assumption of the identity of Richard of York set the king back a step or two. He was forced to face up to this opponent more forcefully as he had some much more powerful support. When Warbeck was finally captured he was placed in the Tower of London with Warwick. The pretender engineered an escape for the two men and upon capture they were both tried for treason and executed in 1499.

Edward Plantagenet only lived into his twenties before his life was tragically cut short. Although he was never guilty of the same extent of treason as his father, he was really the subject of bad luck. He was a legitimate claimant to the throne but was shut away for the whole of his life in order to halt the threat he posed to those that ruled in his place. As a result of his death, the family of the Plantagenets who had produced fourteen kings, was finally destroyed.

MARY QUEEN OF SCOTS

Mary Queen of Scots was unique in the respect that at one point in her life she had legitimate claims to the kingdoms of England, Ireland, Scotland and France. She was also one of the youngest ever monarchs when, at just six days old, she became Queen of Scotland. She had a very regal past and secured her own rights to the English throne by virtue of the fact that she was the great granddaughter of Henry VII. If Henry's children were to produce no heirs then she would be entitled to the English throne, and this aspect was the source of the threat that she posed to Elizabeth. The sixteenth century was fractured by religious unrest and, as a ruler, Elizabeth I was determined to put a stop to this. After a harrowing few years of rule under the brutal Mary I and the short reign of Henry's only son Edward, Elizabeth endeavoured to restore Protestantism to a religiously divided country. As a devout Catholic, Mary Queen of Scots was even more of a threat to the Queen of England and she was held at arm's length for many years.

From her birth in 1542 Mary was thought to be a very desirable marriage match around Europe. Seeing a chance to unite the kingdoms of Scotland and England and put an end to the religious disputes between them, a marriage proposal was set up between the baby and King Henry's son, Edward VI. Although this match was accepted wholeheartedly by the Scottish nobility, the Catholics opposed the plan and took the girl to Stirling Castle, where they officially broke off the talks with England. Not one to take rejection lightly, Henry VIII began an aggressive series of raids on Scotland, known simply as 'the rough wooing', where the King attempted to change their minds by force. The Scots failed to react and turned in the direction of France in order to strengthen their old alliance with the country.

MARY IN FRANCE

A new marriage match was soon drawn up for Mary and she was betrothed to King Henri II's son, François II. In 1548, at the tender age of six, she was sent to France to be raised in the French court. Here she was rewarded with a great education and became well versed in ancient Greek, Latin and French, to name but a few of her talents. She was extremely well received by her future father-in-law, Henri, and was known to be a truly delightful child. When the two youngsters were old enough the alliance was cemented by their marriage in 1558, ten years after her first arrival in France. She became the queen of both France and Scotland when her husband succeeded to the throne in 1559. But Mary's happiness was short lived and within a year the new king was dead. This left her at a loose end and after the death of her dear mother, she decided to return to Scotland.

RETURN TO SCOTLAND

A new problem now arose for Mary. In her absence every shred of Catholicism had been erased from Scotland and, as a devout Catholic, she did not know how she would be received, or even if she would be allowed to practice Catholicism any longer. An agreement was reached which allowed Mary the right to practice her religion in private and she returned to a warm reception in 1561.

The beginning of her reign was well managed and

she was popular among both the people and her advisers. However, the good feeling did not last after her second marriage in 1565 to her second cousin, Lord Darnley. To Mary the match seemed ideal but others could see the man for what he really was; arrogant, buffoonish and extremely impulsive. The pair had a difficult relationship and were unable to trust each other, especially after Darnley and some of his cronies took part in the unprovoked murder of Mary's secretary. Mary's health was somewhat precarious at this point as she was heavily pregnant and in need of the support of her people. Thanks to the disastrous choice she had made in her second husband she found that she had largely alienated those that had been willing to support her, and with the birth of her child to come, the future was looking very bleak indeed.

The relationship between the two did not get much better and there was still a large amount of antagonism between them, even after the birth of their son. The suspicious circumstances which were to follow shortly after were to signal the beginning of Mary's downfall. Her loathed husband Darnley was murdered in very suspicious circumstances when the building that he was staying in was blown up in 1567. His cause of death did not actually come from the explosion but from being strangled afterwards which made Mary look even more guilty. Mary clearly hadn't learned from this experience and made another dubious marriage match. Not only was the Earl of Bothwell generally disliked by the people, he was also heavily implicated in Darnley's murder.

Such a bold move seemed to her Protestant opposition to be very unwise and they decided to confront her army in the summer of 1567. Mary Queen of Scots was forced to admit defeat and to abdicate in favour of her infant son, while she was imprisoned in the Tower of London. Throughout her time in prison Mary made it clear that she believed that she was the rightful Queen of England and posed even more of a threat to Queen Elizabeth by receiving the backing of the Pope in 1570. Although she was sufficiently worried by the risk that she was faced with, the English ruler decided that she should not execute Mary because she was royalty and she would therefore run the risk of serious backlash from the Scottish.

THE BABINGTON PLOT

Having been involved in many unsuccessful Roman Catholic plots to overthrow Elizabeth, Mary Queen of Scots then allegedly became involved in something a lot more dangerous. In 1586 a group of Catholic men revealed to Mary their plans to kill the Queen and to place her on the throne of England. Messages were passed in secret between Mary and Babington, the main plotter, and it was not long before Elizabeth's adviser, Sir Francis Walsingham, got wind of their plans. Mary's involvement in the plot was obvious, though it was more likely that Walsingham had forged her reply than Mary had written to Babington herself. Elizabeth was not able to protect her cousin any longer and under the advice of her ministers she ordered Mary's execution, which took place in Fotheringhay Castle in 1587.

Mary's reliance upon treachery against the Queen of England was spawned from the religious divide which prevailed in England and Scotland. Mary believed that killing Elizabeth was the right thing to do, as this move had been endorsed by the Pope who hoped to restore Catholicism to England. Throughout her life she was criticised for many of the decisions she had made and also the ones that she had been forced into. She held to her convictions that restoring Catholicism was the correct course of action, even if this resulted in the murder of her own cousin. Mary cannot be described as a bad person, but instead one who made many bad decisions and alienated her followers. She tried to do what she thought was right, but in doing so it cost her her life.

SIR THOMAS MORE

Thomas More was fortunate enough to have been brought up in a stable environment within a very respectable family. His father was Sir John More, who had made a name for himself as a prominent judge and was keen to pass his own knowledge onto his son. More made sure that Thomas's every need was catered for and enrolled him at St Anthony's school in London. It was here that More's two greatest passions were nurtured; his interest in law and his desire to serve the Church. His studies suited him well for both subjects and he was an avid scholar of Greek and Latin literature. He remained undecided about which path he should follow and, shortly after he qualified as a barrister in 1501, he decided to join religious orders and become a monk.

After a few years he decided that his duty to his country should be put above his desire to lead a life solely devoted to God, and he left the monastry to enter parliament in 1504. This was a busy year for him; he married for the first time and met and forged a strong friendship with the humanist Erasmus. More's introduction to parliament was not hugely successful as he openly challenged Henry VII about the high rates of taxes that he had been charging the poor under the agency of Empson and Dudley. Sir Thomas More's insistence upon being fair gained him a reputation for being a patron of the poor and secured him the support of the people throughout his life. However, More's policies were risky and put his family in danger. He was forced to withdraw from public life until 1509, when the greatly angered Henry VII had died.

HENRY'S CLOSEST ADVISER

As More reacquainted himself with parliament, his various merits and skills came to the attention of the new king, Henry VIII. His first appointment as Henry's adviser came in 1515, when he accompanied the delegation to Flanders to resolve the disputes surrounding the wool trade. He achieved even greater recognition from the king when he managed to suppress an uprising and in 1518 was rewarded by becoming a member of the Privy council. Clearly, More was a very talented man and his knowledge of politics and law suited Henry VIII perfectly. What most appealed to the king were More's writing skills.

With his assistance the king was able to draw up his 'Defence of the Seven Sacraments' in response to Luther's protestant teachings. As chancellor, More was also asked to spearhead a campaign to enforce laws against heretics, which proved to be quite unsuccessful – only four people ever suffered the penalty for this crime.

More's talents were constantly recognised by Henry VIII and he was duly rewarded. Firstly, he was knighted by the king in 1521 and was then made speaker in the House of Commons in 1523. More's influence helped to establish the parliamentary privilege of free speech, which left politicians free to express their views in parliament. The last of More's promotions came in 1529 when he became Lord Chancellor after Cardinal Wolsey had fallen out of the king's favour. Henry VIII was proving himself to be a frightening opponent to any who spoke against him, and More would have been wise to pay attention to this.

THE BREAK WITH ROME

In 1527 Henry made a decision that Sir Thomas More felt he could not support. He sought to seek a divorce from his wife, Katherine of Aragon, as she had failed to produce an heir and, more importantly, he was in love with his mistress Anne Boleyn. The religious beliefs that More had held so closely to him could not be observed if the king was to allow a divorce between himself and his wife, expressly as a way of legitimising his infidelity. Henry did not act against More at first, but it was noted that the reason behind the politician's resignation was given as poor health. This was unlikely to be the primary cause of his resignation from Henry's service and he made no secret of his disdain for the king's new marriage.

The relationship between the two men became increasingly strained when More refused to attend the coronation of the new queen, Anne Boleyn, in 1533. His absence was enough for Henry to consider him a traitor and, more importantly, acted to undermine the king's authority. Although More had never committed any concrete acts of treason against the king, Henry was now determined to implicate him in a plot against him led by Elizabeth Barton, the nun of Kent. Barton was in great opposition to Henry's decision to break with Rome and she sought to pass a bill through parliament, stressing the sympathy of others to this point of view. Henry's plan to link the innocent More to this plot backfired when the Lords refused to pass the bill until More's name was removed from it.

The king's frustrations grew as he failed to convict

More of any treasonable acts, but More's ultimate downfall came when he refused to swear to the Act of Succession and Oath of Supremacy in 1534, legitimising Henry VIII and Anne Boleyn as the rightful monarchs of England. More tendered his resignation and was forced to relinquish his complete income minus only £100 allowance per year. In addition to this, he was thrown into the Tower of London and reported by the king's solicitor general to have denied parliament's power to confer ecclesiastical supremacy on Henry. Whether or not this conversation actually took place is questionable, but Henry now had the concrete evidence he needed to sentence More to death. On the 1 July he was indicted for high treason at Westminster Hall and sentenced to beheading on Tower Hill. He was executed on 6 July 1535, alongside Bishop Fisher who had also opposed Henry's break with Rome.

More's legacy lived on for many years and he was remembered by the Catholic church by being canonised by Pope Pius XI in 1935. His literature has also stood the test of time with *Utopia* often being read by students around the world even to this day. More can be seen as a man whose morality was dear to him and who was forced to give his life as a punishment for speaking his views publicly.

SIR FRANCIS
WALSINGHAM

As with many of the 'squealers' discussed throughout this book, Walsingham grew up with a very privileged lifestyle. His family was very wealthy and in possession of enough capital to invest in a large manor in Kent. The boy's connections with the royal family came from an early age as they were closely related to one of Henry VIII's ministers, Sir Anthony Denny. Sir Francis Walsingham's interest in politics could have stemmed from his early association with this influential family member, but the boy would surely have been steered towards a career in politics with the influence of his father, who was a renowned lawyer.

Following the death of his father, Walsingham's youth became enriched by more useful connections. His mother was remarried to a relation of Henry Carey, a man closely connected to the Boleyn family, whose daughter Anne would soon become Queen of England. As a consequence, Walsingham spent much of his youth in the company of Anne's daughter Elizabeth, who would ultimately ascend to the throne of England. Brought up as a staunch Protestant, Walsingham stayed true to his religious convictions and imposed a voluntary exile upon himself after Elizabeth's older sister, Mary, ascended to the throne. The new ruler was a very strict Catholic and was well known for her violent execution of 'heretics' who did not follow the Catholic faith. Walsingham was able to use his self-imposed exile to his own advantage by venturing abroad to pursue other avenues not accessible to him in England.

WALSINGHAM'S EDUCATION

For the next five years Walsingham lived abroad and began a rigorous training in both foreign languages and law. His goal was to carve a political career out for himself and to offer his services to the British monarchy. Throughout the period of his training two English monarchs had died; both Queen Mary and King Edward, and the ascension to the throne of Elizabeth, pleased Walsingham greatly. Not only had she been a close acquaintance of his throughout his youth, she also held the same religious beliefs as he did, which meant that he would be free to return to England whenever he desired. Throughout the period of his education Walsingham became deeply interested in the idea of constructing a secret service which would act to expose the plans of enemies of the monarch as soon as they had been formulated. These ideas came into the young man's mind whilst he was continuing his studies in law. He continued to remain abroad in Padua until 1555 when he made the decision to return to his homeland.

Upon return to England Walsingham built up many useful connections which allowed him to rise quickly in the field of politics. He often assisted one of Elizabeth I's most trusted advisers, Sir William Cecil, who gradually instigated the young man's return to the Commons. Due to his excellent education, he was able to assist in matters of great importance regarding foreign affairs, and in 1570 was sent to France by the queen on a very important mission to secure favourable terms for the Huguenots in their negotiations with Charles IX. Following a negative experience with the French king he returned to England with a lasting distrust for the man and warned Elizabeth not to enter into any political agreements with him. His skills at dealing with foreign affairs were duly noted by the queen, and he became one of her principal secretaries of state soon after his experience in France. He also proved himself an invaluable assistant to the queen with his intricately masterminded ability to obtain intelligence from abroad. Clearly he had great talents in the field of secret service and he was frequently able to make a great contribution to Elizabeth's throne by combining information from sources at home and abroad.

WALSINGHAM AND ELIZABETH CLASH

It was never in dispute that Queen Elizabeth held her adviser Walsingham in high regard, but there gradually came a time when the two strong characters began to clash with one another. On one hand, there was the fiercely determined Walsingham, fixed in his opinion that he knew best and that Elizabeth would be wise to adhere to his every word of counsel. The queen on the other hand, felt that her adviser was forcing her to make decisions without allowing her to have any input herself. The queen clearly did not think much of Walsingham's character but was well aware that his master minding of the now well-established secret service in England, had helped her to combat her enemies for the duration of her reign.

As time went on, the pair continued to clash. Firstly there was an issue with some intelligence that Walsingham had received from abroad. He discovered that under the auspices of Felipe II, Spain was preparing to invade England. The motives for this were tied up with the continuing religious disagreements between Catholic Spain and Protestant England. The queen could not agree with Walsingham's advice to fight the advancing Spanish forces, and decided on using peaceful methods to come to some sort of agreement with Spain. Unfortunately for Walsingham he would never have as much backing as the queen and he grew increasingly frustrated that his advice was constantly being ignored. Walsingham did himself no favours by allowing his relationship with other members of the privy council to deteriorate. He found himself disagreeing with the Earl of Leicester and gradually became estranged by him, which left him isolated and alone.

He was undoubtedly devoted to protecting England and clearly believed that he had the queen's best interests at heart with every decision he made on her behalf. In 1581 he was sent to France to forge an Anglo-French alliance in order to unite the two countries against the increasing power of Spain. Elizabeth was encouraged to take François, Duke of

Anjou, in marriage, but stubbornly refused any such union as she believed that it would undermine her authority as a female ruler. Again Walsingham felt exasperated that the queen would not heed his useful advice, and he continued to immerse himself in the work of his secret service. Regrettably for Elizabeth, her status as a ruler was never safe and she was now faced with a threat from Scotland in the form of Mary Queen of Scots. The queen of Scotland held a genuine claim to the throne of England, but this was reliant upon the demise of childless Elizabeth. She was implicated in a number of plots against the queen of England but Elizabeth was not keen on executing her enemy as she was royalty just like herself. Instead she chose to imprison her in the Tower of London for a number of years and believed that this would put an end to Mary's plotting against her.

WALSINGHAM'S FALL FROM GRACE

At this time Walsingham became increasingly paranoid about the threat that Scotland posed to Queen Elizabeth. He became convinced that it was not only Mary Queen of Scots who was conspiring against Elizabeth, but was also persuaded that James VI of Scotland was also in on the plotting. As a consequence, he desired to implicate Mary Queen of Scots heavily in the Babington plot, led by Anthony Babington, which sought to take the life of their ruler. A series of letters were reportedly sent disguised in bottles between the Queen of Scots and the main conspirator, Babington. Walsingham's superior secret service quickly got wind of this plot and set about to bring the conspirators to justice.

There is much dispute regarding whether or not Mary actually had any involvement in this plot, and many believed that Walsingham had fabricated the evidence to render her guilty of committing treason against the Queen of England. Elizabeth did not know what to do. On one hand she felt that she was being pushed into executing her cousin because Walsingham had shown her to be a traitor, and on the other she knew that it would not be a wise decision to murder a royal. After increasing pressure from Walsingham to put Mary to death, Elizabeth finally caved in. However, Walsingham's position as adviser was permanently compromised from this point onwards and he was no longer held in high regard by the queen.

After a lifetime of service to the sovereign he completely lost his political standing and was left with grave financial debts. He died alone and miserable in 1590 and was heavily in debt to the queen.

SIR ANTHONY BABINGTON AND GILBERT GIFFORD

As with many of the medieval traitors mentioned previously, the clash between Catholic and Protestant was the reason behind a plot to assassinate Queen Elizabeth I. Sir Anthony Babington was one such traitor and as a result of his strong Roman Catholic convictions, he sought to take the life of the Protestant queen.

Born in 1561, Babington was brought up within a stable household. Due to the general religious unrest in England from the different rulers, Babington was secretly raised as a Roman Catholic. From an early age he served as a page to the young Mary Queen of Scots and was something of an admirer of the queen's talents and religious devotion. Babington did not begin to rally himself against Queen Elizabeth until 1580, when he moved to London and joined a secret society in support of Jesuit missionaries.

Like Babington, Gilbert Gifford was also brought up in a Catholic family and intended to devote his life to the Catholic church by entering Cardinal Allen's English college at Douai in 1577, with the hope of becoming a missionary priest. The following years were filled with many different relocations abroad as Gifford failed to decide what he wanted to do. In 1582 he returned to Cardinal Allen's college which was now based in Rheims, and was ordained as a deacon in 1585. Gifford's allegiances soon became more sinister when, shortly afterwards, he made the acquaintance of a student named John Savage who was involved in a plot to assassinate the Queen of England. In 1585 he left Rheims again and met one of Mary's agents, Thomas Morgan. He then quickly became involved in the Babington plot, which sought to kill the Elizabeth I.

THE BABINGTON PLOT

As he had in his youth, Babington was able to provide more assistance for Mary Queen of Scots when he arrived in Paris and became associated with her supporters. She was grateful to him for delivering various letters to her and he became an even greater supporter of the Scottish queen. In April 1586 he began to hatch a plan with John Ballard. They aimed to murder Elizabeth I and her ministers, to organise a general Roman Catholic uprising in England to liberate Mary and install her on the throne of England.

The plot proved potentially to be one of the most serious threats to the monarchy in a long time as more and more influential supporters were choosing to support Mary Queen of Scots. One of the most powerful supporters of the plot was King Philip II of Spain, a Catholic ruler who believed that Elizabeth should be killed in order for Catholicism to be reintroduced into England. Babington's plot was soon discovered, no matter how intricate he had made it. Later in the year of 1586 Babington wrote a letter to Mary Queen of Scots, outlining the details of the plot and requesting a token of her appreciation in return. This letter was intercepted by Walsingham's advanced spy network, but it was a while before his forces were able to catch up with the elusive Babington.

Prior to this, Gilbert Gifford had also become involved with the plot and had been made responsible for transporting the messages between

Mary and Babington. He was soon arrested by Sir Francis Walsingham and brought to London for questioning. Babington's plot struck another blow here, as Gifford agreed to preserve his life by acting as a double agent for Walsingham. He seemed to forget all his religious convictions overnight and sought to preserve his life over his own integrity. Gifford then arranged to gain the trust of Queen Mary through taking the role of smuggling secret messages to her by concealing them in beer bottles.

Unaware that they had a double agent behind the scenes, Babington obliviously continued to send messages to Mary detailing his plans for Elizabeth's murder. He was, however, very aware of the risks that he was imposing upon his personal safety and was simultaneously making arrangements to gain a passport to go abroad, under the pretence of spying on refugees. During this time Babington's ally, Ballard, had been caught and detained and finally broke down to betray his comrades when he was subjected to Walsingham's renowned torture methods. Following the delay in the receipt of his passport and with the knowledge of Ballard's confession becoming apparent to him, he decided to try and bargain with Walsingham. He offered to inform him of another dangerous conspiracy to murder the queen but no reply was sent to Babington. As the ports were closed no one was allowed to leave England and the plotter began to realise how serious things were getting.

His freedom was retained and the conspirator was allowed to stay at Walsingham's own residence. Babington's comfort was short lived, however, when he discovered a memorandum about him in Walsingham's house; he quickly disguised himself and fled. Shortly afterwards the man was discovered and imprisoned in the Tower of London. He was tried with all of his accomplices and, when questioned, he cowardly tried to place the entire blame upon John Ballard. Needless to say, no one believed this unlikely allegation and he was promptly sentenced to death for high treason. Ever the manipulator, he then tried to escape his fate by appealing to Queen Elizabeth that she grant him mercy in return for his offering of £1,000. This was quickly rejected and he was executed ten days later.

All of the conspirators involved in the Babington plot were punished by death and Elizabeth was very concerned that this be the case to show that she took a very firm line against those who had betrayed her. Even Gilbert Gifford, who had served Walsingham as a double agent, was not really rewarded. Shortly after the plot he fled to France where he was arrested by the French catholics and left to die in prison. In short, neither man prospered for attacking the British monarchy and each suffered a somewhat tortuous death as a result of their involvement or treachery in the Babington plot.

EARL OF ESSEX

Robert Devereux was born in 1566, the son of Walter Devereux, 1st Earl of Essex, and Lettice Knollys, granddaughter of Mary Boleyn. The young boy's childhood was marred by the death of his father when he was a mere nine years of age. As a result he was adopted as a ward of the queen's trusted adviser and the late Devereux's closest friend, Lord Burghley. Devereux's fortunes were further lifted when his mother remarried Queen Elizabeth's most trusted friend, Robert Dudley, the Earl of Leicester. Such a strong association with the queen proved to be very useful for the young Earl of Essex and he gradually began to win the queen's favour, as both his father and step-father had done in the years previously.

A NEW GENERATION

After the long drawn out celebrations upon the defeat of the Spanish armada in 1588, Elizabeth began to find herself and her government floundering. Not only was the queen suffering problems with health due to old age, she was also forced to face the repercussions of the deaths of three of her closest advisors, Dudley, Walsingham and Cecil. As a result of the queen's isolation, a window opened for a new generation to take on the role of advisors. Among these were the sons of Devereux and William Cecil, Robert Devereux and Robert Cecil. Within a very short period of time Robert had established himself as a favourite of the queen and by 1590 he had impressively built up such a successful relationship with the monarch that he effectively had replaced his late stepfather's own intimate standing with her. Their relationship was not a simple one, mainly because Elizabeth was thirty-four years his senior, and the pair were often found arguing upon matters of foreign policy and even trivial personal difficulties. Despite their differences, they remained great friends and the queen seemed to offer an almost maternal devotion to the young Devereux.

Robert's fiery temper and readiness to cause tensions amongst his rivals also caused trouble for him shortly after he joined the Privy Council in 1591. His direct rival, Robert Cecil had followed in the footsteps of his father and in 1591 had also become a member of the Privy Council. The Earl of Essex was not comfortable with Cecil's growing closeness as adviser to the queen, and was not best pleased when he discovered that Cecil was to be the new Secretary for the State as he was ultimately appointed in 1596. The two men continually fought for Elizabeth's approval and argued over religious and military policy. Luckily for Devereux though, he was clearly Elizabeth's favourite and was bestowed with many important roles, the first being the Master of the Horse. Robert was quick to fall from the queen's favour in 1590 when he was joined in marriage to Frances, the widow of his cousin Philip Sydney, and daughter of the late Sir Francis Walsingham. Elizabeth I was greatly displeased by this union and hoped her annoyance would act as a warning to the impulsive young man.

Later that year he was given the opportunity to prove himself again to the queen, as he was put in charge of an important expedition to encourage the French king Henry IV to reject the efforts of the Catholic league. Early the next year he was able to offer assistance to the Protestant king, acting to forge a strong relationship between England and France. In 1596 the Earl of Essex reached the peak of his military career when he assisted with the command of an expedition that captured Cadiz from the

Spanish. He was greeted in England as a national hero and at this point in his life was most revered by the Queen of England.

THE REBELLION IN IRELAND

As recognition for his impressive victory in Cadiz, Devereux was able to appoint himself as Lord Lieutenant of Ireland in 1599. He had clearly proved his merits in battle and the queen was eager to send him to Ireland in the hope of a similar level of success. However, he was not prepared for the fact that this would actually lead to his eventual downfall. Elizabeth's aim was to use the Earl of Essex to suppress a rebellion led by the Earl of Tyrone. He was backed very well in terms of the military force behind him; 17,000 troops were sent with him. Clearly Queen Elizabeth I viewed the situation in Ireland as being a great threat and she did not expect Robert Devereux to think otherwise.

Unfortunately for this earl, the campaign seemed doomed from the start. Shortly after the departure of his forces, many were overcome by disease and subsequently perished. This meant that Devereux was forced to lead a somewhat less impressive army to Ireland. It was as if he had lost his mind when he directed his party via a tortuous route through Munster which allowed his opposition, the Earl of Tyrone, to greet him face on as he headed northwards. Understandably this put him in a compromising position, but what he did next ensured that he was never to regain the queen's favour. The Earl of Essex entered into a foolish truce with the Earl of Tyrone, not only against the wishes of the queen but also in her own name. Word of this imprudence quickly spread to England and he was summoned by the queen immediately.

She forced him to explain his conduct instantly and he was deprived of all his offices and placed under house arrest. This came as a great blow to the man who had once been one of Elizabeth's greatest friends and he fought for the next year to regain her favour. In 1600 the Earl of Essex felt that he had taken just as much as he could from his old friend. After the queen had refused to renew the lease and patent on his farm wines, he decided to make his own bid for power.

A COUP AGAINST THE QUEEN

In 1601 Devereux rallied various supporters of his scheme, mainly dissatisfied nobles and soldiers but also the more influential support of James VI of

Scotland, who he proposed to be placed upon the throne of England. The group marched into London with the expectation of being greeted by followers of their cause but because no such support was realised, the rebellion collapsed and they were tried for treason. He was sentenced to death later that year and it was with regret that Queen Elizabeth signed his death warrant.

Although the Earl of Essex had been a close friend of the queen for much of her later life, he had also revealed himself to be an impulsive and fiery person and, as a consequence, made some bad decisions which led to his downfall. The queen was forced to take serious action against all those who betrayed her, and the blow fell hardest when she was forced to put her own friends to death. However, Devereux had betrayed her and should have known not to offend the monarch, having been witness to her behaviour for many years.

GUY FAWKES AND ASSOCIATES

Guy Fawkes was born in 1570, the only son of Edward Fawkes of York and his wife, Edith Blake. His background was very religious because his father was a proctor of the ecclesiastical courts. His mother's side had descended from the Harrington family who were aldermen and eminent merchants of York. Fawkes was secure in his connections and had his youth filled with many influential figures. As a young man Fawkes began to develop a very strong religious conviction under the tutelage of John Pulleyn, a devout Catholic whose teachings had a lasting effect upon his young pupil. What also emerged throughout this time was that Fawkes had become an increasingly impulsive and difficult person to be around, and he began to have disagreements with contemporaries, even from his youth. He did not feel a strong allegiance to his country and continuously sought opportunities overseas. After he had come of age in 1591 he hastily sought out chances to spend his generous inheritance and with his cousin he moved to Flanders in 1593. As a devout Catholic, Fawkes was angry that he was not able to worship freely in England under the rule of the Protestant Queen Elizabeth, and he sought opportunities abroad to bring the English government to its knees.

FAWKES IN THE SPANISH ARMY

After a short period of time in Flanders, Fawkes quickly enrolled in the Spanish army under Archduke Albert of Austria, who later became governor of the Netherlands. Guy Fawkes was greatly respected within the Spanish army and proved himself to be both a great fighter and a powerful leader when he was offered a post of command when the Spaniards took Calais in 1596. He also attracted considerable attention with his own appearance; a commanding man with a great frame and flaming red hair, he was marked out from the rest of the Spanish army simply by the way he looked. His dedication to the army was noted primarily through his popularity amongst the other soldiers, as he promptly shifted his allegiance to the Spanish, and more importantly Catholic, side.

Such was Fawkes's dedication that he attracted the attention of some very important backers, Lord Stanley being one of the most prominent. Stanley allowed Fawkes a brief leave from the Spanish army in order to visit the Spanish King Philip II in person, and reveal to him the position of the Catholics in England. King Philip was concerned about the prevalence of Protestantism in England at this time as all evidence of Catholicism had been removed from the country. After a failed attempt to invade England upon the news of the death of Queen Elizabeth, Fawkes was met by the constable of Castile who was on his way to England to discuss a treaty between England and Spain. Peace was temporarily established between the two countries and Guy returned to England.

THE GUNPOWDER PLOT

Following the accession of King James I Scotland, another Protestant, the anger of the Catholics increased. In 1604 Fawkes met with Robert Catesby, Thomas Percy, John Wright and Thomas Wintour at the Strand, where they all agreed under oath to participate in the gunpowder plot. This oath taking took on a religious side as the men renewed their

Catholic vows by performing mass and allowing the re-administration of sacraments performed by a Jesuit priest. In this way they felt that the act that they were preparing to commit, in order to kill the King of England, was justified as it had effectively been endorsed by God. Furthermore, there was general unrest in England due to the arrival of the new ruler James I. Since Elizabeth had neglected to provide an heir, her nearest relative, the King of Scotland finally came to the throne. This united the kingdoms of England and Scotland, but not everyone was prepared to accept this.

As the plan was formulated, the men were careful to cover their tracks and assume new identities to hide their involvement in such a serious plot. All were aware of the risks that such a dangerous mission would entail and none was more careful than Fawkes, who went to great lengths to re-establish his identity as one of Percy's servants. He also removed all previous evidence of having been someone who had defected to Spain in order to fight the Protestants in England. By 1605 the plan had really begun to come into formation and the group had rented out a cellar below the Houses of Parliament. Their idea was to place an enormous amount of gunpowder in the cellar and to disguise the room as a sort of storage facility by hiding the gunpowder beneath some iron bars and faggots. Whilst this was going on Fawkes was nominated to take news of the plot overseas to Flanders, and inform Stanley of their plans.

Upon his return, Fawkes was alarmed to discover that his landlady had suspected him of being a Catholic and he was forced to move out of his lodgings to avoid further suspicion. To make matters worse the progress being made was severely limited as none but Fawkes had been militarily trained and therefore did not possess the same amount of strength. More conspirators were enlisted. This alarmed Fawkes greatly as he was aware that the more people who were involved, the increased risk there was in their plot being exposed. Nevertheless, things fell into place and the plot looked like it was near to completion by the end of the summer of 1605. Unbeknown to the conspirators, however, was the fact that the famous Monteagle letter was soon to come into the hands of William Parker, an influential member of the government, and the details of the plot were no longer a secret.

Oblivious to this, the plotters met on the night of 3 November 1605 and agreed unanimously that the authorities were as yet unaware of any plotting against them. Aside from Fawkes, each man had made plans to make a rapid exit from the country, once the gunpowder had been detonated. Unfortunately for Fawkes, his military service did not stand in his favour this time, since he was the only one who had experience with gunpowder and therefore had been assigned to stay in the cellar and perform the detonation before making a quick getaway.

All seemed to be going to plan until the following day when Guy Fawkes was seemingly caught in the act. The Lord Chamberlain Thomas Howard, the Earl of Suffolk, Monteagle and John Wynniard burst into the cellar and immediately began interrogating Fawkes about the contents of the cellar. Fawkes probably thought he was safe when the four men conducted a brief search of the cellar and discovered only the faggots. The men quickly returned to the king and told him that there was nothing out of the ordinary to be found in the cellar. Not one to take a possible attempt on his life lightly, King James I ordered the men to conduct a more rigorous search. They duly returned and were astounded to find a huge amount of gunpowder concealed in the damp cellar. When questioned, Fawkes claimed that he had no knowledge of the plot and was merely a servant to Thomas Percy. This became harder to believe, however, when he was found with matches on his person. Ultimately it seemed futile to deny his involvement in the plot and instead Fawkes claimed that their motivation was to 'blow the Scotsmen present back to Scotland'.

In January of 1606, and following a difficult few months rounding all the conspirators up, the trial of the eight survivors began in Westminster Hall. The trial was more of a formality than anything else, as the guilty verdict had already been established. Despite this the men refused to plead guilty and instead tried to place the blame upon the Jesuits. Shortly afterwards they were found guilty and hung, drawn and quartered in the old palace yard at Westminster.

Although these men undoubtedly attempted to commit a very serious crime against both the ruler and government of England, they were sure in their convictions that what they were doing was right. As with many of the traitors of the past, Fawkes's religious fervour was what caused his feelings of dissatisfaction regarding the governing of England. He took matters into his own hands in order to change what he did not like and as a result he paid with his life.

CHARLES I

Unlike many of the traitors described in this book, Charles I did not possess the same strength of mind and raw ability as the others. In addition, his case was rather different because he was a monarch and, in fact, the first English ruler to be put on trial. He grew up in a privileged household and was the fourth child of King James VI Scotland, who ultimately became James I of England after his cousin Elizabeth died. Charles's family was very secure in its standing and his mother Anne was the daughter of Frederick II, King of Denmark and Norway. The family had alliances with a number of different countries and held a firm footing in both England and Scotland.

In 1603, at the tender age of three, Charles was named as the Duke of Albany. However, the family were struck down by tragedy in 1612 when Charles's older brother Henry came down with an unexplained illness and died suddenly. This came as a huge disappointment to the king, not merely as he had lost his first male heir to the throne, but more importantly because Charles was a very feeble and frail child. Not only had the youngster experienced problems with his stammer, he also had trouble with his co-ordination, resulting in an inability to walk. After the death of his brother, pressure was put on Charles to overcome these defects and with the help of Lady Carey he was finally able to make some progress in correcting them.

Charles had always sought out a foreign marriage alliance and in his youth he took the arduous journey to Spain in an attempt to court a Spanish infanta. He was not successful in his first quest, but shortly after his father had died in 1625, Charles married the Catholic French princess, Henrietta Maria, daughter of Henry IV. The pairing seemed quite well-matched and they had a number of children. The eldest was Mary who, at the age of nine, was promised in marriage to the Prince of Orange and later became the mother of Great General William III, Prince of Orange. Although this union was successful on a personal level, it proved controversial to the people of England and Scotland. Under the auspices of James I, the religion of the two countries had been stabilised as Protestant and many people were worried that a marriage alliance with a Catholic would cause

Charles to lift restrictions on Roman Catholics. Parliament in particular was opposed to the marriage and vigorously argued against it.

THE FALL OUT WITH PARLIAMENT

Like his father James, Charles was a great believer in the divine right of kings. This meant that a ruler was given almost religious infallibility surrounding the decisions they made because they had supposedly been appointed by God. In effect, a ruler's authority was unquestionable. In 1628 the parliament attempted to protect their status by drafting the Petition of Right, which meant that the king could not levy taxes or impose martial law on civilians without parliament's consent. As a result of their murmuring against his decisions, the king decided to abolish parliament in 1629. Naturally the consequences were dramatic. No one liked the idea of the king becoming a dictatorial figure who did not consider the views of his people, particularly when he had seriously raised their taxes to pay for his own ventures.

The disagreement with parliament was only a tiny portion of Charles's dramatic reforms; it was his religious reform which had the greatest effect upon turning his subjects against him. Initially distrust spread as Charles seemed to be changing his attitude towards the Protestant church. Firstly he had allied himself with controversial religious figures associated with Calvinism and Catholicism, such as Richard Montagu and William Laud. These relationships seemed to spur the king on to make some radical religious changes in a bid to move the Church of England away from Calvinism towards a more traditional and sacramental direction. The bad feeling towards him in Scotland was such that his proposal of a new prayer book resulted in full scale rebellion throughout the country.

THE DECLINE OF THE KING

Charles's biggest problem was that his high ambitions for England and Scotland were not realisable with the limited funding that was available to him. He constantly sought to adopt a very protective foreign policy and in order to achieve this he raised money by selling monopolies and instituting a shipping money tax. When he had demanded these taxes in the years before parliament was dismissed, he had taken swift action to arrest five members of parliament who had previously opposed him. However, after eleven years of ruling on his own, the struggle for supremacy led to civil war within England and Scotland. The civil war began in 1642 and was fought between the supporters of the monarchy, Cavaliers and the supporters of parliament, Roundheads. The first civil war came to a close in 1646 when he was forced to surrender to the Scots and was handed over to the English. In 1648 after six years of fighting had torn the previously united England and Scotland apart, Charles fled to Hurst Castle. This move provoked a second civil war in the country as Charles I was refusing to face the consequences of his actions. Later that year he was brought to trial in Westminster Hall and found guilty of treason by a minute margin of 68 votes to 67. His execution day was set for the start of the next year and his fate was eventually sealed when he was beheaded in Whitehall.

The case of Charles's execution was an unusual one because it resulted in a king being tried for crimes. This showed that rulers were not necessarily infallible and were not above the law. Charles's decision to dismiss his parliament led to widespread unrest through England and Scotland resulting in two civil wars. Undoubtedly Charles seemed to think that he was doing what was best for his people, but his choices ultimately ended up causing more damage than good.

PART THREE

MODERN TRAITORS AND SPIES

BENEDICT ARNOLD

In Saratoga National Historical Park in eastern New York State, stands a monument that resolutely fails to bear the name of the man it commemorates. The famous Boot Monument is dedicated instead to the memory of 'the most brilliant soldier of the Continental Army who was desperately wounded on this spot the sally port of Borgoyne's Great Western Redoubt on 7 October 1777, winning for his countrymen the decisive battle of the American Revolution and for himself the rank of Major General.' The anonymous dedicatee is Benedict Arnold, a man whose name is as synonymous in America with treachery, as that of Norwegian traitor Vidkun Quisling's is in Europe.

The Boot Monument celebrates Arnold's victory in the Battle of Bemis Heights, the decisive final battle of the Saratoga Campaign during the War of American Independence. Arnold's men cut off the British army of British General John Burgoyne, forcing him to surrender on 17 October 1777 and, in the process, Arnold was wounded in the leg and below the buttock. If the bullets had been aimed just a little higher and Arnold had been killed at Bemis Heights, he would have been one of the great heroes of American history. Instead, he is reviled. How did his name become a byword for disgrace? How did he make the journey from hero to zero?

Arnold was born in 1741 in Norwich, Connecticut, to Benedict Arnold III and Hannah Waterman King. He was the last of their six children and one of only two who survived infancy. His great-grandfather, who had died when Arnold was a child, had been governor of the Rhode Island Colony and he could trace his family back to an early immigrant to the New World from England, John Lanthrop.

The family was plunged into debt when Benedict senior made some injudicious business deals and, as his life began to fall apart, he started to drink heavily. With no income coming in and a father often incapacitated, Benedict left school at fourteen and was apprenticed to two of his mother's cousins, Daniel and Joshua Lanthrop. They ran a thriving apothecary and general merchandise business.

A year later, however, Arnold joined the

Connecticut militia to fight the French. They were supported by native Americans and, although he never saw any action, Arnold was sickened by the behaviour of the Indians who massacred several hundred men, women and children at Fort William Henry near Albany. He would hate the French for the rest of his life for their failure to prevent this outrage.

With the death of his mother in 1759, responsibility for the welfare of the family passed to Arnold. By now his father's drunkenness was an embarrassment to the family and he was arrested several times for being drunk in public, eventually dying in 1761. The Lathrops helped Benedict to set up a business of his own, as a bookseller and pharmacist in New Haven, a business that rapidly began to do very well. He was able to buy back the family home, sold by his father to pay off their debts and, together with another merchant, Adam Babcock, bought three ships and started to engage in trade with the West Indies.

When the British Government introduced the 1765 Stamp Act, effectively to raise money to maintain the British military presence in the Colonies, Arnold and Babcock's business was seriously damaged. Ignoring the Act, they continued to trade but Arnold still fell heavily into debt.

In 1775 Arnold had already been involved in

military activity, being appointed captain of a local volunteer force, the Governor's Second Company of Connecticut Guards. When the first fighting of the revolution broke out in April of that year, he went off to fight. On a march northwards, he met the Connecticut lawyer and military leader Colonel Samuel Holden Parsons, and discussed with him the possibility of an expedition to capture Fort Ticonderoga which was situated on Lake Champlain, on the New York State and Vermont border. There were a number of cannons there and the revolutionary force was extremely short of hardware. The Massachusetts Committee of Safety promoted Arnold to colonel and provided the funds for the venture.

At dawn on 10 May, he ordered the attack and the British garrison, taken unawares, surrendered without fighting. He also took Crown Point and Fort St. Johns, although the latter was abandoned when a fresh British force arrived to re-capture it.

Throughout the campaign, Arnold had been at loggerheads with Ethan Allen over who was in overall command. Allen's Green Mountain Boys, the militia of Vermont, had joined forces with Arnold's army. Allen withdrew his men, leaving Arnold in control of the conquests. Soon, however, Colonel Benjamin Hinman was sent to take command, and

Arnold was, understandably, furious. He resigned his commission and went back to Massachusetts.

In June 1775, the Continental Army was formed to fight the war and Arnold joined in a plan to invade Canada and take Montreal, to deprive the colonial forces of a location from which they could launch attacks on northern New York. He was to lead a force to capture Quebec City, believing that once the two principal French-speaking cities of Canada were in revolutionary hands, the inhabitants would join the battle against the British.

Although the British had destroyed most of the serviceable craft, Arnold's army needed to cross the Chaudière River to Quebec and, in spite of the presence of the frigate, *Lizard* (with twenty-six guns) as well as the small sailing warship, *Hunter* (with sixteen guns), Arnold's men succeeded in making the crossing on 11 November. Having estimated the size of the force facing him, however, he sent an urgent request for reinforcements. General Richard Montgomery arrived, having already taken Montreal and their combined army, of just under 1,000 men, attacked Quebec City on the last day of December. It did not go well. While Montgomery's force struggled to even get close to the city walls, Arnold and his men were isolated on the other side of the city and Arnold took a bullet in the leg, remaining on the battlefield, nonetheless, issuing orders and rallying his troops. Around 350 survivors of the attack remained camped outside the city, besieging it, until the spring of 1776 when they were relieved.

Arnold was promoted to brigadier-general following Quebec and was detailed to prevent the British from invading the Hudson River valley. Having successfully kept the British at bay until the onset of winter, he was appointed to command of the Eastern Department of the Continental Army. He defended Rhode Island with a force of only around 2,000 men, facing 15,000 Redcoats. Shortly after, while in New Haven to visit his family, he heard that the British had landed at Norwalk, Connecticut and were marching on Danbury, a major Continental Army supply depot, torching towns as they went. Arnold mustered around 500 local volunteers and this small force harried the retreating British force. During one skirmish, Arnold's horse fell on him, again injuring his leg.

Back in Philadelphia, Arnold assumed command of the forces there, but his position was once more usurped when the Continental Congress appointed Major General Thomas Mifflin as commander, in preference to him. Furious at once again being overlooked, he resigned his commission, but only temporarily. General George Washington had him appointed to the north again, where Fort Ticonderoga had fallen to the British.

The Saratoga Campaign in 1777, culminating in the decisive Battle of Bemis Heights, marked the critical point of the American War of Independence and Benedict Arnold distinguished himself in several of these battles, especially at Bemis Heights where he was wounded. Surgeons decided to amputate his left leg but, knowing that would be the end of his military career, he refused to allow it. With that leg now two inches shorter than the right, he spent the winter recovering at Valley Forge.

In June 1778, the same month that the French critically decided to ally themselves with the settlers, Benedict Arnold was made commander of the military forces in Philadelphia. However, he was very bitter about being passed over so many times for promotion. Plus, he was out of pocket, having funded the expenses of the Canadian invasion with his own money; expenditure for which the Congressional Congress refused to reimburse him.

In Philadelphia he threw grand parties and added to his debts. Congress began to become suspicious and launched an enquiry into his affairs, paying particular attention to some questionable financial dealings in which he was involved. An officer, whom he had stripped of his command at Ticonderoga, saw an opportunity to extract revenge and laid corruption charges against him. Arnold was summoned to a court martial, but they were unable to prove the corruption. Instead, he was convicted merely of two misdemeanours.

In July 1780 he took command of the fort at West Point but by this time, disillusioned by his unfair treatment, he was in touch with both Sir Henry Clinton, commander-in-chief of the British forces in North America and prominent Loyalist, Beverley Robinson. Arnold's second wife, Peggy Shippen, was a Loyalist and a friend of Major John André, head of British Secret Intelligence. With André acting as go-between, Arnold told Clinton he would hand over West Point in exchange for £20,300 and the rank of brigadier. He knew the British would be eager to accept his offer as West Point was of key strategic importance. Its location made it difficult for British ships to travel northwards from New York up the Hudson to meet up with British forces in Canada. In British hands it would separate the north from the south; effectively, and possibly decisively, cutting America in two.

On 20 September, André travelled along the Hudson on the warship, *Vulture*. He rowed ashore at a place called Stony Point to meet Arnold. But, as dawn came up, the Americans began to fire on *Vulture* and she was forced to set sail, abandoning André. Arnold supplied him with a disguise and a passport to help him escape, providing him also with six documents, in his own hand, describing how West Point could be captured. These André hid in his stocking.

On the morning of 23 September, the British major was stopped by three armed robbers – John Paulding, Isaac Van Wart and David Williams. When they discovered he was a British army officer, they immediately took him prisoner and searched him, finding Arnold's papers in his stocking. He was detained at the American Army headquarters at Tappan where Washington convened a tribunal of senior officers to investigate the incident. Needless to say, André was found guilty of spying and sentenced to hang. Meanwhile Arnold, hearing what had happened, and fearing imminent arrest, fled from West Point to the British lines. Sir Henry Clinton refused to hand him over to the Americans in exchange for André and the British officer was executed on 2 October 1780.

Arnold was given the rank of brigadier, as agreed, but, because his plan had failed, he received only a third of the money he had demanded. He did, however, receive a small annual pension.

Following his dramatic defection, Arnold fought with the British, capturing Richmond, Virginia, but in December he left the war behind, travelling to England with his wife and sons. He became involved in trade in Canada for four years, but, returning to England, was unable to obtain the military position he desired and thought he deserved.

Eventually, his war wounds caught up with him. He had gout in his left leg and suffered a great deal of pain in the other. He died of what the doctors diagnosed as dropsy, on 14 June 1801.

After his victory at Richmond for the British, Arnold had asked a captured American officer what he thought the Americans would do to him if they captured him. The officer replied that they would 'Cut off your right leg, bury it with full military honours and then hang the rest of you on a gibbet.'

JOHN WILKES BOOTH

With his jet-black hair and athletic build, he was known as 'the handsomest man in America'. An excellent swordsman, his theatrical performances were filled with energy and presence. And so they should have been. He came, after all, from an acting dynasty. His father, Junius Brutus Booth was an eminent Shakespearean actor and his mother, Mary Ann Holmes also trod the boards. They had emigrated from England to the United States in 1821 and had bought a farm in Maryland, twenty-five miles south of the Mason-Dixon Line, where their son, John Wilkes Booth, was born in 1838. He was named in honour of John Wilkes, the British revolutionary, who was said to be distantly related to them.

Shakespeare, of course, figured large in his education. He attended a local school before going to a military academy, St. Timothy's Hall, when he was thirteen. His acting career began in 1855 when he played the Earl of Richmond in William Shakespeare's *Richard III*. In 1857 he joined Wheatley's Arch Street

Theatre in Philadelphia's stock company, billed as J. B. Wilkes in an effort to carve his own niche away from the glow of his famous family. He began to build a reputation as an actor, becoming something of a star. He would play a theatre for one or two weeks at a time, performing a different play every night – a punishing routine that often involved learning lines for the next play until dawn, when he would go to the theatre for rehearsal.

He was also very wrapped up in the politics of the time, opposing the abolition of slavery. This was a view espoused by most of the white population of the south, and on 2 December 1859, when militant abolitionist, John Brown was hanged for his notorious raid on Harper's Ferry in West Virginia, Booth was there, right at the foot of the scaffold. He had enlisted in the Richmond Grays in order to see the hanging and got himself discharged shortly after. Following Lincoln's election as President in 1860, Booth expressed his support for slavery in a long speech.

When the Civil War erupted on 12 April 1861 Booth's home state of Maryland was caught in the middle. It bordered the south, but remained in the Union, even though many in the state were favourable towards slavery. The new president, Abraham Lincoln, declared martial law in Maryland

and anyone supporting secession from the Union was imprisoned.

The Booth family, like many others in Maryland, was divided, but although he was pro-Confederate, Booth's mother made him agree not to enlist. However, this did not stop him from speaking out against Lincoln as he performed across America, both in the north and the south. On one occasion, he was arrested for denouncing the government.

Of course, Lincoln being a fervent lover of the theatre, and Shakespeare in particular, actually saw Booth perform on several occasions, even watching him once, on 9 November 1863 from the box in Ford's Theatre, Washington; the same box in which Booth would later assassinate him.

Meanwhile, Booth became something of a ladies' man, and in 1861 was slashed across the face with a knife by an actress called Henrietta Irving, who was furious when she found out that Booth had no intention of marrying her.

The north had the war all but won by 1864 and Booth's frustration began to rise to the surface. He concocted a plan to kidnap Lincoln, sharing it with his friends, Arnold and Michael O'Laughlin. He would take the president while he was in residence in the summer at the Old Soldiers Home, just a few miles from the White House. Then he would smuggle him across the Potomac into Richmond. He would be ransomed by the release of 10,000 Confederate prisoners. Around this time, he also began to make the acquaintance of a number of well-known Confederate sympathisers. He met with other Confederates on a trip to Montreal in Canada in October 1864, possibly encountering the director of the Confederate Secret Service, James D. Bulloch. Nonetheless, there is no evidence that the assassination of Lincoln involved any elements of the Confederate government. He returned with a letter of introduction to Dr Samuel Mudd who would become involved with him in the assassination plot.

By the time Lincoln was re-elected in 1864, Booth was involved with a coterie of Confederate sympathisers – David Herold, George Atzerodt, John Surratt and Lewis Powell. They met at Surratt's mother's house regularly to fan the flames of their hatred for the president.

Meanwhile, Booth continued to act. In November 1864, he and his brothers Edwin and Junius, performed *Julius Caesar* at the Winter Garden in New York to raise money for a statue of Shakespeare to stand in Central Park, a statue that stands to this day. However, Confederate terrorist activity burned down a number of hotels that night, including the one next to the Winter Garden Theatre. This activity only served to heighten Booth's antagonism to the north and to Lincoln.

Booth was secretly engaged to Lucy Hale, daughter of the United States Ambassador to Spain, and it was as her guest that he attended Lincoln's second inauguration on 4 March 1865. He remarked later what a perfect opportunity he had to assassinate the president on that day.

On 17 March, Lincoln was due to attend the play, *Still Waters Run Deep*, at a hospital close to his residence at The Old Soldier's Home. This seemed like a good moment and Booth gathered his team, planning to carry out the kidnapping when the president was en route to the hospital. At the last moment, however, Lincoln changed his plans and chose not to attend the performance.

Confederate General Robert E. Lee surrendered at Appomattox Court House on 10 April 1865. Booth was devastated and announced to his associates that he was finished with the stage and from now on the only drama he wanted to present was *Venice Preserv'd*. The reference was lost on his colleagues, but *Venice Preserv'd* is actually a play about an assassination.

Next day, he watched as Lincoln made a speech

outside the White House in which he declared his support for giving the vote to former slaves. For Booth this was the last straw. He stated that this would be the last speech that Lincoln would ever make. In his diary he wrote that night: 'Our cause being almost lost, something decisive and great must be done.'

On 14 April, the newspapers announced that President and Mrs Lincoln would be attending the play *Our American Cousin* at Ford's Theatre. Booth saw his chance and started to make his plans for the assassination of the president. He organised a get-away horse to be waiting outside the theatre and told Powell, Herold and Atzerodt that he was going to kill Lincoln. In a plan designed to throw the country into tumult, he ordered Powell to assassinate Secretary of State Seward and Azterodt to kill Vice-President Johnson. These murders would cause panic through-out the Union and with the top of the government removed, give the Confederate side time to re-group and pursue the war.

Booth's career had made him a friend of many theatre owners and John T. Ford, owner of Ford's Theatre in Washington was one. Booth was able to wander the theatre at will and knew his way around it. On the day in question, he went to the theatre and bored a hole in the wall of the President's box, so that he would later that day be able to ascertain whether Lincoln had actually turned up to see the play.

It was shortly after eight when the Lincolns left for the theatre. Mary, his wife, was wearing a black and white striped silk dress and a matching bonnet and the president wore white kid gloves and a black overcoat made of wool, tailored for him by Brooks Brothers of New York. They took their seats after the play had started, but the performance stopped as the orchestra burst into a rendition of *Hail to the Chief,* in celebration of his presence. The door to the box was then closed but, crucially, not locked. Moreover, unluckily for the President, John Parker, the police guard that night, was a man reputed to be fond of a drink and, true to form, at the interval, Parker abandoned his post in the hallway that led to the President's box and walked across the road to the Taltavul's Star Saloon. When the play's third act began he was not at his post.

Mary sat very close to her husband, holding his hand. She whispered to him, 'What will Miss Harris think of my hanging on to you so?' The president replied, 'She won't think anything about it.' Miss Harris was one of the other guests in the box. It was about 10.15 p.m. and, on stage, actor Harry Hawk was saying, 'Don't know the manners of good society, eh? Well, I guess I know enough to turn you inside out, old gal – you sockdologising old mantrap!'

At this point, the door to the box opened and John Wilkes Booth stepped in, pointed a .44 calibre Derringer at the back of the president's head and pulled the trigger. As Mary screamed and reached out to her husband as he slumped forward in his seat, Booth pulled out a dagger, yelling: 'Sic semper tyrannis!' ('Thus always to tyrants'). He slashed Major Henry Rathbone's arm to the bone and then leapt from the box, catching his spur in a flag and breaking his left shin as he crashed to the stage. He managed to escape through the rear stage door and leapt onto the waiting horse and galloped away.

The unconscious Lincoln had been shot behind the left ear, the bullet tearing through that side of his brain. He was carried across the street to the Petersen House and into the room of a War Department clerk where, breathing heavily, he had to be laid on the bed diagonally as he was too tall for it.

Six surgeons were present, one of whom, a Dr Hall, announced that the President was already, to all intents and purposes, dead, but that he might live another three hours or so. Lincoln had been stripped of his clothes and his face was calm, although, after a while, his right eye began to swell and his face became discoloured.

The Speaker of the Senate and other members of the Cabinet arrived and a guard was posted at the door, as there was a large and excitable crowd gathering outside. This room, like every other room in the house was by now full to overflowing.

Every hour Mrs Lincoln would return to her husband's bedside. At around seven in the morning, she visited his bedside for the last time. Lincoln's son, Robert, stood at the head of the bed, sobbing.

At 7.22 on the morning of 15 April 1865, President Abraham Lincoln expired, still lying diagonally on a strange bed, much too small for his giant frame.

Meanwhile, Booth was being pursued by twenty-five Union soldiers commanded by Lieutenant Edward P. Docherty and Lieutenant Colonel Everton Conger. They followed his trail across the Pottomac to a farm near Port Royal in Virginia, owned by Richard Garrett. Booth had now been joined by David Herold and had been led to the farm by a former private in the 9th Virginia Cavalry, William Jett. They had met him as they crossed the Rappahannock River.

When news of Lincoln's death began to spread – the first American President to be assassinated – there was outrage and Booth was surprised by the depth of feeling. He wrote in his diary:

With every man's hand against me, I am here in despair. And why; for doing what Brutus was honoured for . . . And yet I for striking down a greater tyrant than they ever knew am looked upon as a common cutthroat.

When Jett was picked up by Lieutenant Colonel Conger, he told him of Booth's whereabouts and the soldiers arrived at the farm early in the morning of 26 April. David Herold surrendered almost immediately when they trapped the two men in a barn. Booth refused, however, and the barn was set on fire. Although it is unclear whether orders were given or not, Sergeant Boston Corbett opened fire on Booth, hitting him in the neck and fatally wounding him.

His last words were, reportedly, 'Tell my mother I did it for my country.' He then asked for both his hands to be raised to his face. His spinal chord had been severed by one of the bullets and he was paralysed. He moaned: 'Useless, useless,' and died as the sun came up. He was twenty-six years old.

It took a while to bury Booth. He was firstly taken to the ship USS *Montauk* at the Washington Navy

Yard for an autopsy to be carried out and for the body to be identified. He was then abandoned in a storage room at the Old Penitentiary at the Washington Arsenal, where he remained until the prison was demolished in 1867. He was then moved to a warehouse at the Arsenal before finally being released to the Booth family for burial in the family plot at Greenmount Cemetery in Baltimore in 1869.

Following his death, there were a number of stories that he had not actually been killed and had, in fact, escaped. A man called Finis L. Bates claimed to have met Booth in Texas in the 1870s and that Booth had actually committed suicide in Oklahoma in 1903. He also claimed to have Booth's body and he toured American sideshows with it for many years, as well as writing a book entitled *The Escape and Suicide of John Wilkes Booth*.

Another book, *The Lincoln Conspiracy* claims that Booth escaped to the swamps and *The Curse of Cain* suggests that he escaped to Japan, returning to the United States and killing himself, as in Bates's story, in Enid, Oklahoma in 1903. A man claiming to be Booth was reported to be living in the 1900s in Missouri.

A recent attempt to have his body exhumed so that studies can be carried out was firmly blocked by the courts.

AARON BURR

Remembered today for a treason he may or may not have committed and a duel he probably did not want, Aaron Burr straddles the early years of the fledgling United States as one of its most extraordinary creators. He was a hero of the American War of Independence, a New York State Attorney General, a senator and came within a hairsbreadth of becoming the third President of the United States, losing out only after a remarkable thirty-six ballots to Thomas Jefferson, but serving a term as his Vice President.

Burr was born in 1756 in Newark, son of the Reverend Aaron Burr Snr, a Presbyterian minister and President of the College of New Jersey, later known as Princeton University. His mother was the daughter of a famous Calvinist theologian, Jonathan Edwards. Having taken a theology degree at Princeton, Burr Jr switched to the study of law in Connecticut, but he interrupted his studies to enlist in the army that was fighting the Revolutionary War against the British, marching an extraordinary 500 miles with General Benedict Arnold's expedition into Canada. Burr fulfilled an important role in the battles to take Montreal and Quebec and became something of a national hero.

His reward was a position on George Washington's staff in Manhattan, but Burr longed for action and resigned after only a couple of weeks. He joined General Israel Putnam and again distinguished himself, at one point preventing the capture of an entire regiment. He was angry not to receive a commendation for this particular action from Washington and his relationship with the first President of the United States never really recovered.

By July 1777, Burr was a lieutenant colonel, leading a regiment under the overall command of Colonel William Malcolm in New Jersey, fending off nocturnal attacks by the British. He suffered a reversal in the Battle of Monmouth in June 1778, when his regiment was badly beaten and he suffered a stroke in the terrible heat. However, the next January saw him in Westchester County, where he rigorously imposed martial law and restored order in an area rife with lawlessness before his arrival.

Following his stroke, however, his health was not

good and he resigned from the Continental Army to resume his studies in March 1779, being admitted to the bar at Albany in 1782. The following year, after the British had withdrawn from New York City, he began to practise there, now married to Theodosia Bartow Prevost who would die twelve years later, leaving him with one daughter, also named Theodosia.

Burr's attitude to women was demonstrated in the way he brought up his daughter. He believed that women were the intellectual equal of men and was a devoted advocate of education for women and, during his time on the New York Legislature, even introduced a bill to give women the vote. Theodosia was taught dance, music, languages as well as how to shoot on horseback. Tellingly, a portrait of the proto-feminist, Mary Wollestoncraft, hung in his house.

In 1784, Burr was elected onto the New York State Assembly and, in 1789, he was appointed Attorney General of New York State, his first serious political office. In 1791 he beat the incumbent General Philip Schuyler to the United States Senate. He would remain a senator until 1797.

Burr's defeat of Schuyler had antagonised another political activist, Alexander Hamilton, Schuyler's son-in-law. From then on, their relationship, which had once been good, deteriorated until it imploded ten years later with tragic consequences for both men.

Burr's relationship with George Washington had never recovered from its early setbacks and Burr was disappointed when Washington rejected his request for permission to write a history of the American Revolution. When he also rejected Burr's request to be given a brigadier's commission in the struggle against the French, Burr was devastated. It is probably no coincidence, however, that Alexander Hamilton whose dislike of Burr had by now turned to downright hatred, was at this time close to Washington.

Now part of the New York State legislature, Burr threw himself into the world of New York politics, associating himself with the Democratic-Republicans. He played a critical role in ensuring Thomas Jefferson performed well in New York in his attempt to become President but the rival candidature was championed by Alexander Hamilton and when he lost, the relationship between him and Burr deteriorated still further.

Burr tied with Jefferson at 73 votes each in the eventual 1800 Presidential election. Thirty-six ballots later, a compromise was found and Jefferson became President, while Aaron Burr was appointed Vice President. Throughout the election process, Burr had stated that he wanted Jefferson to be president and he did little to secure his own election, not even leaving Albany at any point during the process. Meanwhile, Alexander Hamilton was constantly working against him.

Jefferson did not want Burr to stand with him in the 1804 election and Burr, instead, launched a campaign to become Governor of New York. He lost, however, blaming his defeat partly on the actions of Alexander Hamilton, who ran a damaging smear campaign against the former Vice President. Burr had by now become tired of Hamilton's statements about him and demanded that he withdraw what he had been saying about him for the last fifteen years. When Hamilton refused, Burr did the only thing he could to maintain his honour – he challenged him to a duel; something not entirely alien to Hamilton, who had already fought twenty-one duels. In fact, one of his sons had been killed in a duel four years earlier.

Duelling being against the law in New York, the two men faced each other on 11 July 1804, outside Weehawken in New Jersey. There are conflicting stories as to what actually happened that day, but the facts are that Hamilton missed with his shot and Burr hit his opponent in the abdomen. Hamilton died from his wound the following day and Burr fled. Although he was charged with a number of crimes, including murder, he was never arrested or brought to trial, eventually returning to Washington to see out what little time remained of his Vice Presidential term.

No longer Vice President, in March 1805, he travelled to Philadelphia and it is there, in collusion with a university friend, Jonathan Drayton, that he is said to have framed the conspiracy that would make him a traitor in the eyes of many Americans, although many historians remain unconvinced as to the truth of the matter. He is accused of plotting to create a massive new nation in America's southwest, incorporating captured Mexican territories and land west of the Appalachian Mountains. The greatest fear was that if this were to happen, America would inevitably descend into all-out civil war.

They were, indeed, fragile times. Spain controlled Mexico, the vast tracts in the southwest and California. The Mexicans wanted to overthrow the Spanish and take control of their own country and the Americans sat waiting in the wings to pick up whatever it could in the event of revolt or war. In the midst of this were the French, Spanish, Indians and disgruntled Americans who lived in the territory known as the Louisiana Purchase, not yet a part of the United States and ripe for the taking, although Burr and his fellow conspirators denied that it was part of their plans to capture it.

Burr had leased 40,000 acres in the Texas part of Mexico, from the Spanish government. He claimed that once settled there with a community of farmers and other settlers, he would have an army available and should war break out, he would use that army to fight for the land and claim it for himself. The war did not come in time for him to carry out his plan, however. It broke out the day he died in 1836.

Involved with Burr in the conspiracy was General James Wilkinson, Governor of the Louisiana Territory and a man who, it was later discovered, was actually in the pay of the Spanish government. Anglo-Irish aristocrat, Harman Blennerhassett agreed to help with the financing of Burr's aspirations. He owned an island on the Ohio River where he had a magnificent house containing a scientific laboratory.

Meanwhile, throughout 1806 'Burr fever' swept the West. Newspapers published reports that he was plotting something; anonymous informants contacted President Jefferson, some claiming Burr was going to invade Washington D.C. Other rumours suggested that he was planning to raise a Native American militia, or buy weapons from a corrupt army fort. Burr did, in fact, write injudicious letters to Wilkinson, referring to 'things improper to letter.'

It was Wilkinson who finally betrayed Burr's

ambitions to President Jefferson as well as to his Spanish paymasters. Throughout most of 1806, the President seems to have mulled it over before finally issuing a warrant for his former Vice President's arrest. Jefferson jumped the gun by declaring Burr a traitor even before he was arrested and tried, biasing any investigation from the start. The first Burr heard of it was when he picked up a newspaper in the Orleans Territory in January, 1807. With federal agents on his trail, he handed himself over to the authorities twice, but each time a judge declared that there was nothing illegal in what he was doing and he was released from custody.

His boats were searched for weapons around this time, as was Blennerhassett's island, but none were found, casting doubts on the assertions that he was about to claim 2.5 million acres of American and Spanish territory.

On 19 February, while he was on his way to Spanish Florida, he was arrested and taken to Fort Stoddert. His incarceration there was initially not difficult and he socialised with the fort's commander and his family. However, damning evidence was soon revealed that changed his position. A secret correspondence was discovered between him and Anthony Merry, the British Ambassador in Washington and the Marquis of Casa Yrujo, the Spanish equivalent. This correspondence revealed that Burr wanted to overthrow the Spanish in the southwest and to found an empire in the former Mexican territory. Merry said that Burr wanted 'to effect a Separation of the Western Part of the United States.' Burr, he claimed, had even requested that the Royal Navy seize the Mississippi during his takeover.

This was not the first time such a venture had been planned. Men such as George Rogers Clark and William Blount had already put together similar expeditions and these were now prevented by law, under the Neutrality Act. However, although Burr's crime was nothing more than a misdemeanour, Jefferson pushed for him to be charged with the much more serious offence of treason.

In 1807, Aaron Burr was taken east in a cage after repeatedly trying to escape from custody and put on trial before the United States Circuit Court at Richmond, Virginia, defended by John Wickham and Luther Martin. Four times he had been arraigned before a grand jury finally indicted him. The only evidence was a somewhat laughable letter that Wilkinson had offered. The letter which was claimed to have been written by Burr, stated that he planned to steal land in the Louisiana Purchase. What made the letter so ridiculous was that it was in Wilkinson's own handwriting. He said he had made a copy because he had lost the original. It was laughed out of court.

The trial, presided over by the United States Chief Justice, John Marshall, opened on 3 August and was watched by numerous well-known people, from Andrew Jackson to Washington Irving. In spite of the fact that the prosecution offered 140 witnesses, most of their evidence was purely hearsay. In addition, the United States Constitution states that for a successful treason conviction, it either has to be admitted by the defendant in open court or proved by an act witnessed by two people. Neither happened in this case. Burr did not confess and there were no witnesses. On 1 September, he was acquitted, to the great disappointment of President Jefferson. When they then tried to convict him on the lesser misdemeanour charge, he was acquitted once again.

Although it seems unlikely that Burr was planning anything more than an invasion of Mexico – he had confessed as much to future president, Andrew Jackson – that was not a treasonable act in itself. However, it was a dangerous plan. The young republic would have been inevitably drawn into a damaging war with Spain and probably France, too, undoing all Jefferson's hard work in maintaining

America's neutrality during the Napoleonic wars.

However, it had been a personal and professional disaster for Burr. Although acquitted, his reputation lay in tatters and there was no chance now of him pursuing any political ambitions in America. Coupled with this was the fact that he was seriously in debt. He fled to Europe, staying there for four years until 1812. While living in London, he befriended the English Utilitarian philosopher, Jeremy Bentham, and travelled extensively to Scotland, Denmark, Sweden, Germany and France. He had still not given up on his ambitions for Mexico and tried repeatedly, but without much success, to raise funds for the venture. Expelled from England, he tried to meet with Napoleon Bonaparte in France, but the great man refused to see him. He returned to the United States, living under the name of Edwards, his mother's maiden name, in order to avoid his creditors.

Finally, in 1834, he had a stroke and was severely incapacitated. He died two years later, aged 80, on Staten Island, and was buried in Princeton Cemetery.

Perhaps Aaron Burr's greatest failing was that he never publicly defended himself or wrote his own version of events for history to judge him. Late in his life he wrote: 'I fear I have committed a great error; the men who knew their falsity are dead, and the generation who now read them may take them for truths, being uncontradicted.'

ZEBULON PIKE

He may have died at the early age of thirty-four, but Zebulon Montgomery Pike Jr's short life can only be described as astonishing. As Donald Jackson, the editor of Pike's letters and journals, wrote: 'Nothing that Zebulon Montgomery Pike ever tried to do was easy, and most of his luck was bad.'

He is a man often remembered merely as a second-rate Meriwether Lewis or William Clark, the explorers who in the early 19th century opened up much of America with their explorations, or for Pike's Peak in Colorado, the mountain that is named for him, but on which he never set foot. But Pike was a great deal more than that. He was a great patriot who worshipped his flag and his country, a determined military commander, a tough outdoorsman, an inspirational leader of men and, above all, a valuable and daring spy for the United States.

He was born into the army life, brought up on a series of Midwestern army posts where his father was stationed. In 1794, aged just fifteen, he enlisted in his father's regiment as a cadet and five years later had risen through the ranks to lieutenant. Reportedly a zealous officer, he was known to lie in wait for his men in bushes outside the fort, trying to catch them drunk. He married in 1801, but his army career was unremarkable until he was picked out by General James Wilkinson, Governor of the Upper Louisiana Territory. Wilkinson, a man later found to be spying for the Spanish and mixed up in Aaron Burr's conspiracy in the southwest of the country, ordered Pike to mount an expedition to locate the source of the Mississippi River.

Setting off from Fort Bellefontaine in August 1805, Pike's mission was also to curtail the illicit fur trade in the north of the Territory, to purchase sites for the building of military posts and to bring back Indian chiefs with whom Wilkinson could hold talks. Whereas the expedition of Lewis and Clark had the distinct aim of finding a practical water route to the Pacific and to establish a fur trading business with northern Indian tribes, Pike's expedition was less organised. Meriwether Lewis was trained to observe flora and fauna as well as Indian customs and culture en route, and had knowledge of cartography and geology. Pike left with twenty men on a seventy-foot boat without a great deal of preparation. There was no one in the expedition who could translate the Indian languages they would encounter, there was no doctor and little in the way of the type of scientific equipment necessary for such an expedition.

Switching to a couple of barges at Priarie du Chien, they met a group of Dakota Indians at the junction of the Mississippi and Missouri rivers and Pike enjoyed some early success when he purchased 155,000 acres of land on which to build a military post. Even more satisfying was the fact that the land was purchased on credit. Eventually, three years later, the Indians received the payment for their land, a mere $2,000. The military post, Fort Snelling was finally constructed in 1819.

Winter hit the expedition hard and the men began to fall ill. Pike divided the party in two, leaving a group behind and proceeding with the others carrying supplies on sleds. They encountered numerous British trading posts and, although these saved Pike and his men from starvation and death, ever the zealous patriot, Pike, informed the British that they were on American soil and ordered them to take down their Union Jacks and leave.

The expedition returned to St. Louis at the end of April 1806 and it had not been successful. They had failed to find the source of the Mississippi, had only moderate success in trying to bring a halt to the illicit fur trade and, in spite of meeting a number of Indian chiefs, Pike had not been able to persuade any of them to travel back to St. Louis to meet Wilkinson.

Wilkinson's immediate reaction was to order Pike to undertake a second expedition. He had barely had time to draw breath.

This expedition was, ostensibly, to escort some Osage Indians back to their homes in the southwest, negotiate a peace treaty between the Kansas and Pawnee tribes and attempt to establish contact with the Commanches who lived on the high plains. Wilkinson also instructed him to explore the Akansas River. The real mission, however, was to find out as much as possible about the what the Spanish were up to on the south-western border of their territories and the United States. And he was to do it without anyone knowing. As Wilkinson wrote, he should 'move with great circumspect, to keep clear of any hunting or reconnoitring parties from that province and to prevent alarm or offense'. It was understood that he was to disguise his men as traders in order to gain information about troop deployments and designs and locations of forts. Neither President Thomas Jefferson nor the War Department had any knowledge of the expedition and had they known they would have been concerned. Tensions were high along the border and many thought that it would not be long before war broke out between the Spanish and the Americans.

Why Wilkinson was ordering such an expedition is unclear to this day. It is thought that it must have been connected to his plan with former American Vice President, Aaron Burr, to separate the American west from the rest of the country and establish another nation there. Knowledge of what lay beyond the Arkansas River was sparse and Pike's expedition would provide valuable intelligence to Wilkinson and Burr.

Spain, on the other hand, jealously guarded its territory. The silver mines of Zacatecas that lay beyond the border were a source of wealth that they wanted to safeguard. In command of the area was Nemesio Salcedo, commandant-general of the Internal Provinces of New Spain. He was assigned to prevent America's westward expansion. Double agent Wilkinson alerted his Spanish paymasters to the fact that Pike's expedition would be passing through their territory.

Pike was completely unaware of what Wilkinson and Burr had been plotting, but from his letters, it is obvious that he was fully aware of the need for him to carry out espionage duties during this expedition. Wilkinson had ordered him to scout as close as possible to the Spanish town of Santa Fe and to be prepared to be captured. In that event, he was to claim to be lost.

He set out in mid-July, 1806, with seventeen men from his previous expedition, two new volunteers, Lieutenant James Biddle Wilkinson, General Wilkinson's son, as second-in-command, a doctor and Baronet Vasquez, as interpreter. Once again, the party was desperately unprepared. Their clothing was unsuitable for the harsh weather they were likely to encounter, they had too few horses, poor maps and again little in the way of scientific equipment.

They stayed with the Osage Indians on the Missouri River for a short while before heading out across the plains of Kansas. Meeting a tribe of Pawnee Indians, they learned that a Spanish expedition was out looking for them, news that Pike seemed pleased to hear, encouraging the view that he wanted to be captured so that he could gain entry to the Spanish Territory. They actually followed the Spanish detachment's trail on leaving the Indian village.

They travelled due south, reaching the Arkansas River where a group led by Wilkinson's son, separated from the main group and set off in canoes to explore the lower reaches of the river. Pike led the remainder up the river, still following the Spanish, even as the weather deteriorated through November.

In late November, they arrived at modern-day Pueblo in Colorado, a location that offered a view of a spectacular peak in the distance. Pike took a few of his men and set out to explore the peak, but it proved too far away and too difficult to get to. After climbing for several days, up to their waists in snow while wearing what was effectively summer clothing, they abandoned the attempt and returned to the main party. Even though he never even managed to get to the base of the 14,110 foot high mountain, it is now known as Pike's Peak in his memory.

They now explored the Arkansas River, but by this time were very short of food and the men were suffering terribly from the horrific cold. They no longer had any blankets, having been forced to convert them to socks, theirs having worn out. The ice on the river was thick enough to support their horses and they worked their way down it, but the source of the river seemed further away than ever. They would have to make a dangerous and difficult traverse of the mountains to reach their next objective, the Red River.

On 17 January 1807, Pike and all except Vasquez

and a private who were left behind to look after the horses, set out in a raging blizzard to find the Red River. Soon nine of the fourteen men had frostbitten feet and three had to be left behind. They crossed the Sangre de Cristo Mountains, barely surviving and unable to hunt. When the men began to complain, Pike told them that if they persisted they would be shot.

Arriving at the headwaters of the Rio Grande, Pike mistakenly presumed it to be the Red River and on 1 February, they constructed a small fort.

Doctor Robinson, the expedition's physician, had some business to attend to in Santa Fe and was given permission to leave the group and hike overland to the Spanish town. Unfortunately, although he told the Spanish Governor, Alencaster when he arrived, that he had been with a hunting party, the Governor immediately became suspicious and sent patrols out to search for Pike's men.

Meanwhile, the members of Pike's party who had been left because of their frostbite, were undergoing a horrific experience in the extreme weather. They were too sick to move and feared he would leave them behind. In an effort to persuade him not to abandon them, they sent pieces of their own gangrenous toe bones back to him.

When the Spanish eventually found Pike and his

men on 26 February, he feigned surprise, claiming that he thought he was at the Red River. They informed him he was on Spanish territory, which was, of course, exactly where he wanted to be.

By this time, the Americans must have been quite a sight. Their clothing had long since fallen into tatters and they looked like mountain men, heavily bearded and wearing furs from the animals they had hunted.

They were taken to Santa Fe where Pike's mission now began in earnest. It was decided to take them to Chihuahua, and as they marched on the long journey south, he memorised everything he saw along the route – forts, garrisons and villages. He spoke to priests and officials, gathering even more intelligence. Amazingly, no one even seemed to realise what he was up to and they made no effort to prevent him from making written notes.

The Spanish began to realise the truth of Pike's mission, but they were reluctant to upset the United States too much. There was little enthusiasm for a war that could do nothing but damage Spanish interests. Consequently, Governor Salcedo gave orders for Pike and his men to be escorted to the border and set free. On the march north Pike again made notes, but more covertly this time, hiding them in the barrels of his men's rifles. Spain had sent a note of protest to Washington, demanding an apology for the incursion into Spanish territory, but Secretary of State, James Madison, denied that Pike had been spying for the United States, claiming he was nothing more than an explorer. Nonetheless, diplomatic relations were broken off and Governor Alencaster was removed from office for releasing Pike too quickly and allowing him to travel further into Spanish territory.

Back home, because of his association with Wilkinson, Pike became implicated in the Burr affair, although he had nothing to do with it. His name was officially cleared, however, when Secretary of War, Henry Dearborn, made a formal statement. However, to his great disappointment, Pike was not treated as a returning hero by his president or his country. Unlike Lewis and Clark's men, neither Pike nor his men received extra pay or land for what they had done. He simply returned to his day-job as an officer in the United States army, promoted to the rank of major in 1810 and colonel in 1812. He published *An Account of Expeditions to the Sources of the Mississippi and Through the Western Parts of Louisiana,* but it was a poor, badly written version of his adventure. Even so, Pike's bad luck prevailed – the publisher went bankrupt and he received no royalties.

In the 1812 war with Great Britain, Pike was a brigadier-general. He was ordered to attack the town of York, capital of Upper Canada, which had a garrison of 800 men with his force of 1,700 troops. On 27 April he led the assault. However, the British had constructed a huge landmine and hidden it on the outskirts of the city. They lured the Americans to its site but it detonated prematurely, killing almost as many British troops as it did Americans. Pike's bad luck returned. A large rock blown into the air by the explosion struck him in the back, killing him.

It would have been no real surprise to the pragmatic and undoubtedly courageous Zebulon Montgomery Pike. Not long before, he had written to his father: 'If we go into Canada, you will hear of my fame or of my death – for I am determined to seek the "Bubble" even in the cannon's mouth.'

VIDKUN QUISLING

It was *The Times* who first coined the word, just ten days after he had seized power in Norway following the German invasion of that country:

> *To writers, the word quisling is a gift from the gods. If they had been ordered to invent a new word for traitor they could hardly have hit upon a more brilliant combination of letters.*

Soon, it caught on, especially in that time after the war when betrayal was shown to have been a common currency during the fighting.

Betrayal, however, was second nature to Norwegian politician, Vidkun Abraham Lauritz Jonssøn Quisling, and not only in his political life. In 1922, when he was thirty-five years old, he fell for a seventeen-year-old Ukranian girl called Alexandra. The pair married, but next year, he met and fell in love with another woman, Maria. He married her as well and, bizarrely, explained away his first wife by claiming she was their adopted daughter. A short while later, he divested himself of any potential embarrassment by sending poor Alexandra to France.

Although he sounds like a fool, the socially inept and diffident Quisling, was the possessor of a brilliant mind. His speciality was mathematics and a proof he found while still a high school student made its way into textbooks. He also graduated from the Norwegian War Academy in 1911 as its best ever cadet, the first for a century to earn a royal citation. In the army he rapidly rose through the ranks, becoming a major. He could speak Russian fluently, using it to good effect when he served as a diplomat and as an aide to Fritjof Nansen, the great Norwegian explorer who became a diplomat and League of Nations High Commissioner. Quisling helped Nansen in his work with Russian peasants in the Soviet Union during the great Russian famine.

Quisling was born into a distinguished family background and he enjoyed success in the first part of his life. For his work in Russia, when he looked after British interests following the cessation of diplomatic relations between the Bolsheviks and Britain, he was even awarded the CBE by the British government. This honour was subsequently revoked in 1940.

He thought of himself as a visionary and, in a project he had taken on while still a boy, had more or less devised an entire philosophy by 1929. The task of writing the book, which was eventually published in 2006, was described by him as 'the greatest which a human being can set himself; namely to ignite a new light for humankind'. It would provide, he went on 'a unitary conception of existence that all will comprehend, and all gather around, so life can once again be lived with united forces.' He called his philosophy 'Universism' but it is nothing more than an amateurish melange of borrowed ideas from numerous philosophies and systems of living, from Taoism to Martin Luther, Neitzche to Schopenhauer. En route, it took in the usual fascist dogma – the superiority of the male over the female, individual will only finding true expression through subjugation to the communal will of society and the purity of one race over another, the Nordic race over the Jewish race.

Returning from Russia, Quisling served as Minister of Defence in the Agrarian Party government, but in 1933, he was dismissed after controversially sending in the army to deal with a strike. His reaction was to found, on 17 May 1933, Norwegian Constitution Day, his very own political party, the fascist Nasjonal Samling (National Union) party, with lawyer, Johan

Bernhard Hjort. Its structure adopted the Führerprinzip, along the lines of Germany's Nazi Party. Quisling, ever willing to aggrandise himself, assumed the title of *Fører*, the Norwegian equivalent of *Führer*. The party adopted the symbol of an encircled St. Olaf's Cross against a red background and consisted of a number of sections. Apart from the National Organisation, there were the NS Kvinne-organisasjon for women; the NS Kamporganisasjon, which was the party's combat wing; the NS Ungdoms-Fylking, which was for young people and the Hird, a paramilitary organisation of about 8,500 members, organised in the same way as the Nazi *Sturmabteilungs* or stormtroopers. He and his party frequently purloined words and symbols from the old Norse Viking era and the *Hird* was the term for royal bodyguards in those days.

In the election of 1933, Nasjonal Samling gained 27,850 votes, around 2% of the total votes cast, with the aid of the Norwegian Farmers' Aid Association who were close to Quisling from his days as a member of the Agrarian Party. It still did not win a single seat in parliament, however.

In 1935, it began to evolve from being a party with its roots in religion and with the support of the Norwegian Church to one with more Nazi sympathies and a clear anti-semitic policy. There was little by way of a foreign policy, although Quisling did attend the Italian sponsored International Fascists Convention in Montreaux in 1935 along with fellow fascists such as Anton Mussert, Frits Clausen and Oswald Mosley.

But Quisling saw himself as a prophet, rarely participating in debates and mainly communicating in writing. This resulted in a party that filled its leadership void with intrigue and in-fighting, leading to a lack of effectiveness. This coupled with its growing extremism, won it even fewer votes than ever in the 1936 election. By then, it was estimated that it had a membership of only around 2,000.

Norway had remained neutral during the First World War, and wanted to do so during the Second World War. However, on 9 April 1940, Germany launched Operation Weserübung, a surprise attack on Norway, by air and sea, although resistance continued for two months which was longer than any other country invaded by the Germans, apart from the Soviet Union. The Germans planned to capture King Haakon VII and the government of Johan Nygaardsvold who had been Prime Minister since 1935. Quisling, who been active in Berlin in encouraging a German invasion, would then be installed as Prime

Minister of a puppet government. Quisling could not wait, however. He and some henchmen broke into the studios of the Norwegian Broadcasting Corporation, taking advantage of the confusion and panic caused by the Nazi invasion and he announced on air that he was taking over the government, becoming the first politician in history to announce a coup d'état on the radio. But the king refused to recognise Quisling's government and escaped with his ministers to form a government in exile, in Rotherhithe in London. In reaction to Quisling's announcement, thousands took to the streets in Norway's second-largest city, Bergen, chanting 'Down with the traitor!' and the Wehrmacht began to report to Berlin that the Norwegian people's hatred for Quisling was making the occupation more difficult to manage. Hitler's enthusiasm for Quisling waned and he was reduced once more to merely leading just the 2,000 members of his party.

Later that same month, however, Quisling again tried to form a government, under the control of hated Nazi bully, Josef Terboven, who had been appointed Reichskommissar, reporting directly to the Führer. Even the Nazis hated Terboven, a fan of mass executions who, on one occasion, had suggested that 10,000 Norwegians be shot as a reprisal for the sabotage being carried out on a regular basis. Inevitably, no prominent Norwegian was willing to serve in this madman's government. Desperate to have a Norwegian in government, the Nazi despot had little option but to abolish the Norwegian monarchy and install the loathed Quisling as head of state, with the title of Minister President on 1 February 1942.

Quisling would grow to hate being answerable to Terboven, repeatedly lobbying Hitler for Norway to be made independent, pleading during a visit to Berlin in January 1944, for Terboven to be recalled to Germany. The Führer, however, was having none of it.

Meanwhile, in classic Fascist leader style, Quisling's megalomania was given free rein. He usurped the royal castle for his offices as soon as Haakon had vacated it, even sitting in the king's chair. He took as his residence a 46-roomed mansion situated on a peninsula on the Oslo Fjord. He looted the Norwegian National Gallery for art and decorated the walls of his villa with, re-naming it 'Gimle', the place in Norse mythology where survivors would live after Ragnarok, the final battle before the destruction of the world. It is now a holocaust museum. Ridiculously, he began to claim that he could trace his Northern Germanic chieftain lineage right back to Odin, the main Norse god.

In January 1945, Quisling was the last foreign visitor to meet Hitler before his suicide in his bunker in Berlin in April of that year. Then, to the delight of the Norwegian people, on 8 May, Quisling handed himself over to the authorities. Along with two other high-ranking Nasjonal Samling leaders, Albert Viljam Hagelin and Ragnar Skancke, he was convicted of high treason, illegal change of constitution and complicity in murder. These charges arose from his unconstitutional seizure of power in 1942, his revocation of the order for mobilisation in Norway after the German invasion, his exhortation to Norwegians to serve in the Norwegian Division of the SS, and his complicity in the deportation of Norwegian Jews and the murder of Norwegian patriots.

The Norwegian government had, controversially, introduced the death penalty for certain charges shortly after the war, in anticipation of trials of war criminals and Quisling was the main victim of this change in the law. He was sentenced to death by firing squad. A good job, too, as it was reported that his prison guards at the Akershus fortress where he was held during his trial, had sworn that if he was not sentenced to death, they would kill him, anyway.

On 24 October 1945, Vidkun Quisling was blind-folded and put against a wall. Ten enthusiastic volunteers raised their rifles and, on command, shot him.

He had been confident prior to his execution that what he termed his 'martyrdom' had some kind of 'deeper meaning' and that he would, as a result of it be 'more dangerous dead than alive'. Sadly for Quisling, however, the only place, where his thinking seems to have had any lasting influence apart from the Q section of the dictionary, where his name remains forever a synonym for 'traitor', is in some strange examples of the extreme Norwegian heavy metal subgenre known as Black Metal.

ALDRICH AMES

Problems were piling up for CIA agent, Rick Ames. His marriage was a mess. He fought constantly with his wife, Nan, and had taken to going on drinking sprees, often ending the night in a lonely hotel room. That all changed when, posted to the US embassy in Mexico, he started a relationship with Rosario Dupuy, an employee of the Colombian embassy. The pair would fly to Acapulco for the weekend, make love on the beach and dine in the best restaurants Mexico City had to offer. Finally, when, under pressure from Rosario, he confronted his wife with a demand for a divorce, Nan informed him that was fine, but she would take him for everything he had.

Meanwhile, Rosario was proving to be an expensive habit. She phoned her family in Colombia on a daily basis and liked to shop. By the end of 1984, Ames was $50,000 in debt. The problem was that he earned only $45,000 a year and was in way over his head. At that point, he recalled that the Soviet secret service arm, the KGB, had once offered one of his colleagues $50,000 to spy for them. He resolved to supply the Soviets with information and thus earn enough to pay off his debts and make a fresh start with Rosario.

Ames typed a note to the KGB resident agent at the Soviet embassy in Washington, in which he informed him that for $50,000 he would sell the KGB the names of three Russian officials who were spying for the USA. Later, Ames would claim that these three men were actually double agents who, although spying for the CIA, were actually still working for the KGB. In giving these names, he reasoned, he would not actually be doing any damage to either country.

Ames was perfectly placed to be a Soviet spy. On his return from Mexico, he had been promoted to the position of Counterintelligence Branch Chief in Soviet Operations. He had access to all of the CIA's Soviet cases, including the identities of all the CIA's 'human assets' currently working in the Soviet Union. He could also get his hands on information regarding Soviet citizens who were working for the CIA. It was two of these that he initially passed on – both KGB officers in Washington. Valery F. Martynov was assigned to the KGB division responsible for obtaining scientific and technical intelligence. Sergey Motorin was a major in the KGB.

The Soviet First Secretary, Sergey Chuvakhin, became Ames's contact and, one day, after the two had lunched together, he handed Ames a bag in which was the $50,000 payment.

A short while after he had provided the information, Ames was shocked when a retired Navy warrant officer, John Walker Jr., was arrested for spying. He had been making a dead letter drop when he was picked up. Ames panicked, believing, wrongly as it turned out, that Walker had been part of a tip-off from one of the men in the embassy, Motorin or Martynov, that he had identified to the Soviets as spies. He instantly felt vulnerable.

He did not hesitate to take action. He invited Chuvakhin to lunch again and handed over seven pounds of CIA intelligence reports that he had removed in his briefcase, unchallenged, from CIA headquarters. Chillingly, he also gave them the name of every 'human asset' that he knew.

Ames did this without even being asked for it by the Soviet Union. He was well aware of what the consequences would be for the twenty-five or so operatives he was handing over. At best, they would be imprisoned after brutal interrogation, and, at worst, they would suffer the fate of many traitors since Stalin's day. They would be marched into an empty room, ordered to kneel facing the wall and would be shot in the back of the head, obliterating their faces in order to make identity impossible. They would then be buried in unmarked graves and their grieving families would not be told where these were. At least ten of the people Ames identified, including Motorin and Martynov, suffered this fate and around a hundred CIA operations were compromised. He later claimed that they knew what they were getting into when they took the work and he would have been thrown in jail if one of them had found out about his activities. 'It wasn't personal,' he said. 'It was just the way the game was played.'

The KGB, under pressure from the Soviet hierarchy, began rounding up the people named by Ames and within a short time, the CIA began to wonder why its agent network in the Soviet Union was disappearing. They stubbornly refused to believe, however, that there was a mole in their midst. Every other agency in the West had been infiltrated apart from theirs and they were reluctant to admit that this was no longer the case. They put it down to a communications coup by the Russians – bugs, perhaps, or maybe they had decrypted one of the agency's secret codes.

Even if they had been persuaded that one of their agents had gone over to the other side, it is unlikely that Aldrich Hazen Ames would have been one of the first people they would have thought of. After all, he had done nothing else but work for the CIA.

Born in River Falls, Wisconsin to Rachel Aldrich and Carleton Cecil Ames in 1941, he later claimed that spying was in his blood and he may have been right. His father had worked for the CIA in Burma in the 1950s, posing as a college professor studying Burmese culture. In 1957, when Rick Ames was sixteen his family connection got him into a summer work programme run by the agency for the children of its employees. He spent the summer at the agency's secret training facility, the Farm, making fake money to be used in training exercises.

Some of his future behaviour and avoidance of the consequences of his actions perhaps began to emerge around this time. He once told a girlfriend, 'Never tell anyone your true feelings. Let them believe an illusion.'

In 1962, his father again pulled some strings when he failed to graduate from the University of Chicago. He persuaded the agency to give Rick a job and he became a case officer in the CIA's Operations Directorate, the covert branch of the agency, based at the Farm. Here, he learned to be a spy, or, as he put it, 'to lie, to cheat, deceive. You could operate in disguise, be anyone you wished.' For a character who had done badly at university mainly because he had devoted too much of his time to performing in the Drama Department, this was a godsend.

His first assignment, however, did not go well. He was sent to Ankara, capital of Turkey, where his mission was to recruit Turks as spies. He only succeeded with one individual and returned to Washington in 1972 not exactly covered in glory. His superiors were distinctly unimpressed and began to doubt that Ames had what it takes to be an effective espionage agent.

He came close to quitting, but instead was sent to the CIA's language school where he became fluent in Russian – a handy skill in those Cold War days. In 1974, he was put in charge of a Soviet diplomat, Alexander Dmitrievich Ogorodnik, who had been blackmailed into spying for the USA. When Ogorodnik was recalled to Moscow to work in the Soviet Foreign Ministry, he photographed numerous secret diplomatic cables that became so useful to the United States that Secretary of State, Henry Kissinger, had them delivered on a daily basis to his office in the White House.

Unfortunately, Ogorodnik killed himself in 1977. He had asked Ames for a lethal pill that he could swallow if he thought he had been detected. Ames gave him a pen with the pill concealed in it and when a Czech translator who happened also to be a Soviet spy, was given a job with the CIA, he exposed Ogorodnik.

Ames was next assigned to New York to handle a nuclear arms expert, Sergey Fedorenko who was part of the Soviet United Nations Delegation. Again Ames secured vital information before Fedorenko was recalled to Moscow. He had also become close friends with Fedorenko and, initially, because of their friendship, Ames did not betray him to the Soviets, but after agonising about it, he decided that he owed it to his Soviet masters and handed his name over. The Russian managed to use powerful political connections in the USSR to keep himself out of trouble. Then, a few years later, Fedorenko contacted his old friend from Canada and asked to see him. Ames organised for the Russian to be smuggled over the border and the two met for an emotional lunch during which Feorenko stated his desire to return to live in America. Ames promised to help him but, instead, betrayed him for the second time. Fedorenko succeeded in escaping for a second time and now lives in the United States.

In 1978, Ames was handling the number two man in the Soviet UN delegation, Ambassador Arkady

Nicholaevich Shevchenko. He had been spying for the United States for several years already and Ames played a big part in his defection. He also consoled Shevchenko when his wife, who had returned to the USSR under duress, 'committed suicide', as the official announcement said.

Then came Mexico City where he did not enjoy a great deal of success and became increasingly frustrated about being passed over for promotion in spite of what he considered had been the good work he had done.

Ames was sceptical about US foreign policy, especially in Nicaragua where he thought his country was being too aggressive, and he was frustrated at his lack of progress in the agency's ranks. He also disliked the way, to his mind, American presidents ignored the advice of the security agencies in order to follow their own particular political agenda. He said later that he considered the CIA to be morally corrupt, aiding the expansion of American imperial power. However, he admitted that he really became a Soviet spy for one reason and one reason only – money. '...the sad truth is that I did what I did because of the money and I can't get away from that,' he said. 'I wanted a future. I wanted what I saw we could have together. Taking the money was essential to the recreation of myself and the continuance of us as a couple.'

And there was lots of it. Rick Ames was the highest paid spy of all time. They paid him approximately $4.6 million for his information, $2.5 million at once and $2.1 million to be held in reserve in an account somewhere until he retired. He had been told they would pay him $300,000 a year and would reserve a piece of land for him in Russia for his retirement.

What did the Russians get in return for such a massive investment?

Amongst others, Dmitri Polyakov who was the highest-ranking officer in the GRU, Soviet military intelligence. In 1988, he was executed after his exposure as a United States spy by Ames.

Another big fish was Colonel Oleg Gordievsky. He was a KGB Colonel, KGB Resident-designate (rezident) and bureau chief in London. He was also a spy for MI6. Ames identified him as a spy, but MI6 managed to implement a plan to get him out of Russia. Gordievsky went for his usual jog, but succeeded in evading his KGB tails, boarding a train to the Finnish border, where he was met by British embassy cars and smuggled across the border into Finland. He was then flown to England via Norway. His wife and children were finally allowed to join him in the UK six years later, but only after extensive lobbying by the British Government, and personal entreaties by the Prime Minister Margaret Thatcher during her meetings with Russian head of state, Mikhail Gorbachev.

In the meantime, Ames passed a couple of polygraph, lie-detector, tests with flying colours. It has since been suggested that he had been trained to beat such tests and he, himself, admits that it is easy to pass them. Some say, however, that he is a socio-path and, as such, is immune to the polygraph.

In November 1986, Jeanne Vertefeuille, a fifty-four-year-old agent with thirty-two years of service with the agency was brought in to re-invigorate the investigation into the 1985 collapse of the Soviet network. She brought in twenty-nine-year-old Dan Payne, an investigator with an accounting back-ground, who immediately suggested that they take a look at agents who seemed to be inexplicably well-off.

Ames by now was completing a stay in Rome. He had put himself forward for the assignment, fearing that things might be getting a little hot in Washington. Rosario, naturally, loved the shopping and when they returned, according to one old friend, Diana Worthen, they seemed to be very wealthy. He bought a Jaguar XJ-6 that cost more than his salary of

$60,000. They purchased a house worth more than half a million dollars that was paid for in cash and his wife's monthly phone bill was $6,000.

Worthen notified the investigators and they began to have a close look at Ames's contacts with the Soviets. When someone suggested, however, that the money could have come from Rosario, who belonged to a prominent Colombian family, Diana Worthen told them that Rosario had told her that although the family were well-known in society, they were not well-off.

Payne began to discover interesting things about the Ames finances – they were spending up to $30,000 a month on credit cards but, critically, when they examined Ames's bank account, they discovered that on each occasion he had made a deposit in his bank account in 1985, he had had a meeting with Sergey Chuvakhin earlier that day. Ames had been cavalier, popping into his bank after lunch, making no effort, whatsoever, to hide the money.

Then, on 6 October 1993, an FBI agent went through the rubbish from Ames's home and found a printer ribbon which, on examination, showed several letters to his Russian handlers. With the evidence building, the FBI were given permission to break into the Ames house and plant bugs. They discovered a huge amount of evidence, including every message he had typed on the word processing programme of his computer. They also found a photograph the Russians had given him of the piece of land they had reserved for him for his retirement.

The next few weeks provided the remaining evidence they needed to nail Ames as well as to implicate Rosario. They had to move quickly as Ames was due to go abroad to attend a conference. They feared that he might take the opportunity to defect.

On 21 February 1994, he was driving out of his neighbourhood when his Jaguar was surrounded by FBI vehicles. Meanwhile, back at the house, Rosario was also arrested. There, they found dozens of designer dresses, hundreds of pairs of shoes and no fewer than half-a-dozen Rolex watches.

Ames immediately tried to do a deal, offering to tell all if they would let Rosario go free. When, the Justice Department rejected his offer, Rosario turned on Ames. It was of little help to her cause, however, and she was charged with conspiracy to commit espionage and tax evasion and sentenced to five years in prison, followed by deportation on release.

Ames was charged with providing highly classified information to the Soviet KGB and its Russian successor. In a frank admission of guilt, he told the court that he had compromised 'virtually all Soviet agents of the CIA and other American and foreign services known to me'. He also admitted to providing the USSR and Russia with 'a huge quantity of information on United States' foreign, defence and security policies.'

He got life and is in the high security US Penitentiary at Allenwood, Pennsylvania.

In cases such as his, his Russian paymasters would normally try to exchange him with someone they held in custody. Ironically, however, the KGB had no one they could exchange for him. Anyone worth swapping he had told them about and they had already killed.

More than $2 million remains in a bank account somewhere, waiting for him. It is unknown how he plans to collect it.

LORD HAW-HAW

'Jairmany calling! Jairmany calling!'

It was a strange accent. It had arrived via Brooklyn in New York, Ballinrobe in Co. Mayo, Galway and London and it crackled through the airwaves from Nazi Berlin, engendering both fear and laughter in its audience, huddled around radio sets in wartime Britain. Six million regular listeners tuned into Lord Haw Haw's *Views On the News* programme, putting up with the offensive comments about Churchill and Stalin, false reports about the progress of the war and spurious warnings of where in Britain the Luftwaffe would strike next, so that they could hear the messages he read out from British prisoners of war.

The man whose voice it was had been born William Joyce in Brooklyn, New York, in 1906 of Irish parents who, like millions of others, had emigrated to America in search of a better life. Three years later, however, the better life not having been discovered, the Joyce family had returned to Ireland, living in Ballinrobe in County Mayo. The family then moved to Galway and the young Joyce was educated at St. Ignatius College.

William Joyce showed treacherous tendencies from an early age, working as an informer for the Black and Tans, one of the two paramilitary forces created by the British in Ireland to suppress opposition during the Irish struggle for independence. He was driven around the city in a military vehicle pointing out the homes of Republican sympathisers. Of course, it was not too long before the IRA found out that he was performing this particular service and his name was put on an IRA hit list. As a result, in December 1921, the family had to flee to England.

Joyce attended London University, gaining a first class honours degree from Birkbeck College in 1927. He also became politically active, allying himself with the Conservative Party and working in the safe Tory constituency of Kensington and Chelsea. If he had behaved himself, he might even have won the nomination for that seat, but he had enjoyed an affair with a Conservative woman and the party's high-ranking officials disapproved.

A few years later, Oswald Mosley was beginning to make waves with his British Union of Fascists and in the mid-1930s, Joyce shifted his political allegiance to this party. He threw himself into the struggle wholeheartedly, indulging in fistfights and skirmishes with the Communists who regularly tried to break up the BUF rallies and meetings. In one of these battles, Joyce was slashed with a razor, leaving a scar that ran from his mouth to his right ear.

A brilliant orator who could both inspire and manipulate an audience, he rose to be Mosley's number two in the party, but in the late 1930s, left the party to found his own, the National Socialist League, eerily echoing the name of Hitler's party in Germany. Mosley later claimed he had got rid of Joyce because of his anti-semitic views and because he was attracting 'the wrong sort of people'. Indeed, Joyce was anti-Jewish and remained so throughout his life.

On 8 August 1939, with war fast approaching, the British government introduced the Emergency Powers (Defence) Act 1939. This act was introduced to enable them to implement emergency powers to prosecute the war more effectively. It contained clauses giving the government wide powers to create defence regulations which controlled almost every aspect of everyday life in the country. There were some bizarre prohibitions such as not being able to loiter on railway bridges or hang out washing in the evenings. Critically for Joyce, however, it also took steps to remove people it believed would pose a threat to security and intern them on the Isle of Man. People with extreme right-wing political views were high on the list and Joyce was one of them.

On 26 August, Joyce received a tip-off, from a pro-fascist MI5 employee, of all people, that he was about to be picked up. He fled the country and headed for the place where he felt he really belonged – Germany.

In Berlin, he found it tough to begin with and he was unable to find work. However, he had a stroke of luck when he bumped into an old contact from his BUF days, Dorothy Eckersley. She obtained for him an introduction to the Rundfunkhaus (radio centre) and there he underwent a voice test. He reportedly did the test with a heavy cold and at one point lost his voice altogether, but was taken on to do radio announcements and write scripts for German radio's English service. Lord Haw Haw's career had begun.

However, the name Lord Haw Haw was, in the beginning given to another man. The term had been coined by the *Daily Express* radio critic who wrote under the pseudonym, 'Jonah Barrington'. Lord Haw Haw had originally been the nickname of the Earl of Cardigan who had led the Charge of the Light Brigade at the Battle of Balaclava and 'Barrington' introduced it partly to reduce the impact the propaganda broadcasts would have on the British people. 'He speaks English of the haw-haw, dammit-get-out-of-my-way-variety', 'Barrington' wrote.

There were a number of broadcasters to whom Barrington could have been referring. Norman Baillie-Stewart, for instance, was a former officer in the Seaforth Highlanders who had been kicked out of the army for selling secrets to Germany in return for sexual favours and a small amount of money. He claimed to be Lord Haw Haw, and did, indeed possess the drawling upper class accent that Barrington described. But the journalist was probably referring to Wolf Mitler, a German national who had been educated in Britain and who spoke English like an upper class English gentleman, or, at least, his impression of what an upper class English gentleman would sound like. Mitler broadcast to Britain in the early weeks of the war.

It was Mitler that Joyce replaced on the airwaves after the German was moved to the Axis Sally programme where he worked with American-born Mildred Gillars. From that moment on, Joyce became the main German broadcaster in English and was known as Lord Haw Haw. He was a very effective speaker and drew a huge audience in 1939–40.

The aim of the broadcasts was to discourage and demoralise British and Amnerican troops as well as the British population at home. They regularly broadcast news of the shooting down of Allied aircraft or the sinking of Allied ships, detailing massive casualty tolls. Ironically, in some cases, these were really the only means by which people could discover the fate of friends or family who, for instance, had not returned from bombing raids over German cities.

Joyce grew in popularity with the Nazi leadership. At Christmas, he would receive a box of cigars from Propaganda Minister, Joseph Goebels and in September 1944, to his delight, he was awarded a medal by Hitler – the War Merit Cross – for his services to German broadcasting.

Joyce's threatening tone is unforgettable to anyone who heard it during those dark days. Of course, much of what he broadcast was nonsense – there was no way the Luftwaffe would have shared their nightly bombing targets with him, after all. He would advise British listeners to 'scurry into your holes like rats' to avoid the nocturnal bombardment. But although much of what he broadcast was pure fantasy, now and then, he came uncannily close to the truth. One broadcast in April 1944, in particular, set alarm bells ringing in British military intelligence when Joyce described floating pontoons in Tilbury docks. The material he described was for Mulberry harbours to be used in the D-Day landings in Normandy. The Germans, seeing them in Luftwaffe photographs, mistakenly thought they were anti-aircraft installations. If they had worked out what they really were, they would have realised that the Allies were planning to land in a location where there were no harbours which would have narrowed down the possibilities.

On another occasion, Joyce surprised fellow broadcaster, Jack O'Reilly by mentioning to him details of a spying mission to Ireland that O'Reilly was about to undertake. O'Reilly was so surprised because this mission had been organised by the SS and was top secret.

The Royal family were strictly off-limits for Joyce and when the Germans suggested the creation of a republican radio station aimed at the British Isles with the objective of destabilising the nation, Joyce was strongly opposed.

Joyce's other job at the station was to write radio scripts. He wrote for programmes such as *Workers' Challenge* that purported to be a left-wing radio station broadcasting from the East End of London, aimed at working class listeners. The programme emphasised the threat of mass unemployment and focused on social ills and there is no doubt that the British government was worried about the effect it was having on morale.

In Germany, Joyce's personal life was no less stormy than it had been in England. During the war he had married his second wife, Margaret, whom he had met at a BUF rally in the thirties. Drink played a large part in the problems of his marriage, as did the liaisons he still indulged in with other women.

Eventually, as defeat for Germany became inevitable, Joyce started drinking heavily and in his last broadcast he slurs drunkenly, praising Hitler and mourning the fact that Britain had rejected the Führer's offer of a peace settlement earlier in the war. The last words he spoke on German radio were: 'Germany will live because the people of Germany have within them the secret of life: endurance, will and purpose. Ich liebe Deutschland (I love Germany). Heil Hitler and farewell.' It was broadcast from Hamburg on 30 April 1945, the day that Hitler committed suicide in his bunker in Berlin.

There had been a plan to get him and his wife out of Germany to Ireland by U-Boat, but it was decided it would prove too dangerous. Instead, even as the news of Hitler's death was being made public, he was heading northwards with forged papers provided by the Germans. In Flensburg, close to the German border with Denmark, he hid out for four weeks, pretending to be a Dutchman, just one of the millions of displaced people all over Europe.

On 28 May 1945 while walking in some woods close to Flensburg, Joyce bumped into a couple of British army officers. They exchanged a few words and one of the officers immediately recognised Joyce's voice as being that of Lord Haw Haw, so distinctive was it. Joyce protested that he was a Dutchman and reached inside his coat for his forged papers. The two British men, thinking he was reaching for a gun, shot him in the hip.

Brought back to London, he was charged with treason, found guilty in September 1945 and sentenced to death by hanging. There was some doubt as to whether he could really be guilty of treason, given that he was American by birth, had Irish parents and had actually become a naturalised German in September 1940. It was argued, however, that when he had been trying to travel to the Nuremberg Rally in 1933, he had 'claimed and asserted the rights to British citizenship' by applying for a British passport.

When Joyce's appeal failed, there were many pleas

for clemency, but they fell on deaf ears. There were many who believed that he had come to embody Nazi Germany by virtue of his radio presence throughout the war, even more than some of the German Nazi leaders. But he continued to maintain that he had 'been guilty of no underhand or deceitful act against Britain'.

On 3 January 1946, Lord Haw Haw was taken from the condemned cell at Wandsworth prison and hanged. It was reported that as he made his way to the gallows, he smiled at the way his knees were shaking. He was thirty-nine years old and was buried in the prison cemetery before being re-interred, after a campaign by his daughter, in the New Cemetery in Galway.

ALGER HISS

The Alger Hiss case was one of the defining moments in post-war American history, creating a fault line through American intellectual life. Where people stood on Hiss's guilt or innocence of spying for the Soviet Union while employed in the U.S. State Department has been described as providing a litmus test of their politics and character. To be sympathetic to Hiss's claims of innocence put you on the side of liberal New Dealism while, to support the view that Hiss was guilty as charged, defined you as conservative and right-wing.

However, Hiss's guilt remains open to question, even half a century later. He went to his grave proclaiming his innocence and numerous books and pundits have debated the case throughout the decades since it first emerged, without the ultimate truth being revealed.

The Hiss case was also a defining moment in that it gave opportunities for advancement to some of its main progenitors. The discovery of a Communist spy at the very heart of the American government allowed Senator Joseph McCarthy to use the atmosphere of hysteria about 'reds under the bed' to launch his campaign – some described it as a 'witch-hunt' – to find Communist sympathisers. Richard Nixon, a member of the House Committee on Unamerican Activities (HUAC) that famously ruined the careers of many people employed in the film industry, came to prominence through the Hiss case, which he pursued zealously and used as a springboard to a seat in the Senate. Within a few years, he was Vice-President to Dwight D. Eisenhower and, of course, he became President of the United States in 1969.

For Alger Hiss, of course, it was the end of a promising and rewarding career. However, native-born, well-educated, patrician and well-connected in government circles, Hiss was far removed from the stereotype Communist spy.

Born in Maryland in 1904, his early life had been overshadowed by tragedy. His father, a grocer, committed suicide two years after Alger's birth and he lost a brother to Bright's Disease when he was twenty-two. Just three years later, his sister, Mary Ann, also took her own life. He earned a law degree from Harvard Law School 1929 and in the same year, married the former Mrs Priscilla Hobson. At law school, he was a protégé of future Supreme Court judge, Felix Frankfurter and also served as a clerk for one of the Supreme Court's most famous justices, Oliver Wendell Holmes.

He started working for President Roosevelt's government as an attorney in 1933, starting in the Agricultural Adjustment Administration (AAA). He served on the Nye Committee, looking into the munitions industry, and then worked in the Justice Department. He moved into the State Department in 1936. In 1944, he attended the Dumbarton Oaks Conference which was responsible for laying the groundwork for the United Nations. In 1945, he attended the Yalta Conference, the meeting of Roosevelt, Winston Churchill and Joseph Stalin, that would establish the make-up of Europe after the war. He served as temporary secretary general of the United Nations when it was founded and in 1947, left the government and became president of the charitable foundation, the Carnegie Endowment for International Peace.

Alger Hiss first found out that he was being accused of being a Communist on 4 August 1948. A headline in the *New York Times* screamed hysterically: 'Red Underground in Federal Posts Alleged By Editor

– In New Deal Era.' it continued, 'Ex-Communist Names Alger Hiss, Then In State Department' The ex-Communist editor in question was Whittaker Chambers, a dishevelled, overweight editor at *Time* magazine.

Chambers had always had literary ambitions, but was thrown out of Columbia University for writing what was alleged to be a 'blasphemous' play. Then, dismissed from his position at the New York Public Library for allegedly stealing books, he joined the Communist Party in 1925. In a world that seemed to be coming apart at the seams, like many, he believed that communism could provide the panacea. He wrote for the Communist newspaper, the *Daily Worker* and the monthly, the New Masses.

In 1932, he began providing information for the Soviet Union. However, like many, he was seriously disillusioned with communism by news of Stalin's purges and his surprise signature in 1939 of a non-aggression treaty with Nazi Germany. He eschewed Communism and went to the other extreme, becoming a fervent Christian and anti-Communist. At the same time, he landed a job at *Time*, going on to become a senior editor of the magazine.

Chambers stated that Hiss was a member of 'an underground organisation of the United States

Communist Party', which became known as the Ware Group and which had the aim of promoting Communist policies in U.S. government. At this point he did not mention espionage and, in fact, would later deny that he or Hiss had engaged in espionage. But his story changed a number of times, and, at the two Hiss trials, he testified that he had committed perjury many times in his earlier testimony.

Chambers had already made his claims about Alger Hiss before he sat in front of HUAC. In 1939, he had approached Assistant Secretary of State, Adolf Berle with his suspicions of what were known as 'fellow travellers' – communist sympathisers – one of whom he named as Hiss. His claims were not investigated. He had also recounted his communist experiences to the FBI in interviews in the early 1940s. Nothing had happened then, either, principally because, by then, the Soviet Union was an ally of the United States in the war against Hitler's Germany.

Things were different in 1948, however. The Cold War was beginning to create a chill in relations between east and west and the American government was seriously concerned about the danger of Communist infiltration of government departments. Investigations had been ongoing since 1947, but had failed to deliver any indictments. The Republicans accused the Democrat administration of being 'soft on communism'.

HUAC spearheaded the investigations and amongst its committee members was the fresh, young and ambitious Californian Congressman, Richard Nixon. Like the other committee members, Nixon knew that Chambers' testimony to it in 1948 was critical to the future of HUAC. If it turned out to be untrue, the committee's credibility would have been struck a killer blow.

Claims made in front of HUAC were protected from libel and Hiss demanded that Chambers make his claims outside the umbrella of the committee so that they could be tested in court. He also demanded the right to reply to the accusation and the day after Chambers had made his claim, Hiss appeared before HUAC, stating the famous line read out by so many accused of communist sympathies: 'I am not and have never been a member of the Communist party.' Moreover, he claimed that he did not even know Whittaker Chambers but said he would very much like to meet him personally. Nixon pressed the case, in spite of Hiss's categorical denial. He demanded that even if Hiss was telling the truth about not being a communist, the committee should still investigate whether he was telling the truth about not knowing Chambers.

Meanwhile, a few days later, Chambers provided more information. Priscilla Hiss was also a Communist, he stated and he described the personal lives of the Hisses, providing details of their homes and cars. He described a Ford Roadster that Hiss had owned and insisted that it had been donated to the communist party by Hiss.

On some counts, Chambers' information was inaccurate. He claimed Hiss was deaf in one ear, which was not true and he said they did not drink, but they did. Much of what he did say, however, was accurate, down to the fact that the Hisses, both keen ornithologists, had been delighted to catch sight of a prothonotary warbler near the Potomac River.

Summoned before the committee again on 16 August, Hiss said, when shown a photograph of Chambers that he was a little familiar. He thought it was possibly a man called he had known as George Crosley who, when he knew him, was surviving by borrowing money and publishing occasional magazine articles. He said he had given Crosley the Ford and that Crosley had once given him an oriental rug in lieu of rent on an apartment Hiss had rented to him. Chambers would later claim to have given oriental rugs to four 'friends of the Soviet people'.

A meeting was organised for 25 August where Hiss

would meet Chambers to confirm that he had known him in the 1930s. Nixon, however, now heading a sub-committee into the Hiss affair, orchestrated a meeting between the two men eight days early, at the Commodore Hotel in New York. Hiss ended the meeting with the words: 'I would like to invite Mr. Whittaker Chambers to make those same statements out of the presence of this committee without their being privileged for suit for libel. I challenge you to do it, and I hope you will do it damned quickly.'

Chambers obliged on 27 August, declaring on the radio show, *Meet the Press*, 'Alger Hiss was a Communist and may be now.' Hiss issued a writ for damages, but, before they got to court, there was a dramatic shift in the accusations being made. Suddenly, it was being asserted by Chambers that Hiss was not just a Communist – he was actually a communist spy.

Chambers had twice denied spying, in front of HUAC and then before a Justice Department grand jury. But now, he dramatically changed his story, claiming that he could provide evidence that Hiss had supplied him with government documents ten years previously that were to be passed on to the Soviet Union. Chambers insisted that he had held on to the documents in case they came in handy at some point in order to protect himself. These documents had been given to his nephew, for safekeeping.

They turned out to be sixty-five pages of State Department documents, four sheets of paper in Hiss's handwriting, two rolls of microfilm containing more State Department documents and a few pages of handwritten notes, all dating from 1938. Chambers initially withheld the microfilm, famously hiding it inside a hollowed-out pumpkin on a pumpkin farm he owned in Maryland. These documents, known as 'the pumpkin papers', he eventually handed over, fearing that he would be found guilty of perjury.

The case exploded in a volcano of newspaper headlines and an orgy of media coverage and, ever-mindful of his image, Nixon flew home from holiday to bathe in the press coverage. Hiss declared that the items were fakes or had come from another source. Nonetheless, he was indicted for perjury for telling a grand jury that he had never handed material over to Chambers. Luckily for him, he could not be charged with treason or espionage as the incident had taken place so long ago and the statute of limitations had expired.

On 31 of May, the circus hit town when Alger Hiss's trial began at the Federal Building in New York's Foley Square. One of the most important pieces of evidence that the prosecution had found was a Woodstock typewriter on which, it was claimed, Priscilla Hiss had re-typed the State Department documents before they were given to Chambers, the originals being returned to the office by Hiss. Indeed, the Hisses had once owned such a machine and had given it to a maid who worked for them. Analysis of the machine and the documents suggested that they had, indeed, been typed on that machine. The defence sought to prove that Hiss had given the typewriter to the maid before the spring of 1938, but the maid could not recall the date and that line of questioning led to a dead-end.

Hiss's defence team relied heavily on character witnesses including Supreme Court judges and Adlai Stevenson, then Governor of Illinois as well as on discrediting Whittaker Chambers as a liar and a 'moral leper'. They claimed that he could have come into possession of the incriminating documents in any number of ways. The handwritten material, they claimed, could easily have been stolen from Hiss's office.

The trial ended in a hung jury, eight of the twelve jurors voting for a conviction. In a second trial, however, in November 1949, Hiss was convicted and sensationally sentenced to five years in prison. He served forty-four months in the Lewisburg, Federal Penitentiary in Pennsylvania.

Two months later, in the wake of Hiss's conviction, the Senator for Wisconsin, Joseph McCarthy, announced that he was in possession of a list of 205 'card-carrying members of the Communist Party' currently working in the United States State Department. The witch-hunts began.

Whittaker Chambers became a hero of the American right and his version of the case, *Witness*, became a bestseller. He died in 1961 of a heart attack, but President Ronald Reagan awarded him a posthumous Medal of Freedom in 1984 and his pumpkin farm became a national historic landmark.

Alger Hiss, on the other hand never gave up trying to clear his name, claiming that he was a sacrificial victim in a much bigger picture. He said he was merely a means 'to break the hull of liberalism'.

There were many doubts and inconsistencies about his conviction. For a start, it was not made known at the trial that during the war United States agents had learned how to reconstruct typewriters to match specific documents. The Woodstock could, conceivably, have undergone such a process. Interestingly, in 1976, White House counsel, John Dean, said he had been told by Charles Colson, President Nixon's chief counsel, that Nixon had admitted that the Woodstock had been tampered with. 'We built one on the Hiss case,' he reportedly said, a statement later denied by Colson.

It is worth pointing out, however, that Hiss did not help his case by being 'secretive and improvised', as one observer described him, in his disclosure of information about the typewriter. He was additionally unhelpful to them in their efforts to locate the machine.

In 1978, after the release of the documents pertaining to the case under freedom of information legislation, Hiss's defence team filed a petition in court of coram nobis – a petition designed to correct an error of a previous court – claiming the FBI illegally withheld the information about the reconstruction of typewriters; that it had ignored an inconsistency between the typewriter's serial number and its date of manufacture, casting doubt on whether it was the actual typewriter used; that there had been an informer on Hiss's defence team, a private detective named Horace Schmal; that the FBI had conducted illegal surveillance of Hiss both before and during his two trials. The Supreme Court rejected the petition then and in 1983.

In 1990, following the collapse of the Soviet Union, Hiss asked former Soviet General Dimitry Antonovich Volkgonov, overseer of Soviet intelligence archives to release any Soviet files on the Hiss case. In late 1992, it was revealed that no evidence whatsoever, had been found that Alger Hiss had ever engaged in espionage on behalf of the Soviet Union. However, it was later suggested that the General had not spent a great deal of time on his search of the archives. Another senior Soviet intelligence operative, General-Lieutenant Vitaly Pavlov, who had been in charge of Soviet intelligence work in North America in the late 1930s and early 1940s wrote in his memoirs that Hiss was never a Soviet agent.

On the opposite side, however, records were found in 1992 in Hungary, in which an American, Noel Field, who had been a Russian spy, but was jailed in Hungary in 1949 for five years on charges of spying for America, named Alger Hiss as a Communist spy. He even said that Hiss had tried to recruit him, but he was already spying for another Soviet network. After his release, Field wrote that he had been tortured and, under interrogation, had been forced to 'confess more and more lies as truth'. It also transpired that ownership of the old Ford Roadster that Hiss said he had given to Chambers had actually been transferred to a dealer who had immediately sold it to a known member of the Communist Party.

In 1995, the decrypted texts of thousands of telegrams sent by agents to the Soviet Union between

1942 and 1945 were released. In these, a Soviet agent codenamed 'Ales' is thought by some to be Hiss. Ales, for instance, definitely attended the Yalta Conference and then travelled on to Moscow afterwards. Hiss did both of these, going to Moscow, he claimed, to look at the subway system. Others dispute the claim, saying Ales worked at the centre of a group and Hiss was thought to have worked alone. Furthermore, Ales obtained military intelligence, whereas only State Department material would have been available to Hiss. At one point Ales was in Mexico when it is known for sure that Hiss was in Washington. Experts have named a United States diplomat, Wilder Foote, as a more likely identity for Ales.

Following the release of the decidedly low-key content of 'the pumpkin papers' in 1975, there was bemusement. Richard Nixon had described these documents as evidence of the 'most serious series of treasonable activities . . . in the history of America,' but they consisted of no more than two fairly indecipherable non-classified navy Department documents, one blank roll of film and two photographs of State Department documents, already seen in court. Following their release, Hiss was reinstated to the Massachusetts bar from which he had been expelled when convicted.

Alger Hiss continued to maintain his innocence and fight to prove it until he died, aged 92 on 15 November 1996. He may well have been innocent as he always claimed. He may also have been one of the greatest liars in American history.

DOUGLAS DEVANANDA

Sri Lanka has enjoyed the longest period of continuous multi-party democracy with universal suffrage in a non-western country – since 1931. Nonetheless, according to the World Bank and Asian Development Bank, it is one of the world's most unstable countries. *The Economist* has described it as a 'flawed democracy' and, in 2007, another influential magazine, *Foreign Policy*, rated the country 25th in its Failed States Index.

The government of Sri Lanka is controlled by rival coalitions led by the left-wing Sri Lanka Freedom Party, led by President Rajapaksa, the comparatively right-wing United National Party headed by former prime minister Ranil Wickremesinghe and the Marxist-Nationalist Janatha Vimukthi Peramuna (People's Liberation Front). Many smaller Buddhist, socialist and Tamil nationalist political parties also operate, but although all of them want regional autonomy and increased civil rights, they all oppose the separatism espoused by the LTTE (the Liberation Tigers of Tamil Eelam, or Tamil Tigers as they are commonly known).

It is against such a background that Kathiravelu Nithyananda Devananda, known as Douglas Devananda operates as a Sri Lankan Tamil politician and a Cabinet Minister in the Sri Lankan government. Devananda is currently the leader of the Eelam People's Democratic Party, Eelam being the Tamil name for Sri Lanka. But Douglas Devanada is a poacher turned gamekeeper, having originally been a Tamil militant himself. In the mid 1990s, he renounced violence as a means by which to achieve Tamil objectives and has, since trading the bullet for the ballot box, been a strident opponent of the tactics of the LTTE and its leader and founder, Velupillai Prabhakaran. The LTTE have not taken kindly to his criticism of them and have tried to assassinate him more than ten times.

Born in Jaffna in 1957, Devananda had an early introduction to politics. His father was a member of the Sri Lankan Communist Party and his uncle, K. C. Nithyananda was a prominent trade unionist.

Studying in Colombo, the young Devananda found himself attracted by the Tamil liberation movement which was emerging at the time. He threw himself into it enthusiastically, joining the Eelam Liberation Organisation (ELO). He would later be a founder member of another Tamil liberation movement, the Eelam Revolutionary Organisers (the EROs).

In 1977, Devananda had his first experience of the political world when his uncle was appointed chairman of the newly formed Palmyrah Development Board. Douglas worked for him as his personal assistant.

A year later, however, Devananda found himself undergoing military training with the Palestine Liberation Organisation on behalf of the EROs. This brought him under constant suspicion of being involved in terrorist activities and he was twice arrested in 1980 under the Sri Lankan Prevention of Terrorism Act. He remained incarcerated until 1983 when, following the anti-Tamil riots of that year, he escaped from prison and fled to Tamil Nadu in India.

The Tamil liberation movement had evolved in 1983 into the Eelam People's Revolutionary Liberation Front (the EPRLF), but by 1986 it was riven by internal strife. Its militant wing and military operations would later be swallowed up by the LTTE.

Tired of the internecine feuding, in 1987, Devananda created his own organisation, the Eelam People's Democratic Party. Around that time, Sri Lanka and India signed the Indo-Sri Lanka Peace Accord, an agreement, that, it was hoped would resolve the Sri Lankan civil war taking place on India's doorstep. Under the terms of the agreement, the government of President J .R. Jayewardene agreed to devolve power to the provinces, Sri Lankan troops were to withdraw to their barracks in the north and the Tamil rebels were to disarm. An Indian Peacekeeping Force was also sent to Sri Lanka.

As a result of this agreement and what it meant for Sri Lanka, Douglas Devananda and his EPDP announced that they were giving up the armed struggle and would engage in the democratic process. The EPDP returned nine members of Parliament including Devananda, in the election of August, 1994 and he was re-elected in subsequent elections in October 2000, December 2001 and April 2004.

In 1994 Devananda became a minister in Chandrika Kumaratunga's administration. He lost his ministerial post in 2001, but he became Minister for Social Service and Social Welfare in 2005 in the government of President Rajapaksa.

The LTTE, which is banned in many countries

including the United States, Canada and all twenty-seven member states of the European Union, see Douglas Devenenda as a traitor and his constant pronouncements, criticising the organisation and its leadership over the years, has done little to endear him to them. Numerous attempts on his life have failed.

In 1994, rebels driving jeeps, carried out a daring commando attack on his residence in Colombo. Four of his security guards died in the ensuing gun battle.

In 1998, Devananda was beaten and knifed inside a jail where he was visiting prisoners. He lost the sight of one eye.

In recent years there have been two attempts by female suicide bombers to kill him – in July 2004 and November 2007. The first of these killed the bomber and four policeman when it was detonated in the Kolluoitiya police station. The bomber had been behaving suspiciously and refused a body search as she tried to get into Devananda's ministry building. The second bomber was horrifically captured on a security camera as she detonated her bomb in Devenanda's office, killing herself and Devananda's personal secretary as well as injuring two security personnel.

Devanada, however, is no stranger to violence. While he was military commander of the EPLRF, in 1986, he had a disagreement with a gang of young men outside his house. When it began to turn nasty, Devananda ran into his house and opened fire on the group from the top floor of the building with an AK-47 rifle. A bullet hit a young man called Aiyaavu, killing him.

There was outrage and condemnation of this killing and Devananda was arrested and thrown into prison. However, he was set free on bail and fled to Colombo. At that point, his fortunes were at their lowest ebb – he had only what he stood up in, a pair of rubber sandals and a backpack stuffed with clothes and documents – and he had little option but to offer to help the Sri Lankan government, to collaborate, as his enemies would have it.

His timing was immaculate because war broke out shortly after, between the LTTE and the Sri Lankan government and Devananda's information and support proved invaluable to the government forces. They were so grateful to him, in fact, that they rewarded him by giving him some islands off the coast of the Jaffna peninsula. Before too long Devananda was a very wealthy man.

Although he and his faction are supposed to have renounced violence, there are a number of instances where they seem to have relapsed into their old habits. In 2000, for example, Mylvaganam Nimalarajan, Jaffna correspondent of the BBC Tamil and Sinhala

Service, was murdered during the hours of curfew in a high security zone in Jaffna. Nimalarajan had been highly critical of the conduct of the 2000 general election in Jaffna, alleging widespread vote-rigging. Devananda, who had complained to the army chief, Lionel Balagalla, that Nimalarajan was an LTTE member, and his men were suspects in the murder and two men, both members of the EPDP were both arrested and charged with the crime. They were later released on bail, however, and the case has never been brought to court.

There had been other similar incidents. In 1995 four EPDP members turned up at the home of A. Nicholas, the Assistant Government Agent on the island of Delft and took him away for what they described as questioning. They brought him back dead, claiming he had committed suicide. There were no arrests and no investigation ever took place.

When Nadarajah Atputharajah, editor of *Thina Murasu*, an EPDP publication was gunned down while travelling in his jeep in 1999, it was widely believed that Devananda was behind the shooting. The dead man was alleged to have been giving support for the LTTE in his publication.

In 2001, a gang of EPDP members, armed with T56 assault rifles, swords and knives, attacked a group of rival candidates and their supporters who were canvassing in Naranthanai for the general election. Two of them were killed. One MP and another senior member of the EPDP were arrested and charged with murder.

Douglas Devananda, now fifty years old, lives in a state of heightened security in an upmarket suburb of the Sri Lankan capital, Colombo. He is the most heavily guarded Tamil politician in the country, living, effectively, in a fortified bunker. To get to the building, a checkpoint guarded by sandbags and armed men has to be negotiated. The building itself is protected by high walls and security cameras. When the tall metal gates swing open, the visitor is confronted by ranks of armed men before being body-searched. Mobile phones are prohibited and equipment such as cameras or tape recorders has to be vetted.

Inside the building, an ante-room to his living and working space is decorated with pictures of EPDP members who have been killed by the Tamil Tigers and Devananda claims that forty-five died in the first three years of the cease-fire.

A heavy, fortified door opens onto the large room in which he works, eats and sleeps. The room bristles with activity and there are radios, television sets and banks of computers.

He has nothing but contempt and downright hatred for his former colleagues. 'They should just be annihilated,' he says. 'There is no other way.'

When asked about the way he has to live, Devananda has said: 'I have become used to this bunker existence. And they won't get me.'

It will not be for the want of trying, however, one imagines.

CAMBRIDGE FIVE

The Cambridge Apostles is a highly secretive, elite, intellectual, undergraduate society – exclusively male until the 1970s – founded at Cambridge University in 1820. Essentially a discussion group, the Apostles met once a week and one member generally gave a prepared talk that was thrown open to discussion. Oddly, members used to traditionally eat sardines on toast – known as 'whales' – during meetings. Becoming a member involved taking an oath of secrecy and listening to the reading of a curse composed by an Apostle in 1851. It had all the makings of a wonderful organisation for spies, then, or future spies. At least two of the Cambridge spy-ring that scandalised Britain's security services after the Second World War, were Apostles – Guy Burgess and Anthony Blunt.

They might not all have been Apostles, but all had been to Cambridge and all of them, apart from

Anthony Blunt, had been recruited as Soviet spies whilst there. Blunt, a committed Marxist, was recruited during a visit to Russia in 1933, by the Narodnyy Komissariat Vnutrennikh Del – the NKVD. He was an unlikely Russian spy, born in genteel Bournemouth in 1907, the youngest son of a vicar and a third cousin of Queen Elizabeth, the Queen Mother. He was also gay.

Blunt read Mathematics at Trinity College, Cambridge, changing to Modern Languages in his second year. He graduated in 1930 and became a French teacher. A Fellow of Trinity in 1932, he would go on to become one of the greatest and most respected art historians of the 20th century, Slade Professor of Fine Art at Cambridge, Director of the Courtauld Institute, as well as Surveyor of the Queen's Pictures.

At the outset of the Second World War, Blunt joined the British Army but was quickly seconded to MI5, the department handling British military intelligence. He passed on information to his Soviet handlers gleaned from messages that had been decrypted using Enigma machines. After the war, Blunt's art history career took off and he was knighted in 1956.

Michael Whitney Straight, an American related to

the wealthy Whitney family, had been recruited by Blunt at Cambridge – where he was also an Apostle – in the 1930s. Straight had worked for the United States Department of the Interior on his return to America in 1937, writing speeches for President Roosevelt and, in 1940, he was moved to the eastern division of the US State Department. After the war, he pursued a career as a writer and magazine editor. Worried that his past would come back to haunt him, when he was given the opportunity, in 1963, to work for the government once again, he confessed his Communist leanings while at Cambridge to Arthur Schlesinger Jr., a family friend as well as an assistant to President Kennedy. In these conversations, it emerged that Sir Anthony Blunt had been a leading light in a Cambridge spy network.

MI5 hauled Blunt in and although he confessed to being a Soviet spy in April 1964, his confession was not made public for another fifteen years when Prime Minister, Margaret Thatcher, named him in Parliament in 1979. He was stripped of his knighthood and lost his position as an Honorary Fellow of Trinity College. It emerged that a writer, Moura Budberg, known as the Russian Mata Hari, who had been the mistress of secret agent and diplomat, Sir R. H. Bruce Lockhart, Russian writer Maxim Gorky and historian and science fiction writer H. G. Wells, had all informed MI5 in 1950 that Blunt was a Communist and they had taken no action. Sir Anthony Blunt died in disgrace in 1983.

Blunt had played an important part in recruiting a number of other spies for the USSR. Among those who had come into his circle at Cambridge were Guy Burgess and Donald Maclean.

After attending Eton, Guy Francis De Moncy Burgess had gone to the Royal Naval College at Dartmouth, following in the footsteps of his naval officer father, but it had not worked out. At Cambridge, he became an Apostle and first met Anthony Blunt. Like Blunt, Burgess was gay, but, unlike Blunt, he was indiscreet and was often accused of inappropriate behaviour, either because of his sexual proclivities or his heavy drinking.

After Cambridge he worked as a journalist, writing for the *Times*. He then became producer of the BBC radio programme, *The Week in Westminster*, before spending time in Spain during the Spanish Civil War. It was when he landed the position of secretary to Hector McNeil, when he became Minister of State at the Foreign Office in 1946 that Burgess really became useful to the Russians. He passed countless documents to them during this time.

In 1950, he was transferred to the British Embassy in Washington where he shared a flat with another member of the Cambridge spy ring, Kim Philby, who was the MI6 representative in the US capital. Burgess's boorish behaviour was unrelenting, however, and he was described in an FBI file as 'a loud, foul-mouthed queer with a penchant for seducing hitchhikers.'

When Kim Philby warned Donald Maclean in 1951 that he was under investigation, Burgess, although he was not under suspicion, disappeared with Maclean. They turned up in Moscow five years later. But Burgess's life in Russia was miserable – he made little effort to learn Russian and although he lived with a state-sanctioned lover, the Soviet Union was never very tolerant of his homosexuality. He died in Moscow, in 1963, probably of alcoholism.

Donald Maclean was another Trinity alumnus. Son of the Liberal Party Leader after the First World War, Sir Donald Maclean, he was recruited by Blunt in his last year at university and carefully coached by him to pass the Civil Service examination and interview. He was given a job at the Foreign Office and was controlled by the Soviet GPU resident, Anatoil Gorsky. When war broke out, he was at the British Embassy in Paris, marrying the American, Melinda

Marling there. They returned to England shortly before the Germans arrived in the city.

As the war progressed, Maclean continued to supply the Soviet Union with information, amongst which was material concerning uranium and atom bombs being developed by British scientists.

It was after the war that he provided his most useful information. Posted to Washinton from 1944 to 1948, he handed over material concerning communications between the British Prime Minister and US President and minutes of British Cabinet meetings regarding the atom bomb. Such invaluable information allowed Soviet scientists to predict the number of bombs the Americans were capable of constructing and contributed to the construction of the Russians' own atomic bomb. It is possible that, knowing exactly the American atom bomb capability, Stalin felt confident about blockading Berlin in 1948 as well as arming North Korea, action which led to the Korean War in which 30,000 US and Allied troops died.

Walter Krivitsky was a Soviet spy from Poland who hated Stalin's methods and finally defected to the United States in 1940. He was later found dead in the Bellevue Hotel in New York with three suicide notes by his bed, although suspicions linger that he was murdered by Soviet intelligence. It is thought that

Krivitsky had tentatively identified Maclean as a Soviet agent in discussions with MI5 in 1941. He claimed that there was a mole in British intelligence whom he described as 'a Scotsman of good family, educated at Eton and Oxford [sic], and an idealist who worked for the Russians without payment'. However, no action was taken against Maclean.

Maclean provided vital information that Stalin put to good use at the Yalta and Potsdam Conferences and reported to his handlers that the true objective of the Marshal Plan was to gain economic domination of Europe for the United States.

When an FBI agent discovered in 1949 that an agent known as 'Homer' was communicating with the USSR, Maclean was one of the three suspects in the British intelligence service. Kim Philby, another of the Cambridge Five, became concerned that if Maclean was arrested, it was possible that the names of the other members of the Cambridge network would be revealed. Philby organised, therefore, for Guy Burgess to return to London and warn Maclean. On the day he returned to Britain, he was stopped for speeding three times as he rushed to give the warning to his fellow spy.

It was presumed that Maclean's room at the Foreign Office was bugged. The plan was, therefore, for Burgess to simply hand him a note containing details of where they could meet. It was decided that he would have to flee and Yuri Modin, his handler, organised the defection of an extremely nervous Maclean. He was so afraid, in fact, that he refused to go alone. The KGB ordered Burgess to accompany him to Moscow.

Meanwhile, the FBI and MI5 investigation continued and they set a date of 28 May 1951 for an interview with Maclean. Maclean did not turn up, of course. On the previous Friday, his thirty-eighth birthday, he and Burgess took a ferry to France and vanished. Philby had warned Burgess that under no circumstances should he accompany Maclean. When he heard that he had in fact gone with him, he was certain he simply would drop him off and return immediately. He did not, of course, and it is presumed that the Russians thought that he had outlived his usefulness as a spy, but did not want him to return and be interrogated by MI5 sometime later.

Maclean adapted well to life in the Soviet Union. Unlike Burgess, he learned the language and worked as a specialist in Western economic policy. To show their gratitude, the Russians awarded him the Order of the Red Banner of Labour and the Order of Combat. His wife had joined him with their children, but she later had an affair with Kim Philby when he arrived in Moscow and moved in with him in 1966. She eventually returned to her native United States. Maclean died of a heart attack in 1983, aged sixty-nine.

John Cairncross also attended Trinity, studying Modern Languages. Born in Leshmahagow in Scotland, he worked in the Foreign Office after graduating. However, in 1937, he had joined the Communist party.

Cairncross went to work in the famous code-breaking operation at Bletchley Park in 1942, all the while passing top-secret material to the Soviet Union. It is thought that the material he provided helped the Russians in the Battle of Kursk and was invaluable to them in their war against the Germans on the Eastern Front.

In 1951, he confessed to being a spy when incriminating documents were discovered in his possession. Nothing came of it, however, and he was never prosecuted, leading, inevitably, to accusations of a cover-up. When Kim Philby was outed as a spy in 1963, there were rumours of still another spy in the Cambridge network – the infamous 'Fifth man'. However, it took until 1990 to establish his identity when Soviet defectors Yuri Modin, handler of the

Judas Iscariot here depicted in The Last Supper *by Rubens, was the the Apostle who betrayed his Divine Master.*

Lord Chancellor of England, Sir Thomas More (1478–1535), disapproved of Henry VIII's schism with Rome and his refusal to recognise any other head of the Church than the pope led to his execution for high treason.

John Wilkes Booth (1838–1865), was the man who assassinated the 16th President of the United States, Abraham Lincoln.

Four members of the Cambridge Five, graduates of Trinity College, Cambridge, who passed information from British Intelligence to the Soviet Union in the 1940s and 1950s. Clockwise from top left, Anthony Blunt, Donald Duart Maclean, Kim Philby and Guy Burgess.

Traitor and CIA agent Aldrich Hazen Ames, who sold-out his colleagues to the Russians for money.

Iva Toguri d'Aquino, a.k.a. 'Tokyo Rose', who was arrested for speaking out against the US during World War II, looks out a jail cell window.

After testifying against the Dapper Don, Sammy 'The Bull' Gravano was relocated out west, courtesy of the witness protection programme. It was there that Gravano resumed his life of crime and had this mug shot taken by the Maricopa County Sheriff's Office.

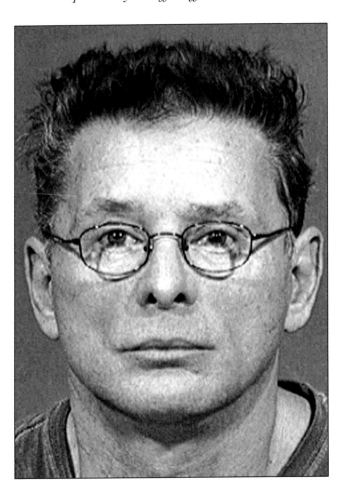

Former MI5 agent David Shayler was arrested on allegations of violating the Official Secrets Act, which requires that serving or former members of the intelligence agencies do not divulge information about their work without official authority.

Cambridge Five from 1944 until 1955, and Oleg Gordievsky, former KGB bureau chief in London, named Cairncross.

Cairncross always denied ever passing any material harmful to Britain, among the 5,832 documents with which he supplied the Russians. He claimed he was only trying to help the USSR defeat the Nazis. He also resolutely denied that he was the 'Fifth man'.

Moving to Rome after his confession, he worked for the United Nations there and died in the south of France, where he had retired in 1995 at the age of eighty-two.

The greatest enigma of them all, and probably the most effective of the Cambridge spies, was Harold Adrian Russell Philby, known as 'Kim' after the character in Kipling's novel of the same name. Yuri Modin said of Philby in 1994:

He never revealed his true self. Neither the British, nor the women he lived with, nor ourselves [the KGB] ever managed to pierce the armour of mystery that clad him. His great achievement in espionage was his life's work, and it fully occupied him until the day he died. But in the end I suspect that Philby made a mockery of everyone, particularly ourselves.'

His father was the army officer, diplomat, explorer, author and Orientalist, St. John Philby, who had converted to Islam and was adviser to King Ibn Saud of Saudi Arabia for many years.

Philby went to Trinity College, Cambridge, aged sixteen, in 1928, to study economics and, whilst there, became a Communist. He is reported to have asked one of his tutors, Maurice Dobb, who specialised in the interpretation of neoclassical economic theory from a Marxist point of view, how he could best serve the Communist cause. Dobb put him in touch with the Comintern Underground in Vienna and Philby was, consequently, recruited by Soviet intelligence.

In 1936, he was ordered by Moscow to begin to act as if he was pro-fascism. He attended the appropriate meetings and rallies and began editing a pro-Hitler magazine. In 1937, he went to Spain to report for the *Times* on the Spanish Civil War from the perspective of the Republican leader, the fascist Francisco Franco. Franco ultimately awarded him a medal for bravery.

It was Guy Burgess who gained him an *entrée* into British intelligence, obtaining an introduction for him to Marjory Maxse an MI6 officer. He was appointed head of counter-espionage for Iberia and did well, obtaining the important role of head of the brand-new Section IX – responsible, ironically, for counterespionage against the Soviet Union. This was, obviously, the ideal position for a Soviet spy.

Defections of Russians to the West were a grave danger for Soviet spies. The risk of exposure increased with every defection. In August 1945, Philby's cover was almost blown when an NKVD officer, Konstantin Volkov, made it known that he wanted to defect to Britain. There was a possibility that he would disclose the names of Soviet agents in the British secret service, Philby among them. But, of course, Philby was ideally positioned to deal with such a problem. He received the report and manipulated matters so that he was given the assignment. He made the Russians aware of Volkov's plans and the Russian was kidnapped, taken to Moscow and executed.

After the war ended, Philby worked in Istanbul under the cover of First Secretary to the British Embassy and then, in 1949, he was sent to Washington in the same role, liaising between the British Embassy and the newly created CIA. He received and passed on material that the United States was sharing with the United Kingdom, such as the results of one of the most top-secret postwar initiatives, the Venona project, the decrypting of thousands of communications between Soviet agents in the United States and Moscow.

Philby was invaluable to the Soviet Union. On one occasion, the CIA tried to organise a revolution in Soviet-influenced Albania. Every time the revolutionary force tried to make a landing on the Albanian coast, the Russians and Albanians were waiting for them, thanks to Philby. Similarly, in the Ukraine, a revolution was blocked, thanks to him.

For a year, while Burgess was sharing his flat in Washington, Philby made sure his self-destructive fellow spy did not get himself into too much trouble. Then, when Burgess disappeared with Donald Maclean, Philby himself finally came under suspicion. He was forced to resign and was denied his pension until an investigation was completed. He was then questioned for several years, never once breaking under interrogation. Surprisingly, on 25 October 1955, he was publicly exonerated as the 'Third Man', in the House of Commons by Foreign Secretary, Harold Macmillan. 'While in government service,' he said, 'he carried out his duties ably and conscientiously, and I have no reason to conclude that Mr. Philby has at any time betrayed the interests of his country, or to identify him with the so-called "Third Man", if indeed there was one.'

In 1956, he was asked to work for MI6 again, posing as a middle-east correspondent in Beirut for

The Observer and *The Economist*. He was actually working on Operation Musketeer, the British, French and Israeli plot to attack Egypt and depose Egyptian President, Gamel Abdel Nasser.

Suspicion still hovered around him, however, and in 1963, constantly in fear of being exposed by each new defector, he was confronted with new information by his friend, Nicholas Elliott, sent to talk to him by MI6. Philby, who had been drinking heavily and whose behaviour had become increasingly erratic during the previous few months, knew the game was finally up. He boarded the Soviet freighter, *Dolmatova*, on 23 January 1963, and sailed for Moscow.

Russia was a disappointment to him, however. He had believed he would be given the rank of colonel in the KGB, but he was largely ignored and did not actually enter KGB headquarters for ten years. He still drank heavily and seduced Donald Maclean's wife who lived with him for a while, his own wife having abandoned him in 1965.

He recovered enough to start training young agents about to be sent to Britain, Australia or Ireland and married Rufina Ivanova Pukhova, a Russian woman, twenty years his junior. Following his death in May, 1988, he received a hero's funeral and a great number of honours and accolades by a grateful Soviet Union.

But who was the 'Fifth Man'? A number of men have been suggested as the fifth member of the Cambridge spy-ring over the years. Guy Liddell, MI5's Director of Counterespionage during World War Two, who died in 1958, was anonymously accused in 1949. His career was ended by the accusation, even though his superiors wrote it off as Soviet disinformation. However, he was subsequently named in a death-bed confession by Guy Burgess's close friend, Goronwy Rees. Rees confessed to spying and claimed that Liddell was also a member of the group.

Victor Rothschild, Third Baron Rothschild, was a member of the Cambridge Apostles with Burgess and Blunt and it has been alleged that he had spied. James Jesus Angleton, long-serving chief of the CIA's counter-intelligence operations, is also mentioned in this context.

One of the most surprising names that emerged as a possible 'Fifth Man' was Sir Roger Hollis. Hollis had been head of MI5 from 1956 until 1965, but rumours spread that he had been the person who had alerted Kim Philby to his imminent arrest. There was also a suspicion that there was a mole in the highest echelons of the British secret service. This arose from the fact that MI5 operations still failed, even after Burgess, Philby and Blunt had stopped having access to classified operational information. Some within the agency, notably Peter Wright and Arthur Martin, became convinced that the source of the leaks was either Hollis or his assistant, Graham Mitchell. When Mitchell was cleared and the focus fell on Hollis alone, the Director-General of MI5, Martin Furnival Jones, refused to sanction an investigation.

Martin and Wright could not persuade anyone else in the organisation that their conclusions about Hollis were correct. Wright, living in Australia and furious at being denied a pension for his thirty years of service, wrote the book *Spycatcher* which was banned in the United Kingdom, but published elsewhere. In the book, Wright claims that Sir Roger Hollis was a Soviet agent.

EMAD SALEM

'You were informed. Everything is ready. The day and the time. Boom! Lock them up and that's that.'

That is what FBI informant Emad Salem had thought would happen. Thanks to the incompetence of the FBI, however, it did not and six people lost their lives in the 1993 bombing of the World Trade Centre.

In January, 1993, the biggest and most complicated terrorism trial ever to come before an American court, opened in Lower Manhattan. There were twelve defendants, mostly Arab-speaking Muslims, the most important of which was Sheik Omar Abdel Rahman, a blind, Egyptian-born religious leader. They were charged with plotting a *jihad* or religious war against the United States and their plans included the blowing up of the Lincoln and Holland Tunnels, the United Nations, the Federal Office Building in lower Manhattan as well as other well-known landmarks in New York City because of America's support for Israel and the Egyptian government.

Rahman and the other defendants had been held in custody following the 1993 bombing of the World Trade Centre in New York. In their 'war of urban terrorism' they were also found to have been involved in the assassination, in 1990, of Rabbi Meier Kahane, founder of both the controversial Jewish Defence League and Kach, an Israeli political party which became outlawed in Israel because of its extremist policies. Kahane was assassinated after giving a speech in the Marriott Hotel in New York. El Sayyid Nosair was arrested but acquitted of his murder. But, although he was found guilty and sent to prison on gun-possession charges, Nosair still masterminded many of the group's actions from his prison cell. He stood in the dock alongside Rahman as one of the twelve defendants.

The key witness in the trial was Emad Salem, a former Egyptian Army officer who had succeeded in infiltrating Rahman's group at the Jersey City mosque where the blind man preached. Salem, who had been placed in a witness protection programme in July 1993, was described as an Egyptian intelligence official. He had entered the army as a private and during his seventeen-year career had fought in the

1973 war with Israel and had been pensioned out as a senior officer while continuing to work for the Egyptian intelligence services. The woman he married, after re-locating to the United States from Cairo in 1987, Barbara Rogers, claimed he was in fact an Egyptian double agent. His stories to Rogers, however, that he worked in intelligence and was one of President Sadat's bodyguards were made up to impress her, he later claimed. He had served in the Egyptian Army for seventeen years, though, and had left behind in Egypt a wife and two children. But Salem found life to be tough in America. 'I was like a big shot in Egypt, and all of a sudden I became just an immigrant,' he said. He earned a living driving a taxi or working as security in department stores.

He told plenty of other lies to Nancy Floyd, the FBI agent who recruited him to work as an informer. He claimed, for instance, that he knew Muammar el-Qaddafi, President of Libya, President Sadam Hussein of Iraq and King Hussein of Jordan. Like his stories of working for the Egyptian intelligence services, these were pure fabrication.

The FBI had first approached Salem in 1990 after the death of Rabbi Kahane, to ask him to infiltrate Sayyid Nosair's circle of associates at the Jersey mosque. Initially, he refused. In October, 1991, however, he lost his job as head of security at the Best Western Woodward Hotel in Manhattan and had little option but to take a job with the government. They paid him $500 a week, plus expenses.

In June, 1992, Salem met the imprisoned Nosair. He and an associate, Ali Shinawy, told Salem that their group planned to blow up twelve Jewish buildings in New York, including temples and banks. Within a few days, Salem was introduced by Nosair's cousin, Ibrahim El-Gabrowny, to 'Dr. Rashid' which was the alias of Clement Rodney Hampton-El, a New Jersey hospital technician, who had fought the Russians in Afghanistan. He had access to bomb-making material, but told them that he was unable to get the remote bomb detonators the group needed, but could buy ready-made pipe bombs for around $1,000 each as well as guns. Salem and Shinawy were delegated to locate a warehouse in which the bombs could be built.

At this point, the FBI were finding it difficult to corroborate what they were being told by Salem. Their own surveillance, such as listening in on Nosair's phone calls from prison was beginning to confirm what he was telling them, they insisted that he wore recording equipment. Salem, who, after all, was being paid only $500 a week, was outraged and told them it would be far too dangerous.

The FBI became impatient and decided to withdraw their payments to Salem, later justifying this action by saying they did not believe what he was telling them. At the same time, they were worried that Salem might be working for Egyptian intelligence. Their doubts about him did not decrease when he showed them what he described as a small explosive device that was nothing more than a powerful, easily obtainable firecracker. The surveillance of the Jersey mosque group was effectively ended, a decision that has been heavily criticised ever since.

'That case is something we all try to learn from,' said an FBI official, later. 'You don't blow off that kind of information coming from an informant unless you've got some other way to keep an eye on the suspects involved.' Salem was the only eye they had.

Several months later, a massive car bomb was detonated below Tower One of the World Trade Centre. It consisted of 1,500 pounds of the high explosive fertiliser commonly used as an industrial explosive, urea nitrate and was supposed to knock Tower One into Tower Two, bringing down both towers and killing 250,000 people. It failed to bring the towers down and succeeded in only killing six and injuring 1,042. Up to that date, however, it was the most destructive terrorist attack on American soil.

The FBI were stunned and Salem was re-employed in March 1993, paid $1 million to infiltrate the group again and help in the investigation into the attack.

Salem taped more than 1,000 conversations during his time within the terrorist group. He monitored their activities as they collected firearms, bought the ingredients needed to make bombs and discussed their plans to kidnap prominent people and bomb important buildings.

Critically, however, Salem had also bugged the FBI, taping all his telephone conversations with them and raising the question of the extent to which the FBI were aware of the plans to bomb the World Trade Centre, but did nothing to prevent it.

Salem also described how, during a journey by van to Detroit in late 1993, Rahman had told him that his period in the Egyptian Army had been a waste of time and that to make up for it, he should assassinate Egyptian President, Hosni Mubarak. It is believed that Rahman had issued the fatwa approving the 1981 assassination of Egyptian President Anwar Sadat.

Many people have questioned whether the FBI were actually responsible for the bombing, utilising informant Salem as an agent provocateur, or was it simply that it failed to prevent an independent Salem and his associates from carrying out the attack?

Salem said the FBI were involved in building the bomb, but had told him they would provide fake explosives to ensure nothing came of it. In December 1993 James M. Fox, the head of the FBI's New York Office, denied that the FBI had any foreknowledge of the attacks.

In one taped conversation, Salem is trying to get some money out of the agency, but it also seems to indicate the FBI's full knowledge of what was going on. He is speaking to FBI Special Agent, John Anticev.

ANTICEV: But ah basically nothing has changed. I'm just telling you for my own sake that nothing . . . that this isn't a salary, but you got paid regularly for good information. I mean the expenses were a little bit out of the ordinary and it was really questioned. Don't tell Nancy I told you this. (Nancy Floyd was the FBI agent who had recruited Salem)

SALEM: Well, I have to tell her of course.

ANTICEV: Well then, if you have to, you have to.

SALEM: Yeah, I mean because the lady was being honest and I was being honest and everything was submitted with receipts and now it's questionable.

ANTICEV: It's not questionable, it's like a little out of the ordinary.

SALEM: Okay. I don't think it was. If that what you

think guys, fine, but I don't think that because we was start already building the bomb which is went off in the World Trade Centre. It was built by supervising supervision from the Bureau and the DA and we was all informed about it and we know what the bomb start to be built. By who? By your confidential informant. What a wonderful great case! And then he put his head in the sand I said 'Oh, no, no, that's not true, he is son of a bitch'....Okay. It's built with a different way in another place and that's it.

ANTICEV: No, don't make any rash decisions. I'm just trying to be as honest with you as I can.

SALEM: Of course, I appreciate that.

Salem's tapes could conceivably have become a gift for the defence attorneys, providing evidence of entrapment and collusion on the part of the FBI with Salem in the implementation of the bombing. Defence Attorney, Ron Kuby said at the time: 'The mastermind is the government of the United States. It was a phoney, government-engineered conspiracy to begin with. It would never have amounted to anything had the government not planned it.'

Salem may have connected with the individuals arrested for the bomb, and have convinced them that he was sincere in his intention to blow up the WTC and they became involved in the plot. Then Salem handed over his fellow conspirators. The real target in all this, of course, was Rahman whom the FBI wanted very badly.

For their part, the defence claimed that Rahman was 'an innocent man wrongly accused'. He had been framed by the Egyptian government for whom, they alleged, Salem was working. They claimed that Salem had manipulated the FBI into going after Rahman, who had been trying to overthrow the Egyptian government for a very long time and had become something of a thorn in its flesh. 'You have seen the great and powerful FBI succumb and lie down with Emad Salem,' one defence lawyer said 'He was the sole controlling factor in this investigation. He ran it. They did what he wanted.'

As well as Salem's testimony, there were more than 200 witnesses. The most compelling piece of evidence, however, was a taped conversation between Salem and the blind cleric in which Rahman told him not to bomb the United Nations and a Manhattan Federal building, but, instead, to find a plan to 'inflict damage on the American Army.'

Sheik Rahman was found guilty and sentenced to life in prison, while his co-defendants were given sentences ranging from twenty-five years to life. Before sentencing, Rahman gave a rambling 100-minute speech in court, in which he railed against America, calling it 'an enemy of Islam' and protested his innocence in what he described as an 'unlawful trial'.

Emad Salem disappeared immediately after the arrests. He is presumed to have entered the Witness Protection Programme.

GEORGE KOVAL

On 2 November 2002, Russian President Vladimir
Putin made a surprise announcement that a man
named George Koval was to receive, posthumously,
the highest award available in Russia – Hero of the
Russian Federation. The announcement was greeted
by puzzlement. Who was George Koval? Putin's
announcement went on to explain that Dr George
Koval was the only Soviet intelligence officer to
infiltrate America's Manhattan Project's secret plants.
His work, Putin went on to say, 'helped speed up
considerably the time it took for the Soviet Union to
develop an atomic bomb of its own.'

In short, he was one of the most important spies of
the 20th century.

In the early 1900s, Abraham Koval, from the town of
Telekhany, in Belarus, emigrated to the United States
to seek his fortune. Behind him, he left his fiancée,

Ethel, promising to bring her to America as soon as he had saved enough money and as soon as he had bought a house for them to live in.

Abraham knew only one person in the entire United States, a friend who lived in Sioux City in Iowa. In 1910 he arrived there and began to work as a carpenter, quickly learning English. He worked hard, prospered and, a year later, had saved enough to bring his fiancée to America. They married and had three children, the second of which was a boy, born in 1913 whom they christened George.

The Kovals had remained in close contact with their family back home and became involved with an organisation called the Yidishe Kolonizatsye Organizatsye in Rusland (Organisation for Jewish Colonisation in Russia) that had been founded by Jewish Communists in 1924. Abraham became secretary of the organisation's Sioux City branch in the 1920s. When the Soviet Union created a Jewish Autonomous Region in Birobidzhan, located on the Trans-Siberian railway, close to the Chinese border, in response to the Palestine project of the Zionist movement, the Koval family who were still living in Russia, moved there.

In 1932, Abraham Koval decided to move his family back to the USSR, to join his family in

Birobidzhan. He would not be short of work, after all, as the region was developing fast and in need of carpenters. He joined the Communist Party, a pre-requisite for finding employment, and was given a job and a place to live by the Birobidzhan commune. Anyway, when the Bolsheviks had come to power in Russia, George's mother had been delighted. She had worked in a factory in Russia from the age of ten and had been politicised by her fellow workers, espousing the cause of socialism, even though her father was a rabbi who disagreed with the atheist views of the Communists.

George was eighteen years old when the family returned to the Soviet Union. To begin with, he worked at a local sawmill, but he was a clever lad and in 1934, after working at the mill for two years, he was enrolled at Moscow University's Mendeleev Institute of Chemical Technology. He excelled in what was a very difficult subject, graduating with honours. That same year, 1939, he got married and was accepted into a graduate programme at the university.

At this time, the Red Army officer corps and the NKVD – the Soviet Union's repressive secret police – were recruiting, following the damage that had been done to their numbers by Stalin's purges in the 1930s. The NKVD had conducted mass executions without trial, it ran the Gulag system of forced labour and handled mass deportations of peasants and ethnic minorities to outlying, unpopulated regions of the country. It conducted espionage and political assassinations abroad, was responsible for subversion of foreign enemy governments and enforced the policy of Stalin within Communist movements in other countries.

George Koval was a perfect recruit and, following the customary background check, he was inducted into the Glavnoje Razvedyvatel'noje Upravlenije, the GRU – the Main Intelligence Directorate of the General Staff of the Armed Forces of the Russian Federation. The GRU's main New York bureau coordinator was Arthur Adams, known by the codename 'Achilles'. Achilles had been a victim of one of Stalin's purges and had been recalled to the Soviet Union and sentenced to forced labour, a sentence that few survived. Koval, born in the United States, with a flawless American accent and a perfect grasp of English, was the perfect candidate to replace Achilles. He began his training and was given the codename 'Delmar'.

Unfortunately for George, Achilles was made of strong stuff and was unexpectedly discovered to still be alive. Naturally, it made more sense to return him to his post, rather than introduce an inexperienced agent to what was difficult work. Koval was, instead, given an assignment of less importance. He was to be sent to America to gather information on United States research into chemical weapons.

He was fairly ineffectual until 1943, the year that he was drafted into the United States Army. He had been provided with forged documents showing that he had an Associates Degree in Chemistry from a local community college, a qualification that impressed the army sufficiently to send him to the City College of New York to learn how to maintain the equipment for handling radioactive materials.

Koval graduated in 1944 and was sent by the army to Oak Ridge, Tennessee. Oak Ridge National Laboratory had been established in 1943 as part of the Manhattan Project to develop an atomic bomb. American scientists feared that the Nazis were developing their own atom bomb and Oak Ridge was built in record time on isolated farmland in the mountains of East Tennessee. It was a secret city the rest of the world did not even know existed even though within two years it boasted a population of more than 75,000. It was the perfect place for a spy such as George Koval. However, security was so tight that he was only able to pass on information to Moscow when he left Oak Ridge twice a year to go on holiday.

His information was very useful to the Russians

and Oak Ridge would become the model for the military research towns the Russians began to build after the end of the war. Towns such as Chelyabinsk-70, a closed city, now known as Snezhinsk, which is built around a major scientific research institute – the All-Russian Scientific Research Centre of Technical Physics – Federal Nuclear Centre, which is one of two centres of the Russian nuclear programme, the other being Sarov.

Delmar's reports described the procedure for producing plutonium and polonium, the scientific and security procedures and measurements of quantities and quality of the materials involved.

He was promoted to Staff Sergeant in 1945 and transferred to Dayton in Ohio. There, in the Health Physics branch of the Medical Department, he was assigned to Unit III of the Dayton Project. This was another of the sites involved in the Manhattan Project. Its task was to develop the neutron-generating devices that triggered the nuclear detonation of the bombs once the critical mass had been assembled by the force of conventional explosives. At Dayton, Delmar had even greater access to information on the Manhattan Project. He was able to provide Moscow with information about the numerous smaller facilities involved in the project across the United States.

After the dropping of the atom bombs on Hiroshima and Nagasaki brought an end to the war, Koval was demobilised, but was offered the chance to remain employed at Dayton as a civilian. His Russian masters were keen for him to accept their offer and to continue to gather information. But Koval was becoming increasingly worried about the danger of exposure. A Soviet agent, Igor Guzenko, had recently defected to Canada and the United States had learned from him that the Russians had been obtaining copious amounts of information about the Manhattan Project. Security at United States nuclear research facilities had been tightened even more as a result, and the possibility of capture seemed much greater to Koval. It has also been reported that around that time, United States counter-intelligence agents found Soviet literature describing the Koval family as 'happy immigrants' from the United States, when they returned to Russia in 1932. In 1948, Koval had finally had enough and fled back to the USSR.

On 29 August 1949, at 7.00 a.m. local time, at Semipalatinsk in Kazakhstan, the USSR exploded its first nuclear test weapon, the RDS-1, also known as Joe-1 in tribute to Joseph Stalin. The bomb's yield was 22 kilotons of TNT, similar to the United States' bombs. At the insistence of Lavrenty Beria, head of the Soviet nuclear programme, it was similar to the design of the American 'Fat Man' bomb that had been dropped on Nagasaki.

By now, the Americans were aware that George Koval had been spying for the Soviet Union, but, to avoid embarrassment, they kept it secret. Koval was, by this time, studying again, receiving a PhD in Chemistry and becoming a professor at his old university. He retired sometime in the late 1970s and led a quiet, solitary life, spending his time communicating with fellow scientists around the world by letter and email.

Historical accounts have downplayed the role of espionage in the development of the Soviet nuclear bomb. Beria, in particular, distrusted the information provided by Soviet spies, but there is no doubt that George Koval's contribution was enormous. No one had gained the kind of access to American nuclear plants that he did. One of his former Oak Ridge colleagues, Dr. Kramish, noted, 'He had access to everything. He had his own Jeep. Very few of us had our own Jeeps. He was clever. He was a trained GRU spy.'

Dr Kramish described him as the 'biggest' of the atomic spies. 'You don't get a medal from the President of Russia for nothing,' he is reported to have said.

George Abraham Koval is remembered by his

neighbours towards the end of his life, as polite, respectful and private. He died quietly in his Moscow apartment on 31 January 2006, aged ninety-two, one of the greatest heroes of the Soviet Union.

JOHN DEAN

G. Gordon Liddy, who, along with E. Howard Hunt, masterminded the break-in at the Watergate Hotel that would ultimately bring down the presidency of Richard Nixon in 1974, once said that he would like to kill John Dean by shoving a pencil through his neck.

He felt so strongly quite simply because it was Dean who brought down the whole pack of cards that was the Nixon White House. It was Dean who described to Nixon the lies surrounding the Watergate Affair as 'a cancer on the presidency'; it was Dean who first laid the blame for the cover-up of the break-in firmly at the door of the Oval Office.

John Wesley Dean III was just thirty-one years of age when he arrived in the White House in July 1970. His job was to work for President Richard Nixon as White House Counsel, a role in which he advised the President on all legal issues that concerned both him and the White House. Born in Akron, Ohio, Dean had been educated at Colgate University, studying English Literature, before taking a degree in Political Science in 1961 at the College of Wooster. His law degree came from Georgetown University from which he graduated in 1965 and his first job was with a law firm in Washington D.C.

Dean became involved in politics when he was appointed chief minority counsel to the Republican members of the Judiciary Committee of the House of Representatives, one of the two chambers of the United States Congress, the other being the Senate. He was appointed associate director of a National Commission on Crime in 1967 and helped Nixon on crime issues during his 1968 presidential campaign. In 1969, when Nixon had been elected President, he became Associate Deputy in the Attorney General's office and in 1970, he replaced John Erlichman as Counsel to the President.

Watergate is the generic name for what was really a series of related scandals involving the Nixon administration. These took in campaign fraud, political espionage and sabotage, illegal break-ins, improper tax audits, illegal wiretapping and a secret slush fund laundered in Mexico which was used to pay those who were involved in these operations.

Critically, this secret fund was also used as hush money to buy the silence of the seven men who were indicted for the June 1972 break-in.

It all began when a security guard at the massive Watergate Hotel and apartment complex in Washington DC spotted tape covering the locks on some of the doors in the complex. He called the police and they found five men, to become known as the 'plumbers', inside the office of the Democratic National Committee. Virgilio González, Bernard Barker, James W. McCord, Jr, Eugenio Martínez and Frank Sturgis were arrested and charged with attempted burglary and attempted interception of telephone and other communications. They were indicted by a grand jury in September of that year for conspiracy, burglary and violation of federal wiretapping laws. By this time, the number of men charged had risen to seven, E. Howard Hunt Jr and Gordon Liddy having been added to the roster. All of the men charged were employees of Richard Nixon's Campaign to Re-elect the President, CRP, but universally known as CREEP.

The target for their activity was Larry O'Brien, the Chairman of the DNC, who had been appointed by Vice-President Hubert Humphrey as director of his presidential campaign. Humphrey and several others were trying at the time to supply Nixon with misinformation regarding firstly a $205,000 loan his brother Donald had received from billionaire recluse, Howard Hughes and secondly, a cash contribution of $100,000 to the presidential campaign that Nixon's shady friend Bebe Rebozo had received from Hughes.

Nixon was worried that the Democrats had documents supporting these activities and that they would release them prior to the election, seriously denting his chances of re-election. The Democrats, who did not actually have the material, were keen for Nixon to believe that they did. It is thought that this may have been the reason Nixon's men broke into the office, to enable them to listen in to communications from the Democrats to discover if they were going to let the genie out of the bottle before the election.

Nixon easily won the election in November 1973, but his seven employees had been tried and convicted in March 1973, receiving stiff fines and imprisonment. However, a letter shortly after the convictions, from James McCord to the judge in the trial, John Sirica, lit a touch-paper that extended all the way to the White House. McCord raised the issue of his own personal safety for disclosing some new facts. 'Several members of my family have expressed fear for my life,' he wrote, 'if I disclose knowledge of the facts in this

matter, either publicly or to any government representative. Whereas I do not share their concerns to
the same degree, nevertheless, I do believe that
retaliatory measures will be taken against me, my
family and my friends should I disclose such facts.
Such retaliation could destroy careers, income and
reputations of persons who are innocent of any guilt
whatever.' In spite of these fears, he went on to tell
Sirica that, 'There was political pressure applied to
the defendants to plead guilty and remain silent'. He
claimed that perjury had been committed and that
people involved in Watergate were not identified in
the trial.

In the meantime, Acting Director of the FBI,
Patrick Gray had appeared in February before the
Senate Judiciary Committee as part of the process of
applying to replace long-standing FBI Director, J.
Edgar Hoover, who had died the previous May.
Committee chairman, Sam Ervin, Senator for North
Carolina, asked Gray about the Watergate files that
the media were suggesting were in the possession of
the White House. Gray told him he had given the
reports to John Dean and had talked to Dean on
many occasions about the FBI investigation into the
Watergate affair. He had linked Dean to the
Watergate affair and did not even get the job.

As the pressure began to mount, Dean began to suspect that he was going to be made the scapegoat for the Watergate disaster. He felt increasingly excluded from the inner circle of Nixon and his two close associates, White House Chief of Staff, H. R. Haldeman and John Erlichman, Assistant to the President for Domestic Affairs. Then Nixon sent him to the presidential retreat, Camp David, to put together a report containing everything he knew about Watergate and Dean began to smell a rat. Although he went to Camp David, he never compiled the report. By now he was talking to investigators and had hired a lawyer.

Dean was asked for his resignation on 30 April, the same day as Haldeman and Erlichman, but refused to resign and was, instead, sacked. He immediately released a statement in which he said he refused to be a 'scapegoat in the Watergate case'.

On 25 June, at the Watergate hearings, he was the first person from Nixon's administration to actually accuse the President of being directly involved in the Watergate break-in and the consequent cover-up. Among officials also accused of involvement was John Mitchell who had been Attorney General. Nixon vigorously denied all of Dean's accusations and, although they were damaging to his credibility and honesty, there was no legal basis to them. It was Dean's word against his.

Then it came to light, during the testimony of White House Aide, Alexander Butterfield, that tapes had routinely been made of every meeting in the White House. Senate Counsel, Fred Thompson, explored the possibility of the existence of the recordings and it emerged that Nixon had ordered the installation of a taping system in February 1971. There were line-taps on all of the telephones, and tiny microphones had been installed at various locations around the rooms. Special Counsel, Archibald Cox, in charge of the investigation, immediately subpoenaed the eight tapes that would confirm John Dean's testimony.

Initially, Nixon refused to release the tapes on grounds of national security. Then, under pressure, he offered to let the Mississippi Senator John Stennis listen to them and provide a summary. When Cox rejected this approach, Nixon ordered the Attorney General, Elliot Richardson to dismiss Cox. Richardson and his Deputy, William Ruckelshaus resigned instead and it was left to Solicitor General Robert Bork to get rid of Cox.

The House Judiciary Committee subpoenaed the tapes in April 1974, but Nixon only gave them edited transcripts that dealt with political opponents and the halting of the investigation into Watergate. The committee rejected these. Judge Sirica then subpoenaed the tapes of sixty-four conversations involving the President for use in cases against the officials accused of wrongdoing. Again Nixon refused. When new Special Counsel, Leon Jaworski, took the case to the Supreme Court, they voted unanimously that Nixon should hand over the tapes.

In July the tapes were released, the so-called 'smoking gun' tape amongst them. In that tape, Nixon is heard to agree that the Director of the CIA should be asked to stop the investigation because the break-in was a national security matter. That was the clincher – by agreeing to this, Nixon had entered into a criminal conspiracy to obstruct justice. That was a felony and enough to get him impeached. Nixon finally bowed to pressure and resigned on 9 August 1974, to be replaced by Gerald Ford, his Vice President. President Ford controversially gave Nixon a full pardon.

John Dean, the man who had first implicated Nixon, had already been in court. On 30 November 1973, he appeared before Judge Sirica and admitted to paying 'hush money' to the 'plumbers'. He also revealed the existence of Nixon's 'enemies list'. Dean was sentenced to one to four years in a minimum-security prison. Strangely, however, he was released into the custody of US Marshals and held at Fort Holabird in Maryland in a special safe house used mainly for holding witnesses testifying against the Mafia. He was in a Witness Protection Programme. He testified in the trials of the other Watergate conspirators, John Mitchell, Haldeman, Erlichman, Robert Mardian and Kenneth Parkinson. When these trials ended on 1 January 1975, Dean's lawyer moved to have his sentence reduced. The motion was granted and Dean was freed.

Dean became an investment banker until his retirement in 2006. In 1992, he successfully sued Gordon Liddy who had claimed in a book that Dean was, in fact, the mastermind behind Watergate. Liddy was supporting an incredible theory put forward by two other authors, Len Colodny and Robert Gettlin, that the target of the break-in was not, in fact, material damaging to Nixon's election campaign, but information that implicated Dean and his then fiancée, Maureen Biner, in a prostitution ring.

Dean now writes and gives lecture tours. He is heavily critical of George Bush and his administration and his most recent book was titled *Worse than Watergate: The Secret Presidency of George W. Bush.*

PART FOUR

FEMMES
FATALES

YOSHIKO KAWASHIMA

She was known as Eastern Jewel and was one of the most extraordinary women of the 20th century, helping to foment war between China and Japan. Working as a spy, throughout her life she seduced countless men, many of them rich and powerful. Not for nothing was she known as the eastern Mata Hari.

She was born a Manchu princess in 1906, fourteenth daughter of Prince Xu who ruled Inner Mongolia and claimed to be descended from the emperor who founded the Qing Dynasty in 1616. However, she was adopted by one of the Prince's Japanese advisers, Naniwa Kawashima, who changed her Chinese name, Jin Bihui, to the Japanese Yoshiko Kawashima. Educated in Japan, learning judo and fencing, she effectively became Japanese, forgetting her origins and being taught to hate China. When her father died in Port Arthur, her mother, deprived of a position in society, committed suicide. Eastern Jewel was reported to be unmoved on hearing the news.

She did begin to demonstrate some odd behaviour, however, at the age of seventeen, when she started wearing men's clothing. It is said by some that she began to do so after being raped by her adopted father. However, by now, she was a striking woman – like a film star, some said, with a strong personality.

The Japanese decided to dispatch Yoshiko to Manchuria to marry a Mongol prince, Kanjurab. They surmised that with her there, they would have a grip on what happened in Manchuria. Unfortunately, however, the marriage was short-lived. Eastern Jewel tired of her new husband after just four months and left Mongolia for the Chinese coast before returning to Tokyo, where she lived in the student quarter. There, she adopted yet another identity, calling herself Yang Kuei Fei.

Tiring of Tokyo, in 1928 she persuaded a member of the Japanese ruling elite to take her with him to Shanghai where, at a New Year party, she bumped into the Japanese Major General Takayoshi Tanaka, of the Shanghai Special Service. Eastern Jewel, in her customary garb of riding breeches, black knee-high boots, army jacket and riding crop, pushed Tanaka into a back room and proceeded to make love to him. To their delight, the couple discovered that they shared a fetish for boots and he was never allowed to take his off. They began a passionate affair.

Tanaka worked for Major-General Kenji Doihara, a man known as 'Lawrence of Manchuria' because of his knowledge of that country. Doihara had established an intricate network of spies in China and Eastern Jewel was perfect for it, especially as she was acquainted with the boy-emperor, Pu Yi, who would be the 'Last Emperor' of China. The Japanese wanted Pu Yi to return to his homeland, Manchuria, to allow them to use him as a pretext for invading the country. She was, after all, close to him and he had told her that his home was her home.

First, however, she was engaged by Tanaka in 1931 to create enough of a disturbance in Shanghai to justify an invasion by Japanese troops to keep the peace. She was given $10,000 which she used to pay thugs to attack Japanese businesses. The Japanese army duly arrived to protect Japanese interests and citizens. They were eventually forced to withdraw when diplomatic pressure was brought to bear by countries around the world.

At this point, Doihara decided to make use of Eastern Jewel's friendship with Pu Yi. She was told to persuade him to move to Mukden in Manchuria, where the Japanese would install him as a puppet emperor who would fully support their move into the country. They believed that he would be so fed up with his treatment in China at the hands of Sun Yat-sen, leader of the Kuomintang that he would do anything to take revenge.

Eastern Jewel's first effort was to tell him that his life was in danger if he did not move, but he refused to go. She then orchestrated assassination attempts that she thwarted – finding poisonous snakes in his bed or discovering bombs in a basket of fruit. Still, he would not move. It is reported that, frustrated at the delay, Doihara arrived in Tientsin and asked to see Eastern Jewel. She turned up disguised as a man and fooled the Major General until she spoke to him. He and Eastern Jewel decided that the best way to frighten Pu Yi was to have Chinese terrorists attack his Japanese guards at his villa. She hired the attackers and, at last, the emperor was frightened into leaving for Mukden.

He was installed as Emperor of Manchuko and almost immediately, the Japanese launched their invasion, claiming that the emperor had requested it 'to preserve peace'. Eastern Jewel, meanwhile, was rewarded for her work. She was appointed commander and was given the right to wear the full dress Japanese uniform commensurate with her rank. Needless to say, given her penchant for dressing in men's clothes, she was delighted.

On 23 February 1932, as Shanghai burned under an onslaught of Japanese bombing, Eastern Jewel was flown over the city by the Japanese Air Force. She was said to have laughed and clapped her hands as she looked down on the devastation and horror below her. The massive loss of life seemed to mean nothing to her, a fact emphasised by her laughter with Japanese officers as she later stepped over the dead bodies of men, women and children as she walked in the streets. It meant nothing to her, but her callousness meant a great deal to any Chinese who witnessed it. It would not be forgotten.

She continued her work for the Japanese. In Manchuko she became the mistress of Major General Hayao Tada, Pu Yi's chief military adviser, and in 1932 she created an 'Anti-Bandit Force'. She recruited between three and five thousand former bandits to hunt down the lawless bandit and guerrilla groups that were running wild. She commanded this force for a number of years.

When the Japanese army captured Beijing in 1937, she went to live there with orders to spy and report on local activity. She took money from prominent people to ensure that they would not come under suspicion of collaboration with the forces of Chiang Kai-shek, who had taken control of the Kuomintang following the death of Sun Yat-sen in 1925. If they failed to pay she would report them as agitators or spies.

By the end of the war, however, Eastern Jewel was a shadow of her former self. Her beauty had faded and she was haggard and bloated. Her sexual practices were legend, reportedly sleeping with as many as twelve men at one time, including very often members of the Japanese guard assigned to protect her. When she was bored she would send the guards to the local theatres as she had developed a liking for handsome young actors.

She had claimed that she had been raped by her foster father and foster grandfather when she was just fifteen and that her father had forced her to have sex with Japanese officers. She also blamed her behaviour on her rejection by a young Japanese officer named Yamaga. Her extravagant love life was her revenge on him, she claimed.

Her promiscuity had its penalties, however, and she was now riddled with syphilis, her body covered in running sores. She drove around Beijing in an abandoned army truck, causing disgust amongst passers-by.

The re-capture of the capital was the worst possible news for Eastern Jewel. Her money was gone now, spent on protection during the war years and she went into hiding, changing her name and living in a run-down hovel. On 11 November, 1945, a news report announced that 'a long sought-for beauty in male costume was arrested in Peking by the Chinese counter-intelligence officers.'

In 1948 Eastern Jewel was tried before a military court for treason, espionage and war crimes. The chief prosecutor reminded the court of her callousness on the day she flew over the ravaged capital. 'This woman deserves death as a traitor,' he said, 'but most of all because she rode in Japanese airplanes over bombed-out villages and laughed.'

She was sentenced to death but demanded that, as a Japanese soldier, she should be executed by firing squad. The court rejected her demand, however, and on 25 March 1948, she was led outside where her head was put on a wooden block. As had happened to countless thousands of Chinese people at the hands of the Japanese, she was beheaded with a sword.

Yoshiko Kawashima was executed under her Chinese name, Jin Bihui.

MATA HARI

As was customary, the detachment made as much noise as they could as they walked along the corridor to the condemned woman's cell. It was preferable for her to be awake when they arrived, rather than be startled into consciousness with the knowledge that they had come for her. For, she had not known the date of the execution. The authorities considered it inhumane to make the condemned prisoner aware of the date of his or her demise.

However, in spite of the stamping of their feet on the cold stone floor, Mata Hari was not awake that morning of 15 October 1917, as they approached the cell. The previous night's sedative had not worn off and she had to be stirred from her sleep. Captain Pierre Bouchardon, the man who had interrogated her so many times, told her to be brave and informed her that her request for clemency had been rejected by the President of the Republic. The time had come for her execution. 'It's not possible!' she said disbelievingly while two nuns who had been with her during the months she had spent in prison tried to comfort her. Calming down, she turned to one of the nuns. 'Don't be afraid, sister,' she said, 'I shall know how to die.'

She bravely held her head high as she walked out onto the site of her execution, refusing a blindfold when it was offered. Twelve soldiers facing her, nervously took aim and as they did so, extraordinarily, she blew a kiss at them. The order to fire was given and twelve shots rang out. She fell to the ground, a bullet through the heart that had loved so much. An officer walked over to her and, as was the custom, delivered the coup de grace – a single bullet in the side of her head. Mata Hari, dancer, courtesan and spy, was dead.

She had been born Margaretha Zelle in 1876 in Leewarden in the Netherlands, the second child of a successful hat manufacturer, Adam Zelle and Antje van der Meulen. Her three siblings were all boys and their unusually dark-skinned, dark-eyed and black-haired sister was known to them as M'greet. She stood out in a family whose colouring was generally fair and blonde and it was suggested that she must have had Jewish or even Javanese blood. M'greet played on these exotic looks, inventing fantasies with which she would regale her schoolfriends. She was popular with both teachers and pupils and was bright, showing a particular facility for languages.

Everything changed for the Zelle family when M'greet was thirteen. Her father had made some injudicious investments on the stockmarket and was declared bankrupt. Suddenly, they were forced to move from their comfortable house in a good area to a small, shabby home in one of the poorer sections. Adam Zelle went to Amsterdam to try to re-build his fortune, leaving Antje to bring up the children alone. It was hard for her and she became became depressed and fell ill. She tragically died two years later, when M'greet was fifteen.

Adam Zelle did not want to look after the children and, instead, distributed them amongst other family members and friends, M'greet being sent to lodge with her godfather in the small Dutch town of Sneek.

Aged fifteen, she was very tall for the time – five feet ten inches, far taller than the average Dutchman, making it difficult for her to find a likely candidate for marriage so that she could escape from her dependency on her godfather and his family. It was decided, instead, that she should train to be a kindergarten teacher. She was sent to train in Leyde in a school run by a man called Wybrandus Haanstra. Not only was she not a very good teacher – she found it hard to maintain discipline in a classroom – but she also had an affair with Haanstra. She was forced to leave the school in disgrace.

She was taken in by an uncle in The Hague, carrying out domestic chores for him and his family. She was now eighteen, and although not classically beautiful, was certainly an attractive girl with grace and style.

One day, reading a newspaper, M'greet read a curious advert. It read: 'Officer on home leave from Dutch East Indies would like to meet girl of pleasant character – object matrimony,' and had been placed by the friends of a thirty-eight-year-old army officer, Rudolf MacLeod, without his knowledge. MacLeod, whose Scottish ancestors explained his distinctly un-Dutch name, agreed to meet M'greet and the two instantly liked each other. She had always been attracted to men in uniform and when he proposed to her, she enthusiastically accepted. Married on 11 July 1895, M'greet gave birth to her first child, a boy they named Norman John, in January 1897.

Unfortunately, however, Rudolf MacLeod was reluctant to give up the habits he had enjoyed as a bachelor and M'greet not only had to endure her husband's serial infidelity, but also his alcoholism. At the same time, he was subject to violent jealousy and would fly into a terrible rage if another man so much as looked at his wife. Given her attractive good looks, that was a regular occurrence and he would become violent towards her, abusing and beating her, even when she was pregnant.

When MacLeod was posted with his family to Java, M'greet was excited, possibly believing that this change in their circumstances would lead to a better life for them all. They settled in Abawara and M'greet immediately fell in love with Java's lush vegetation and graceful, beautiful people amongst whom, with her dark looks and olive skin, she felt at home.

However, the change of scenery did little to change Rudolf's behaviour or his terrible temper. He took a native woman as a mistress and did little to hide the fact from his wife. He told her it was customary in Java and she would just have to get used to it. She had a second baby in May 1898, but her husband was disappointed that it was a girl. She was given the Malay name, Non.

When Non was one year old, Rudolf was sent to Sumatra and he left M'greet and the children behind, depositing them at the house of the comptroller for the island and making M'greet feel once again like an interloper in a strange house, just as she had felt after the death of her mother. Eventually, Rudolf summoned her to their new, spacious home in Medan, where he had been promoted to garrison commander.

She excelled in the role of garrison commander's wife, throwing large parties and socialising with her customary ease and style. She spoke Dutch, German, English and French to visitors, Malay to servants and dressed in the latest fashions imported from Amsterdam. She played the piano and, needless to say, danced superbly. For once, Rudolf seemed proud of his beautiful, gracious wife.

Tragedy struck, however, on the night of 27 June 1899 when both their children suddenly fell ill. Norman, the elder of the two, died before the doctor arrived and Non was rushed to hospital where she was successfully treated. They had been poisoned, although it was never discovered by whom. Eventually, a disgruntled servant was suggested as the perpetrator.

The child's death made a bad marriage worse and Rudolf began to drink heavily, while M'greet sank into a deep depression. She succumbed to typhoid and MacLeod resented the cost of caring for her. She could not take it any more and wrote letters home, pleading without success with her family to send the money that would allow her to escape and travel home.

Eventually, even MacLeod had had enough and the family returned to Europe in 1903. There, he beat M'greet for the last time and walked out, taking Non with him. She divorced him and won custody of the child and maintenance payments which were, of course, never forthcoming. Unable to find work, she was forced to return Non into the care of Rudolf. She was left with nothing.

She did have her dreams, however, and, although an initial trip to Paris did not provide her with the theatre or modelling work she had been hoping for, a second trip gave her everything she desired and more.

Mata Hari, Malay for 'the sun', was 'born' on 13 March 1905 at the Musée Guimet. She had been performing as a circus horse rider, using the name Lady MacLeod and had also worked as an artist's model. Gradually, she had begun to earn a reputation as an exotic dancer, an art that was also being championed at the time by dancers such as Isadora Duncan and Ruth St. Denis. She had become the mistress of the millionaire Lyon industrialist, Emile Etienne Guimet, founder of the museum.

That night the improvised stage was set with a large carving of the four-armed Indian god, Siva, a bowl of oil burning at his feet. She entered looking like a vision, clad in items from the museum's oriental collection – bracelets dangled on her legs, arms and wrists, an Indian belt, covered in precious stones encircled her waist, holding up her translucent sarong. Conscious of her small breasts, the jewel-encrusted metal breast cups she wore were stuffed with cotton wool. She cast off her shawls one by one until, illuminated only by the light of the burning oil, she removed her sarong, her naked body writhing with desire for the god. She bent low, touching the statue's feet with her forehead and her four dancing partners approached and draped a gold lamé cloak across her body, allowing her to stand up and receive the rapturous applause of the audience.

On that night, M'greet became Mata Hari, a huge star who made striptease respectable, almost an art form, although she wore a skin-toned body stocking and was never actually totally naked on stage. She began to perform across Europe – Spain, Monte Carlo and Germany.

She created a mythology for herself. When asked where she had come from, she would reply that she had been born in India and that her mother had been a temple dancer who had died giving birth to her. She had been brought up in the temple of Siva and her life and her art were dedicated to him. Her gullible audience fell for it hook, line and sinker.

Mata Hari enjoyed a fabulous career until, approaching forty, life started to become difficult. She was not as fit as she once was and her figure was no longer that of a young girl. She began to spend her life more as a courtesan than a dancer, enjoying the company of rich and influential men – often military men – who gave her the lifestyle she desired. There is little doubt she was an expert in satisfying the needs of the men with whom she enjoyed relationships, but one thing remained constant. Even when making love, the breast cups remained firmly in place. She laughed it off saying that her brute of a husband had bitten off both her nipples.

Still performing occasionally, she appeared in a show in Germany in May 1914 which was attended by the police as a result of complaints that the show was indecent. That night, she is said to have met and begun a relationship with a high-ranking German policeman, Traugott von Jagow, who, it is suggested, was the head of German espionage.

Von Jagow, knowing of her connections, is believed to have asked her to spy on France. Some say that she even attended a German spy school in Antwerp in Belgium and that, while learning about codes, ciphers, communication methods, the use and manufacture of chemicals, maps, charts, photography and enemy weaponry, she was given the code name 'H 21' that was later to play a major part in her demise. Of course, there is no real evidence that she did attend the school and she certainly denied it.

Two days after war broke out between France and Germany on 4 August 1914, Mata Hari went to Switzerland, but was sent back to Germany due to a problem with her passport. Eventually she made it to Amsterdam before returning to Paris, a city at war whose authorities and people worried about spies in their midst. Mata Hari, with her recent German connections, came under immediate suspicion and was put under surveillance.

Around this time, she met the man she would love above all others, a handsome twenty-one-year-old Russian officer, Vladmir Masloff, known as Vadim. Although Mata Hari was almost twice his age, they fell deeply in love. But, tragically, Vadim was sent back to the front where he was wounded, losing the sight in his left eye. However, it only served to make their relationship even more intense.

Vadim was recovering from his wound in a hospital

near Vittel and in order to visit him, she required a permit. With her record that was not going to be easy. In her efforts to obtain a permit, she was introduced to Captain Georges Ladoux, an officer in charge of French espionage. Ladoux, knowing her connections with high-ranking Germans, asked her if she would spy on the Germans for the French. She agreed to do it and, in return, was given the permit. The job was lucrative, which was fortunate, as she and Vadim were in sore need of funds.

The plan was for her to use a connection in Brussels, a man who supplied food to the German army, in order to gain access to General Moritz Ferdinand von Bissing, who was in command of the German occupation of Belgium. She would seduce von Bissing and find out what she could from him.

As the war made getting to Belgium through northern France impossible, she first had to travel to Spain before sailing to Britain. She would then cross to Holland and, eventually, Belgium. But, on arriving in Britain, she ran into trouble. Firstly, the British were convinced she was a German spy and secondly, they suspected her of being someone else entirely; a woman for whom they had been looking for some time – the German spy, Clara Benedix. Mata Hari bore a vague resemblance to Bendix and that was enough for the British, who arrested her immediately her ship docked and took her to Scotland Yard for questioning. Eventually, she persuaded them she was not Bendix but, instead of letting her sail to Holland, they sent her back to Spain, isolated and penniless. It was December 1916.

Ever resourceful, in Spain she had a brief fling with a German major, Arnold Kalle. She was convinced she had obtained some German secrets and would be paid handsomely for them by her French masters. Unfortunately, her information was old news to the French and it is also likely that Kalle, suspicious of her intentions, had deliberately fed her old information to see if it made its way back to the French. Returning to Paris and learning there would be no money for her information, she awaited her next assignment, certain that she could gain access to someone much more important than Kalle.

It was not to be, however. In January 1917, the German military attaché in Madrid transmitted radio messages to Berlin describing the helpful activities of a German spy, code-named H-21. H-21 was, of course, Mata Hari. Although what was communicated in the message was fairly innocuous, the fact that Mata Hari had a German code name interested the French. It suggested that she had been spying for Germany, before being recruited by Ladoux. The Germans were perfectly aware that the French had broken the code they were using to send these messages and the only conclusion has to be that they fully intended the French to intercept and understand them. Mata Hari was a double agent and they were giving the French the responsibility of dealing with her.

On 13 February, she was arrested and interrogated at length while incarcerated in Saint-Lazare Prison. She maintained her innocence throughout, but it was not enough and at her trial on 24 July 1917 a huge crowd thronged the streets around the courtroom, hoping to catch a glimpse of the infamous sex symbol. And she was a sight to behold. Although the prison had afforded her no personal comforts – no bath and only fifteen minutes of exercise a day, and despite the fact that she was, by now, overweight, she was immaculate in a beautiful blue dress and a hat with a lace mantilla sweeping across her face and dropping down over her slim shoulders. In spite of the heat of mid-summer, she wore gloves, folded into a large fur muff.

The trial was held in secret and there was only one outcome – she was found guilty and condemned to death: 'The Council unanimously condemns the named person, Zelle, Marguérite, Gertrude, as mentioned above, to the punishment of death.' Cruelly, they also required her to pay court costs.

She awaited a reprieve, but none arrived and on that fateful morning, Mata Hari blew her last kiss and died.

CHERYL HANIN

Former Mossad director, Meir Amit, once said: 'A woman has skills a man simply does not have. The history of modern intelligence is filled with accounts of women who have used their sex for the good of their country.' To that history can be added the name of Cheryl Ben Tov, née, Hanin, the woman who used her charms to ensnare former Israeli nuclear technician Mordechai Vanunu.

Vanunu was born in Morocco, immigrating to Israel with his family in 1963. He harboured ambitions to be an Israeli Air Force pilot, but failed the exams and opted to join the army instead. He had the chance to make the army a career, but felt that he wanted to pursue his studies. However, he failed the entrance exams for a university physics course and returned home to Beersheba in southern Israel. There, he was accepted as a trainee at the Negev Nuclear Research Centre in Dimona. He signed the

Israeli Official Secrets Act and began a crash course in nuclear physics.

Construction of the centre had begun in 1958 and ever since then, there had been rumours that it was not there simply to exploit nuclear energy for peaceful use. People said that its work was also to make nuclear weapons.

Vanunu made a decent career and not bad money at the centre. He earned trust and worked in increasingly sensitive areas. In the meantime, he took a philosophy degree at Ben-Gurion University, but began to become involved in student politics, expressing support for Palestinian causes, sympathies upon which the authorities did not look favourably. But Vanunu sympathised with them as an outsider. As a Jew born in an Arab country, Morocco, he felt that the Israeli Jews of European descent looked down on him.

His superiors at the centre repeatedly instructed him to refrain from his political activities, but he paid no attention to their warnings. Additionally, the nuclear issue weighed heavily on his mind. He was conflicted by the destructive capability of the weapons he was helping to construct.

Finally, he had had enough and decided to leave, but before he could resign, they told him they were making him redundant. Before he left, he took dozens of photographs inside the centre, photographs which included different types of bombs that were being made. He thought they might come in useful one day.

It was early 1968 and, like many young people at the time, he decided to go travelling, taking his rolls of undeveloped film with him. He went to Sydney in Australia, where he earned a living driving a taxi. Curiously, he also began to attend an Anglican church, converting to Christianity. At that time, in this particular church, they were involved in a debate about nuclear weapons. Vanunu brought his first-hand experiences at Dimona into the debate.

A Colombian, Oscar Guerrero, who had been painting the church, became friendly with Vanunu. He immediately recognised that the information Vanunu was sitting on was priceless. Evidence of Israel's nuclear programme could be gold dust. He convinced Vanunu that he could sell the story for a lot of money and Vanunu finally had his Dimona films processed. Guerrero offered the pictures to the news organisations. At first, he received only rejections, from *Newsweek* and other publications. In 1986, however, things began to look up when the *Sunday Times* in London began to show an interest. Peter Hounam, an investigative reporter, was assigned to find out if there was any truth in what Guerrero was selling.

A British physics professor, shown the pictures, said that they appeared to be genuine and the newspaper sent Hounam to talk directly to Vanunu. Vanunu managed to convince him of the veracity of what the pictures showed and explained that, in fact, the Israeli weapons programme was even more extensive than first imagined.

Vanunu was flown to London to meet experts who grilled him and then kept him waiting for a decision. He was promised around £50,000, not for the information he was giving the newspaper, but for a book deal and serialisation in a German magazine.

The waiting continued and Vanunu, alone in London, became bored. He tried to occupy his time, but in spite of insistence that he remain in his hotel room, he started to go out and wander around London. One day he caught the eye of a slightly plump, attractive blond in her twenties, walking through Leicester Square. She returned his gaze and he spoke to her, asking her if she was a tourist. She answered in an American accent, telling him her name was Cindy and that she was a beautician on holiday from America. They seemed to get on and she suggested that they could meet next day at the Tate Gallery. Vanunu, interested in art, was delighted to have met a like-minded soul, and an attractive one at that. He readily agreed to meet her. What he did not know, of course, is that Cindy was no beautician. She was, in actual fact, an agent of Mossad, the Israeli secret service, planted specifically to catch Vanunu in a 'honey trap' operation.

She was no ordinary agent, either. Cheryl Hanin had grown up in some luxury in Florida, the daughter of Stanley Hanin, the very wealthy owner of a tyre business that he would later sell for $32 million. Cheryl had thrown herself into the study of the Jewish religion in 1977, on the advice of her rabbi, as a way of dealing with the acrimonious divorce of her parents. Part of her studies was a three-month residential course in Israel, funded by the World Zionist Organisation. Shortly after completing the course, and after graduating from high school, she left America, aged just seventeen, and joined the Israeli army. Her work was partly military and partly agricultural and it was while working on a kibbutz that she met, fell in love with and married Ofer Ben Tov, an Israeli soldier six years older than her, who would also later work for Mossad.

Mossad had been created in 1951, three years after the state of Israel came into being and quickly became one of the world's best and most daring intelligence agencies. Its capture of Nazi war criminal, Adolph

Eichman and the famous 1976 commando raid at Entebbe that freed a hundred Israelis held hostage on a hijacked French passenger plane, had helped to create its reputation.

Cheryl's intelligence and American background made her an ideal recruitment target for Mossad and she was taken on and trained. She learned such things as how to shoot someone from a distance of 100 yards, how to use radio equipment, navigate speed-boats and spot when she was being followed. She would have been sent on training missions such as breaking into an occupied hotel room and stealing documents from an office. She would have learned how to pick up men in clubs, being observed all the while by her teachers. Her training over, she joined a Mossad unit that worked with Israeli embassies around the world, posing as the wife or girlfriend of other agents.

In September, 1986, she was given a proper assignment when she was summoned to Mossad head-quarters in Tel Aviv and ordered to fly to London under the name of Cynthia Hanin, the name of her sister-in-law. The agency's deputy-chief, Beni Zeevi was assembling a team in London to carry out an important operation, so important that instructions had come directly from the office of the Israeli Prime

Minister, Shimon Peres. Mordechai Vanunu was be kidnapped and brought back to Israel at all costs. The Israeli government was incensed that the lowly technician had exposed Israel's nuclear capacity to the world, something they had been denying for years.

The *Sunday Times*, now ready to publish Vanunu's revelations, but still frustrating him by not giving him a publication date, had warned him to be careful and, above all, not to go abroad. They were sure that the Israelis would not risk a major incident by kidnapping him in Britain, but could not be so sure about other countries. Nevertheless, when 'Cindy' invited him to Italy where her sister owned a flat that happened to be unoccupied, he jumped at the chance, as well as at the business-class ticket she had bought him.

Peter Hounam was suspicious of this girl Vanunu was seeing so much of. He even suggested to him that she might be an Israeli agent. Vanunu told him not to worry, that she was just a tourist and was even critical of Israel. All the same, the *Sunday Times* invited Vanunu and his new girlfriend to dinner to check her out, but Vanunu called to cancel, saying he was 'going out of the city'.

On 30 September, they left for Rome on British Airways Flight 504. They were met at the airport by a friend who drove them to Cindy's sister's apartment. No sooner had they entered than two men pounced on Vanunu, pinning him to the ground and tranquillising him with an injection.

Unconscious, he was driven to a speedboat and then transferred onto an Israeli Navy ship off the Italian coast, which was disguised as a Panamanian-registered cargo vessel. All the while, he was accompanied by Hanin who was later reported by crew-members to have been rude, selfish and bossy. Within a week, Vanunu was languishing in a cell at Mossad headquarters in Tel Aviv.

On 5 October, even though their source had vanished into thin air, the *Sunday Times* published the story with a front-page photograph of the Dimona reactor and a further three pages revealing that Israel possessed as many as 200 nuclear devices, ranking it as a major nuclear power, the world's sixth and the first after the non-proliferation treaty of 1968, which Israel had not signed.

When news broke of the kidnapping of the man who had revealed the story, there was outrage around the world, but there was nothing that could be done. The Israelis did not deny the story, refusing to say anything at all about Vanunu. The first confirmation of his capture came two months later, in December, when he appeared in court. In the dock, he held up his hand on which he had written in black ink the words: 'Vanunu M was hi-jacked in Rome. ITL. 30.9.86. 21.00. Came to Rome by fly BA504', explaining to the world how they had taken him.

He was charged with treason which could have resulted in the death penalty, but he was, instead, sentenced to eighteen years in prison. Having spent the first twelve in solitary confinement, he was released in 2007, but only on condition that he remained in Israel and did not speak to the media. He failed to uphold the conditions of his release, however, and is now back in prison.

Cheryl Ben Tov and her husband now work as estate agents in Florida. They have two daughters and also have a home in Israel in Netanya.

She was undoubtedly good at her job. When Vanunu was released, he denied that 'Cindy' was an agent of Mossad. 'She was either an FBI or a CIA agent,' he said. 'I spent a week with her. I saw her picture. Cindy was a young woman from Philadelphia.'

To millions, she is a hero who helped to bring a traitor to justice, while to others, Mordechai Vanunu is a hero who tried, in his own way, to bring a halt to things that he believed endangered the world, by exposing Israel's gigantic nuclear arsenal to global scrutiny.

KATRINA LEUNG

Sex, money, politics and a spy with the codename 'Parlour Maid'. It was the stuff of fiction. Katrina Leung, a venture capitalist and Republican Party fundraiser and donor, had affairs with two FBI agents while acting as a double agent and spying for China.

How did she do it, and for so long, many have asked? The blame can be laid fairly and squarely at the door of an FBI department whose workings had developed systematic flaws over a period of years. The decentralised nature of the culture in the Los Angeles Chinese counterintelligence programme, in which there was little management or command of agent handlers, only 'support', led to a lack of accountability. It also enabled agents to fob their superiors off with whatever they wanted them to believe.

This was certainly the case with agent James J. 'J.J.' Smith. Smith had many years' experience in Chinese counterintelligence and this gave him a somewhat privileged position in the agency. His superiors effectively thought he knew more than they did and, consequently, they would defer to him on whatever he told them. Over the years, this allowed him to manipulate or simply ignore bureaucratic procedures, allowing him to maintain a twenty-year sexual relationship with Katrina Lleung, aka 'Parlour Maid'. Little did he know that she was using that relationship to gain information about United States intelligence and was passing it to the People's Republic of China.

Katrina Leung's origins are hazy. She was born on 1 May 1954 in Guangzhou in the south of China and in 1970 emigrated to the United States, on a Taiwanese passport. She enrolled at Washington Irving High School in New York, graduating in 1972 in the August of which she became a resident alien. Having obtained a degree from Cornell University in 1976, she went to the University of Chicago, where she obtained a Master of Business Administration.

Leung's first contact with the security services occurred around this time, when the FBI asked for information about some of her acquaintances, but in 1980 she blotted her copybook when she formed a relationship with a Chinese activist that the FBI believed to be smuggling technological information from the United States to China. Leung, at the time general manager of an import-export company, came under investigation by the FBI, who began to suspect her of being a Chinese spy. When she left the job, however, the agency closed down the investigation.

The Chinese activist had been arrested in China by this time but agent J. J. Smith wanted a bit more information about him. He reopened the file on Leung and was immediately impressed with her, especially her contacts in the top echelons of the Chinese government; contacts that could prove very useful to the FBI. He decided to convert her into an FBI agent, and in December 1982 she became an FBI 'asset' with the codename 'Parlour Maid'. Six months later, they were lovers and, in 1984, Smith used his influence to obtain United States citizenship for Leung.

The FBI's plan was for Leung to be recruited by the Chinese Ministry of State Security (MSS) and work as a double agent, spying for the USA and in June 1984, she duly became an agent of the Chinese with a handler known by the codename 'Mao'.

Meanwhile, she was becoming successful in other areas. Towards the end of the 1980s, she was a well-known figure in the West Coast Chinese community. As well as being president of her successful business consultancy, she was also a director of the Los Angeles World Affairs Council. She was on hand to welcome Chinese diplomats to Los Angeles and hosted functions for visiting Chinese digitaries. She even befriended Chinese President, Yang Shangkun, who took a shine to her. An indication of how highly they thought of her and trusted her was her appointment to the role of adviser when they were looking for a new location for the Chinese consulate in Los Angeles.

Her work, checked and approved by a Chinese defector at the agency, was also highly regarded by the CIA and the FBI. She was even sent to China to report back on the country's political situation following the massacre in Tiananmen Square in 1989. Around this time, however, she began an affair with yet another FBI agent, Bill Cleveland, the San Francisco office's supervisory special agent for Chinese counterintelligence and son of a former Assistant Director of the agency. Cleveland had been with the FBI since 1969.

Leung's problems began when the FBI came into possession of a tape of a woman, identifying herself as 'Luo', speaking with a man identified on the tape as 'Mao'. When Bill Cleveland was called in to listen to the tape, he immediately identified Luo's voice as that of his lover, Katrina Leung. In the tape, Leung provided details of a trip to China Cleveland she had recently made on behalf of the State Department. During that visit, Cleveland and his colleague I. C. Smith had become suspicious when they had noticed that they were followed by more than the usual number of Chinese security agents. Cleveland contacted J. J. Smith who, according to an FBI report, was 'visibly upset' when he was told about the agency's suspicions. A meeting, involving Parlour Maid's two lovers – neither of whom knew about the other, of course – was convened at FBI headquarters in Washington.

A top-level FBI analyst, who also attended the meeting, concluded that the information Parlour Maid was providing to the FBI far outweighed in value the information she was passing to China. Naturally, Smith also came out in support of her, using the full weight of his thirty years of experience to convince his superiors that she was still a valuable FBI asset.

When J. J. confronted her in private, however, she confessed to him that in mid-1990, the Chinese had discovered that she was also working for the FBI and had threatened her. She said that at that point she provided Mao with information concerning the FBI. She would later tell an FBI interviewer: 'If you ask me, like, worst day of my life, that must be the day that, you know, J. J. confronted me.'

Smith made her apologise in person to Cleveland and her work continued, as did her affairs with both Smith and Cleveland.

Suspicions lingered, however, and in November 2002 the FBI monitored a hotel room in Los Angeles where Leung and Smith met. Electronic surveillance revealed that they were, indeed, having a sexual relationship. That same month, when Leung was on her way to China for a visit, the FBI intercepted and searched her luggage at Los Angeles Airport. They discovered a fax from Smith to Leung containing the photographs of six agents, taken at a meeting of the Society of Former Special Agents for the FBI. Two agents, on active FBI duty, were amongst the pictures. They searched it again on her return at the end of the month and found that the photos of the agents were missing, presumably handed over to authorities in China.

To make matters worse, the next month they discovered that she had covertly copied a top-secret document that had been checked out of the office in Smith's name. This had been passed to Mao, her MSS handler.

J. J. Smith was interviewed in December 2002 about Leung and admitted to probably telling her too much about FBI operations in the course of his work as her handler. He additionally admitted making trips with her to Hong Kong and to London, but when asked whether he was having an affair with her, he at first refused to answer the question and then flatly denied it.

When Leung was interviewed around the same time, on the other hand, she admitted the affair and confessed that it had begun in the 1980s. She voluntarily provided the FBI with a document detailing phone conversations between her and her handler, Mao. Then, on 12 December, the FBI searched her house and found an FBI telephone directory containing details of Los Angeles FBI counterintelligence agents, a telephone list relating to the 'Royal Tourist' investigation at Lawrence Livermore National Laboratory where Bill Cleveland now worked, a secret FBI document about Chinese fugitives and an FBI directory containing the names and phone numbers of the FBI's legal attaché offices abroad.

In numerous interviews during the next few months, Leung admitted everything. She described how she would take documents from Smith's open briefcase and photocopy them without his knowledge and how she kept notes of their conversations about FBI matters, all of which was passed to her MSS handler. She also admitted passing information to the

Chinese about Cleveland's 1990 visit to China and that she withheld information from both the FBI and the MSS over the years, deceiving both agencies. She confessed to receiving $100,000 from China, claiming it was given to her because the Chinese President was fond of her.

When Cleveland was hauled in, he finally admitted to having an affair with Katrina Leung. However, he told his questioners that he had relied on Smith to deal with Leung's disclosure of information regarding his 1990 Chinese visit. Smith had assured him it had been properly dealt with.

In 1990, Bill Cleveland had left the FBI and went to work as head of security at Lawrence Livermore National Laboratory near San Francisco. Leung had begun an affair with Cleveland two years earlier, in 1988, an affair that had cooled but was re-kindled in 1997. Coincidentally – or not, as the case may be – 1997 happened to be a critical year in the investigation known as 'Royal Tourist' into the Lawrence Livermore scientist, Peter Lee, who was suspected of passing classified information regarding US nuclear weapons to China. Interestingly, the Cox Report, a classified 1999 investigation of China's covert operations in the United States, severely criticised Lawrence Livermore National Laboratory, alleging that security had been compromised and Chinese agents had succeeded in stealing classified information. Had Leung obtained that information from Cleveland, in the same way that she had from Smith? She was later found to have a document relating to 'Royal Tourist' in her possession, but Cleveland denied under oath that he had been the source.

J. J. and his Parlour Maid were both arrested on 9 April 2003. Katrina Leung was picked up at her San Marino home and charged with Unauthorised Copying of National Defence Information with Intent to Injure or Benefit a Foreign Nation. This charge was used rather than Treason or Espionage because prosecutors did not feel they had enough evidence to support those charges. She was denied bail because they feared she would disappear. She spent three months in jail and was then released on $2 million bail.

She was lucky, however. When the case finally made it to court, US District Judge Florence Marie Cooper dismissed it because she found that Leung's constitutional rights had been violated when her counsel had been denied access to information regarding the case from J. J. Smith.

The State appealed against the decision and entered into plea negotiations with Leung concerning illegal tax returns she had made which had emerged during the trial. She pleaded guilty in December 2005 to one charge of lying to the FBI and one of filing a false federal tax return. Her plea agreement meant that she had to cooperate fully in debriefings about her activities as an agent of the FBI and she also received three years' probation, 100 hours of community service and a $10,000 fine.

Smith pleaded guilty to lying to the FBI about his affair with Leung and agreed to cooperate in the ensuing investigation of her activities. More serious charges of mail fraud and mishandling of classified documents that could have sent him to prison for ten years, were dropped in exchange.

There is little doubt that Katrina Leung did untold damage to the security of the United States during her twenty years as a double agent. However, this duplicitous, manipulative and undoubtedly very clever woman did not do too badly out of it, in the end. Her fine was $10,000, but over the years the US government had paid her some $1.7 million. Not a bad profit, really.

LINDA KASABIAN

She spent eighteen days in the witness box, describing the horrors she had witnessed in graphic detail. Meanwhile, Charles Manson and his co-defendants, the ragged bunch of hippies who had worshipped him and still did, tried their best to disrupt proceedings, to put her off her stride. Every now and then, Manson, himself, would look hard at her across the courtroom, threat oozing from every pore, and draw his finger across his throat in a slitting gesture. There were shouts of 'You're killing us!' from Susan Atkins. Kasabian coolly responded, disgust in her voice, 'I am not killing you. You have killed yourselves!'

On another occasion, Manson suddenly held up a newspaper to the jury. MANSON GUILTY, NIXON DECLARES its headline shouted. President Richard Nixon had made some comments about the proceedings to members of the press. Manson wanted to create a mistrial, but the judge was having none of it, in spite of the best efforts of Manson's legal team.

The defence tactics were simply to discredit Kasabian's testimony. They focused on her LSD use and her shambolic lifestyle. They picked holes in her story. But she remained strong, desperate to get her story out and hoping, perhaps, to exorcise some of the demons that had taken up residence in her head. It all started one August night at 10050 Cielo Drive when Voyteck Frykowski appeared in front of her at the door of the house rented by film director, Roman Polanski, and his beautiful young actress wife, Sharon Tate, covered in blood.

Then, when they were all found guilty, her testimony contributing hugely to the prosecution's success, she suffered even more, and even stranger intimidation during the penalty phase of the trial, when the judge would pass sentence. The defendants trooped into the dock, a gruesome sight – their heads were shaved and they had carved swastikas into their foreheads. They now claimed that it had not been Manson who had planned the killings, but Linda Kasabian.

Naturally, the judge and jury rejected these incoherent and inconsistent ramblings.

She had been born Linda Darlene Drouin in Biddeford, Maine, in 1949 and endured a fairly troubled childhood in a broken home, with a stepfather she never got along with. Finally, she had had enough and took off westwards towards California, 'looking for God' she said.

Like many teenagers in the love and peace years of the 1960s, she wandered from commune to commune, soaking up the hippie culture as well as a lot of acid. She got married, divorced and married again, to Robert Kasabian and in 1968, gave birth to a daughter, Tanya. Once again, however, the marriage did not work out and Kasabian returned home to live with her mother. Robert Kasabian suggested they try again and suggested she joined him on a sailing trip with a friend, Charles 'Blackbeard' Melton, to South America. She travelled to Los Angeles with Tanya and hooked up again with her husband.

When her relationship with Kasabian once again seemed doomed, she took the opportunity to accompany a friend, Catherine 'Gypsy' Share to a ranch where a band of hippies lived. Share told her that these hippies believed there was a hole in the ground through which they could escape to paradise and avoid the social upheaval that they believed was imminent. Intrigued, Kasabian, with baby Tanya in tow, went with her.

The Spahn Ranch had once been owned by silent movie star, William S. Hart and many westerns had been filmed there, including Bonanza and The Lone Ranger. Situated in Chatsworth, in the Santa Susana Mountains, the ranch was now owned by dairy farmer, George Spahn. The hippies lived there rent-free in exchange for some housekeeping chores and sex with Spahn.

Kasabian was instantly welcomed into this group that called itself the Family. At its centre was Charles Manson, a small, dark-haired, bearded man with piercing eyes and a charismatic personality. Thirty-four-year-old Manson had been a career criminal, spending less than half his life outside approved school and prison. In 1967 he had been released from a ten-year prison stretch for transporting an underage woman over a state border for immoral purposes.

Charles 'Tex' Watson, who had been introduced to Manson by Beach Boy, Dennis Wilson, was the Family member Kasabian warmed to most and they developed what each has since described as an intense sexual and personal relationship. Watson persuaded her to steal money from her ex-husband's friend, 'Blackbeard' Melton and when she handed it over, the Family members accepted her as one of them, a devoted follower of Manson.

She described Manson as Christ-like in appearance, no accident, one imagines, on his part, and on the day she first met him, she was entranced. That night she and Manson made love in a cave close to the ranch. She has said that she felt as if he could 'see right through her'. Like the other Family girls, she fell completely under his spell and was prepared to do whatever he asked of her.

The Family would undertake regular expeditions known as 'Creepy crawls' in which they would break into houses in Los Angeles while the owners were in bed asleep. They lived on what they stole in these operations and Kasabian was soon participating in them. She had no qualms about stealing because Manson had told them in one of his many quasi-spiritual campfire lectures, 'Everything belongs to everyone.'

One of Manson's main beliefs was that an apocalyptic war was imminent. 'Helter Skelter', as he called it, after the Beatles song of that name, would be a result of racial tension between blacks and whites. He wanted to make an album of music that would contain subtle, hidden messages that would help start the war. In the summer of 1969, when the album did not look like happening, he decided to show the way. On 8 August he announced that it was time for Helter Skelter.

Kasabian was the only Family member with a driving licence and on that night she was instructed by Manson to collect a knife and a change of clothing and drive 'Tex' Watson, Susan Atkins and Patricia Krenwinkel to a house in Cielo Drive that was being rented by respected film director, Roman Polanski, and his acress wife, Sharon Tate.

On arrival at the quiet, secluded house, the group cut the telephone wires and climbed a fence into the grounds. When they saw the headlights of a car approach, Watson hissed to the girls to hide in the bushes. As the car approached slowly, Watson pulled a gun and shot the driver, killing him. Eighteen-year-old Stephen Parent had been visiting his friend, William Garretson, the caretaker, who was living in the property's guesthouse.

Watson cut a hole in a screen at an open window. He told Kasabian to wait in the car and keep lookout while he, Atkins and Krenwinkel disappeared into the house through the window.

Sitting in the car, Kasabian began to hear horrible screams emanating from the house. She clambered out of her seat and began running towards the noise. 'I knew they had killed that man (Parent), that they were killing these people. I wanted them to stop,' she said later. She was frozen in her tracks on the driveway, however, by the sight of a man staggering out of the door. '...he had blood all over his face and he was standing by a post,' she would testify 'and we looked into each other's eyes for a minute, and I said, 'Oh God, I am so sorry. Please make it stop,' The man collapsed into some bushes.

Inside, Polanski's friend, Wojciech Fryowski, had been asleep on a couch in the living room. He awoke to find Watson standing in front of him. 'I am the devil, and I'm here to do the devil's business,' he chillingly announced. The other occupants of the house were rounded up from various bedrooms – Tate, Jay Sebring, America's top men's hair stylist and twenty-five-year-old Abigail Folger, heiress to a coffee fortune.

Watson tied Tate's and Sebring's necks together, throwing the other end of the rope over a beam so that if they tried to escape they would choke. Folger went to get her purse and they took the seventy dollars she had in it. Watson then stabbed Folger frenziedly. Frykowski had freed his hands from the towel they had used to tie him up and made an attempt to escape. Watson hit him on the head a number of times with his gun and then shot him twice.

At this point, the shocked Kasabian burst in, telling them that someone was coming, in an effort to stop the slaughter. They told her it was too late and Kasabian, in a state of shock, ran back to the car and started it up, considering fleeing to seek help. But she realised her daughter, Tanya, was still back at the ranch and she worried about what would happen to her.

Folger, still alive, had run outside to the house's pool area, but Krenwinkel, who had followed her, caught up with her and stabbed her, Watson joining in. Frykowski, trying to crawl across the lawn was also stabbed by Watson. Meanwhile, in the house, Sharon Tate was pleading for her life and that of her unborn baby. Atkins told her she did not care about her or her baby and she and Watson stabbed the beautiful actress sixteen times. Then, before leaving the house, they left a sign, just as Manson had ordered them to. Atkins grabbed a towel and wrote the word 'pig' on the front door in Sharon Tate's blood.

The following night, Manson, Steve 'Clem' Grogan and Leslie Van Houten joined them when they drove to a large house in Los Angeles' Los Feliz area. It belonged to Leno LaBianca, a supermarket executive, and his wife, Rosemary. Manson and Watson broke in and tied up the LaBiancas. They emerged from the house and Manson ordered Watson, Krenwinkel, and Van Houten to go inside. Manson, Kasabian, Susan Atkins and Grogan drove off.

Watson began to stab Leno LaBianca with a

chrome-plated bayonet, but in the bedroom, Rosemary was putting up a fight. Watson stabbed her, however, and she fell. Returning to the living room, he carved 'war' on Leno's stomach. In the bedroom, Krenwinkel was stabbing Rosemary repeatedly with a kitchen knife and Watson ordered the watching Van Houten to join in. Rosemary LaBianca received a total of forty-one stab wounds.

Krenwinkel then wrote 'Rise' and 'Death to pigs' on the walls and misspelled 'Helter Skelter' as 'Healther Skelter' on the refrigerator door, using the couple's blood. She stabbed Leno's corpse a further fourteen times, leaving a carving fork sticking out of his stomach. She finished by sticking a steak knife in his neck.

Their grisly business was not over for that night, however. Manson decided he wanted to kill a Lebanese actor acquaintance of Kasabian's, Saladine Nader. Kasabian was sent to his apartment to knock on the door, while Atkins and Grogan waited to jump him. However, she deliberately chose the wrong door on which to knock and when that door was opened, she apologised and walked away, undoubtedly saving that person's life.

When asked later in court why she had gone with them, fully aware this time of what was going to take place, Kasabian would say that when Manson had asked her, she was afraid to say no.

A few days later, Kasabian fled the Spahn Ranch with Tanya, returning to her mother's house in New Hampshire.

Meanwhile, the police rounded up the Manson Family for car theft, not realising that they had the Tate-LaBianca killers in custody. It was only when Susan Atkins carelessly boasted to fellow cellmates about the murders that the truth emerged.

Atkins was offered a reduced sentence – life instead of the death penalty – if she would become a witness for the prosecution and tell all before a grand jury and she agreed. Suddenly, however, the strange grip that Manson held over people reinstated itself and she gave up this opportunity. By now, Linda Kasabian, pregnant with her second child, had voluntarily handed herself over to the authorities in New Hampshire and had been extradited back to California. They offered her immunity in exchange for turning state's evidence. Although it was reported that she would have helped even without a deal, 'to get it out of my head', she had said, she agreed, under instruction from her attorney.

Her deal did not happen, however, without a great deal of controversy. On one side, it was argued that she had not prevented the murders and had not gone to the police until she really had no other option. On the other side, she had not actually entered the houses where the killings had occurred, it was argued, and had not physically taken part. It helped that she had been shocked by what happened and had seemed reluctant to be a part of it all. 'I'm not you, Charlie, I can't kill anyone,' she had reportedly screamed at Manson. She was also the only member of the Family to express remorse and suffered a serious emotional breakdown when they took her back to 10050 Cielo Drive to retrace the events of that night.

On 25 January 1971, Manson, Krenwinkel and Atkins were found guilty of all seven charges of murder and Leslie Van Houten was found guilty of two counts of murder. Watson was found guilty on all seven counts at a separate trial later in the year. They were all sentenced to death, but their sentences were commuted to life after the US Supreme Court declared the death penalty unconstitutional in 1972.

But, at least they had been stopped before their mayhem was able to spread further. Susan Atkins told her cellmates that other celebrities on their list included Richard Burton and Elizabeth Taylor, Frank Sinatra, Steve McQueen and Tom Jones.

Linda Kasabian returned to New Hampshire with

her husband and two children, escaping the glare of the media that now followed her around. She lived in a commune and worked as a cook. She testified at 'Tex' Watson's trial, as well as at the two re-trials of Leslie Van Houten in 1977. She divorced Robert Kasabian and married for a third time.

Her life, however, has continued to be troubled. She committed numerous traffic violations and was then partially disabled in a car crash. She was charged after interfering with firefighters trying to extinguish a bonfire. Then, following former Manson Family member, Lynette 'Squeaky' Fromme's attempted assassination of President Gerald Ford in 1975, she experienced constant monitoring harassment by the Secret Service. She moved to the state of Washington and, there, got into further trouble for possessing drugs.

SHI PEI-PU

It would be almost impossible to make up a story such as the one involving Bertrand Boursicot and the Chinese opera singer, Shi Pei-Pu. It is a story of both tragedy and farce, spy story and love story. Above all, it is utterly unbelieveable!

Bertrand Boursicot travelled to China in 1964, to work in the French Embassy in Beijing as a clerk. But that was irrelevant to the good-looking and well-built young Frenchman. To him China was a land of secrecy and intrigue and he was looking for adventure. He was also looking for love and, perhaps, if he could find it, sex. He had never been with a woman, never even been in love. At boarding school, there had been the usual schoolboy sex, but he had resolved to stop sleeping with boys when he turned eighteen.

It was not easy, however, and he was unable to even find a girl who would go on a date with him. He did not have a great deal to offer – much as he liked to put on the airs and graces of a diplomat, there was no escaping the fact that he was merely a clerk with a not very good education, who had been hired on a thirty-month contract.

In December 1964, he joined the Beijing ex-pats' party circuit and was excited when he met a blonde British secretary who agreed to give him her phone number. He invited her to a party just before Christmas at the home of a French Embassy official, but realised pretty quickly that there was someone at the party who interested him more than his date.

He was a short, slightly-built Chinese man, the only Chinese present at the party. He was aged around twenty-five and was dressed in the usual Mao suit that all Chinese wore in those days, and he was speaking fluent French. Boursicot went over and introduced himself and, before the end of the party, he had obtained the man's address and phone number.

His name was Shi Pei-Pu and Boursicot contacted him and invited him to dinner shortly after they had met. Shi told him that he had been an actor and singer when younger and was currently writing plays about the workers. His late father had been a university professor and his mother, with whom he now lived, was a teacher. He had two older sisters and had learned French as a boy. He had a degree in literature from the University of Kunming.

The two men became good friends. Shi took Boursicot to places off the beaten track, where few foreigners would ever be able to go and he told him wonderful stories of old China. He was a terrific storyteller and Boursicot loved listening to him talk of the roles he had played during his performing career and of the loneliness of his childhood. They shared secrets with each other that they had never told anyone else.

The relationship was short-lived, however. For a number of years, Boursicot had been trying to obtain an invitation to join an expedition that was travelling to the Amazon jungle. Finally, in mid-March 1995, it arrived. He called Shi to let him know he was going to resign but before he left, Shi invited him to his house. This was very unusual and even slightly dangerous – foreigners did not visit the homes of Chinese people in Mao Tse-Tung's China. Then a few days later, Shi told Boursicot a remarkable story.

He told him that his mother had had two daughters before he was born and reminded Boursicot that, in China, sons were more desirable than daughters. Shi's grandmother declared that if Shi's mother's next-born was not a boy, Shi's father would have to take a second wife. Shi's parents were distraught and when Madame Shi gave birth to another girl, Pei Pu, they were aghast at the thought of the break-up of their marriage. They made a spur-of-the moment decision – they would tell the grandmother that the new baby was a boy and raise it as such.

So, Shi Pei-Pu had lived his life as a male, even though he had been born a female. Amazingly, Boursicot accepted the story, unquestioningly. He promised to tell no one.

Eventually, Boursicot realised that he had fallen in love with the strange Shi Pei-Pu and asked her to sleep with him. Sex between them was never entirely satisfactory, however, and Boursicot was surprised by Shi's minute breasts. Shi told him that in order to keep up the pretence, he had been taking male hormones for a number of years to make him appear more masculine.

Boursicot left China at the end of December 1965, but before he did so, Shi had yet another surprise for him. She told him she was pregnant. He told her that if it was a boy, it should be called Bertrand and, if a girl, Michelle. He left, promising he would return.

By the time Boursicot returned to work as an archivist at the embassy, a couple of years later, China was in turmoil, in the throes of the Cultural Revolution that was to tear the country apart. While he had been away, he had had an affair with a French woman and had undertaken the expedition to the Amazon. However, he was afraid of getting in touch with Shi, given the difficult political climate. Shi had moved house and it took him a while to find her. He firstly travelled there in a pedicab, but was too frightened to knock at the door and returned to his hotel. Eventually, he disguised himself in a Mao jacket and a worker's cap, borrowed a bike and cycled there.

When he finally met Shi again, she told him how difficult life had been and that it was dangerous for the Frenchman to be there. She told him that she had had a son who looked a lot like him. But the boy had been sent to be looked after away from the city where it would have been too dangerous to keep him. Boursicot returned a few days later, but during this second visit there were problems when the neighbours in the block of flats where Shi was living, appeared at the door shouting about the foreigner who was inside. Some men in uniform also turned up and Boursicot told them he was a 'friend of the Chinese people', and was learning from Shi Pei-Pu about the Cultural Revolution.

Frightened of what might happen to Shi, he stopped visiting her, but cycled around her neighbourhood in his disguise several times a week hoping to see her. Eventually, he saw her out walking and Shi managed to whisper to him that she would meet him on the corner of Wangfujing and Changan Avenue every Thursday at two o'clock.

Unable to meet and talk, the two began to arrive there every Thursday. They could not even sit at the same bench and so would sit looking longingly at each other from different seats. Shi eventually broke their silence by obtaining permission, through her unit boss at the Writers' Association, for them to meet officially to discuss the *Thoughts of Chairman Mao* twice a week at her apartment.

They continued in this way for several months until Shi informed him that a man from the government was going to continue with the lessons. Two men arrived on his next visit and proceeded to teach him about the glories of Chairman Mao's China. Before long, they told him, however, that if he was to continue to see Shi, he was going to have to provide them with information from the embassy.

And so, Boursicot's career as a spy began. He had no access to military information, but did see all the mail that entered the embassy. He provided reports from the French Embassies in Moscow and Washington, useful material for the Chinese. He justified his actions by telling himself that he was doing no harm to his own country; the information was all about China's great enemy – the USSR.

Meanwhile, his relationship with Shi entered a tricky phase. She complained constantly and their sex life was still far from satisfactory. They made love rarely and when they did it seemed to Boursicot to be rushed. He was barely allowed to touch his partner and Shi merely satisfied him with her hands and her mouth.

In spring 1972, Boursicot's contract ended and he left China. He returned briefly in November 1973, however, and on this visit, finally met his son. But, he was there only for a few weeks before returning to France.

Back home, Boursicot struck up a relationship with a twenty-three-year-old man called Thierry. They moved in together and were very happy. In 1975 the two relocated to New Orleans in the United States, Boursicot having rejoined the diplomatic service. When he was not working in the passport section of the French Consulate, he accompanied Thierry on cruises of the city's gay bars and bathhouses.

However, back in China, things were changing. The Chinese Premier, Zhou Enlai had died and the old leadership was beginning to fail. The Cultural Revolution, too, was coming to an end. Boursicot decided he wanted to go back and bring Shi and Betrand back to Paris. However, the only diplomatic opening he could find was in Ulan Bator, the capital of Mongolia. It would be cold and miserable, but it was only thirty-six hours by train from Beijing and he would have to make that journey on a regular basis to take documents to the embassy in the capital.

The work in the embassy in Ulan Bator was all-encompassing. He was accountant, mail clerk as well as secretary to the Ambassador. Accessing material to take to his Chinese masters proved relatively easy, but the material itself was very low-level and when he met his Chinese contact in Beijing, he had nothing much to show. This was especially disappointing as the Russians were at the time massing on the Chinese border and the Chinese were keen to stay informed about troop movements.

Women came and went in Boursicot's life in Ulan Bator and Thierry came to visit. Every six weeks he would take the train to Beijing where, inevitably Shi would complain about his absence. He was no longer sexually interested in Shi, but they continued to make love in the usual way.

By 1982, Boursicot had been transferred to Belize, but he had finally succeeded in obtaining an invitation from a French government institute for Shi to go to

France on a three-month cultural visa. Thierry welcomed Shi and Bertrand to Paris and they moved into the apartment he shared with Boursicot. Shi gave lectures and performed traditional Chinese opera and even appeared on television. He was given a one-year extension to his visa and Boursicot, who had returned from Belize, was delighted. However, no one knew that the two had a relationship, let alone a son.

Their discovery was the result of a stroke of bad luck. Agents of the French Directorate of Territorial Surveillance, the agency that investigated threats against France emanating from abroad, were routinely examining the Chinese diplomatic representation in Paris when they came upon a relationship between 'a civil servant at the Ministry of Exterior Affairs posted abroad' and 'a Chinese national...later identified as Shi Pei-Pu'.

On 30 June 1983 Boursicot was hauled in, questioned for two days and charged with espionage. The following day, agents interviewed Shi at the apartment. Boursicot had already told them Shi was a woman, but they reported meeting a person who seemed neither masculine or feminine. She complained that she was not well, but when they called for a doctor, she refused to be examined. She denied knowing anything about Boursicot's espionage, but five days later, she was arrested and charged with complicity in the delivery of information to agents of a foreign power. Shi continued to deny the charge.

The judge ordered a medical examination to determine if she was male or female and to see if she had undergone surgery. In the meantime, she was sent to the hospital wing of the men's hospital at Fresnes. A few days later, when Boursicot learned that Shi was in the same prison as him, he was surprised and thought that she must have refused an examination and had been sent to a male prison because of that.

On 13 July the findings of the medical examination on Shi were made public. Boursicot heard the announcement on the radio in his cell. 'The Chinese Mata Hari, who was accused of spying, is a man,' it said. He refused to believe it.

They underwent interrogation by the examining magistrate separately for six months before they were questioned together in January 1984. During the questioning, to his horror, Boursicot heard Shi admit to being a man. Shi then lied about what he had told Boursicot. 'I never told Bernard I was a woman,' he said. 'I only let it be understood that I could be a woman. At the time I thought I was a woman, since I did not have any male genital organs. I had a hole – although I must say it did not resemble or was not exactly like one I had seen on an actress once when I was taking off my makeup at the Beijing theatre.' The Frenchman said that Bertrand could not, therefore, be his son but Shi replied that he had been born using artificial insemination. Tests would later prove, however, that this was another lie.

At their trial in 1986, Shi's lawyer, Francois Morette said: 'This is the story of two beings, both of whom are psychologically fragile and exalted, who entered into the same dream where each will believe what the other is saying, because they both want to believe it.'

They were each sentenced to six years in prison, but, after serving less than a year of his sentence, Shi Pei-Pu was given a pardon by President Mitterand. His imprisonment was reported to be an embarrassment to the Chinese government and the French did not want to damage relations between the two countries for what presidential adviser, Regis Debray described as 'an unimportant case'.

When Shi Pei-Pu was being examined, he told the doctor he would like to explain something. He proceeded to push his testicles up into his body cavity. The skin of the scrotal sack consequently hung slack. He then pushed his penis between his legs, toward his back, bisecting the skin of the scrotum, and squeezed his legs together tightly, concealing the penis and leaving the skin of the scrotum resembling the vaginal lips, beneath a triangle of pubic hair. Pushed between the empty scrotal sac, the penis had created a small cavity so that shallow penetration would have been possible.

Whoever said 'love is blind' must have been thinking of Bertrand Boursicot when he said it.

SISTER PING

In the early hours of 6 June 1993, two police officers
were surprised to see two Asian men flagging down
their car, in an obvious state of distress on a road
adjacent to Jacob Riis Park in Queens, New York.
Climbing out of their car, they were startled by
screams coming from the beach. Running towards the
sounds, they saw a 150-foot tramp steamer, the name
Golden Venture on its bow, that had evidently run
aground about a 100 yards offshore. On the ship they
could see countless people crowding its deck and
watched in horror as dozens of them slipped over the
side into the cold water of the Hudson. Some struck
out for shore while others flailed around in the water
in obvious difficulty. The officers radioed in for help.

The *Golden Venture* had set out from Thailand,
many months before, sailed to Kenya, negotiated the
Cape of Good Hope and then crossed the Atlantic
Ocean to its final destination, New York. Its cargo was

a human one, consisting of 300 illegal Chinese immigrants, mostly adults, who had paid to come to the United States to make their fortunes. They were emaciated, having been incarcerated in the ship's hold for months on end, with nothing to eat but rice and peanuts and purified salt water to drink. The heat had been intense and the hapless souls flailing in the freezing cold waters of the Hudson were clad only in their underwear. Many were in great difficulty, some suffering heart attacks when they hit the water. People who arrived to help were horrified and one Coast Guard officer said, 'I could feel the gristle of their bodies, the cartilage. They walked out of the water, collapsed on the beach and died.'

Ten of them died that bitter morning, but it was not the first time such suffering had been endured by a shipload of immigrants. In 1992, more than a dozen ships, smuggling people in this way, had disgorged their pathetic cargoes on American shores. American Coast Guards had intercepted a ship, the *Mermaid 1*, off the Bahamas, carrying 237 illegal Chinese immigrants. A month later, the *Pai Sheng* had dropped another 250 Chinese on a pier in San Francisco. Officials at the United States Department of Justice were becoming worried about the scale of the smuggling.

The Chinese had begun to arrive in America in the mid-nineteenth century. They originated mainly from the counties that bordered the Pearl River delta, near the southern city of Guangzhou. Smugglers had emerged in the 1960s and 1970s, helping mainland Chinese to get out of China to the much more affluent Hong Kong which was, at the time, still under British control. The gangs of smugglers were known as 'snakeheads' because when the smuggled people crawled through the wire fences that necklaced the borders, the shape looked like a snake.

The morning of the *Golden Venture* disaster, not far from the beach where the immigrants lay dying or gasping for breath, a middle-aged woman sat in a small shop at 47 East Broadway, in Manhattan's Chinatown, watching the story unfold on TV news channels as it was beamed from helicopters hovering noisily over the grim scene. Cheng Chui Ping was small and fat. Her hair was cut short and she had wide, dark eyes. Known in the neighbourhood as Ping Jia – Sister Ping – she dressed simply, almost like a Chinese peasant. Her English was sparse and her education had been minimal. She ran a shop selling clothes and goods from China and a small restaurant, enterprises which seemed to take up much of her time. She chopped vegetables, served food and washed the dishes in her restaurant and when she was not doing that, she was dragging huge bales of clothes down the street and into her clothes and general merchandise shop.

Sister Ping, however, was no ordinary shopkeeper, scraping a living from her small business. Not only did she own the shop and the restaurant next door; she also owned the entire building in which they were located. She had paid $3 million for it in cash and it was handily situated right across the street from the Bank of China.

There were those who said she provided a better service than the bank across the street. She utilised her extensive network to smuggle money back to their families in China from those who had settled in America. The bank took weeks and gave a bad exchange rate and delivered the money in the Chinese currency – yuan. Sister Ping took a matter of hours, charged less and paid in much more desirable US dollars. Business was good and the Bank of China had to start offering incentives such as colour televisions to people to use their service. Still, however, they preferred Sister Ping's.

In fact, Sister Ping was a fabulously wealthy woman – a *shetou* or snakehead, who ran one of the most sophisticated international people-smuggling operations of its kind. She had helped in the purchase of the *Golden Venture* and with it had smuggled thousands of Chinese, mostly from the Fujian province of China. Described as 'the mother of all snakeheads', she depended upon an intricate global network to make her operation successful. It also required a callous attitude to human life. In fact, in 1998 one of her ships capsized off the coast of Guatemala, killing fourteen people.

However, by the late 1980s, she was one of China-town's most revered figures. Everyone owed her something. Still, however, there were no big houses or expensive cars for her or her husband, Cheung Yick-tak. They rode the subway and worked in their businesses every day.

She, herself, had entered the country illegally. She had been born in 1949 in the farming village of Shenhmei in the province of Fujian and had made her way, like thousands of others, to Hong Kong, arriving in the United States in 1981. She opened a shop and became an American citizen, bringing her husband and children over from China. She began her people-smuggling business by helping friends and family to get to the United States. But she realised that it was a perfect time to launch such an enterprise. Relations were thawing between China and the USA and trade opportunities were opening up between the two countries. She put together her extraordinary network with associates who worked with her and for her in China, Hong Kong, Thailand, Belize, Kenya, South Africa, Guatemala, Mexico and Canada.

Her method was to buy off corrupt immigration officials and anyone else necessary and to use fake papers and passports. She charged up to $60,000 a trip and only demanded a small down-payment, the remainder to be paid on arrival in the USA. If friends or family were unable to pay when the immigrant arrived, he or she was put to work in catering or in garment factories until the debt was paid off, with interest, in instalments. Astonishingly, she was estimated by the FBI to have amassed a fortune of around $40 million over the two decades she was in business.

In 1989, she was arrested for bribing an undercover policemen to smuggle Fujianese immigrants through Canada to New York. Already that year, she had been found to be carrying $50,000 and the phone numbers of safe houses around the world. She was found guilty and served four months in prison. Her husband had not been so lucky a few months previously, when a raft he was using to smuggle some people across the Canadian border close to Niagra Falls, capsized. Four people drowned and he went to jail for nine months.

However, 1989 was also the year of the Tienanmen

Square riots in China and they provoked a boom in the number of people wanting to escape to America. George Bush Sr. also announced an amnesty to illegal Chinese immigrants in the United States, instantly creating a huge number of people who could afford the cost of bringing over their relatives. Smuggling people was less dangerous than smuggling drugs and, consequently, many new gangs emerged. These gangs brought new rules. Immigrants were recruited en masse and, once arrived, if they were unable to keep up their payments in recession-hit America, they were often kidnapped, tortured or killed.

Snakeheads joined together in the purchase of old ships and the journeys became unbearable. The *Golden Venture* was one such ship. It had been won in a poker game by the leader of a New York Fujianese gang. He, Sister Ping and several other snakeheads packed it out with immigrants and sent it to disaster.

By 1994 the enquiry into the *Golden Venture* disaster was getting very close to Sister Ping, and she was, therefore, relieved to receive an invitation to an anniversary celebration of the Communist Party in China in the company of other VIPs of Fujianese descent. In Beijing, however, there was a surprise awaiting her when she was arrested. She bribed her way out of custody, but America was now off-limits.

She went back to her home village of Shengmei which had in recent years greatly benefited from her activities. Meanwhile, in the United States, she was indicted in her absence for people-smuggling and illegal money transfers. Shengmei, filled with beautiful houses and buildings, courtesy of immigrants who had found success in America thanks to Sister Ping, protected its most famous inhabitant and even Beijing could not get at her.

Sister Ping went back to work, exploring new routes and techniques and travelling the world on her three passports – American, Hong Kong and Belize. She pioneered a new route through Belgrade to Europe and the United States and may have joined other snakeheads in introducing cargo containers as a means of smuggling people.

She was on the run for five years and lost to the authorities when Interpol began checking the passenger lists of flights from Hong Kong to New York. When they spotted the name of Sister Ping's son, they staked out Chek Lap Kok airport. Sure enough, she turned up to meet him and they pounced.

Even after she had been arrested, however, and the full horror of what she had been responsible for had been laid bare, there were still people who worshipped her and it is not difficult to see why.

Stories abound displaying the ways she helped people in trouble. One man, a restaurant worker, told of how he injured his legs and was unable to work. She gave him $2,000 and told him to pay her back when he could. When she was arrested, he still owed her $1,200, but she had never asked him for the money. Ping's younger sister, Sue said, 'My sister was just thinking of helping others. How would she know it would get her into trouble?'

She was tried in June 2005 in New York on a number of counts – conspiring to commit alien smuggling, hostage taking, money laundering and trafficking in ransom proceeds. She was found guilty and, before sentencing, pleaded for more than an hour for a lenient sentence. She was only a simple, hard-working immigrant, she said, who loved America and had been terrorised by Chinese gangs.

The judge, Michael Mukasey, dismissed her speech as 'simply incredible'. Evidence at the trial, he said, had shown conclusively that she was a leader of a ring that took millions of dollars from hopeful immigrants, transported them in inhumane and dangerous conditions, and used violent gangsters to collect debts and ransom.

He gave Sister Ping the maximum penalty allowed by law, thirty-five years imprisonment. She has so far been unable to smuggle herself out of prison and is currently incarcerated in Danbury in Connecticut, due for release in 2030.

TOKYO ROSE

It was the most expensive court case in United States criminal history, costing $750,000 and taking sixty-one days to get through all the witnesses and evidence. Even then, the jury failed to reach a verdict. The judge, however, was not having it and insisted that they arrived at a verdict. Eventually, Tokyo Rose – Iva Toguri D'Aquino – was cleared of seven charges of treason and convicted of one – speaking 'into a microphone concerning the loss of ships'.

She was sentenced to ten years in prison and fined $10,000 a large sum of money in those days. At last they had punished Tokyo Rose. There was just one small problem, however. She was not really Tokyo Rose. In fact, no one was.

There were around twenty women broadcasting Japanese propaganda over the airwaves to American troops serving in the Far East during the Second World War, American, Ruth Hayakawa and

Canadian, June Suyama – the 'Nightingale of Nanking' – among them. Iva Toguri, as she had been named when she first arrived in Japan from the United States, had been a secretary at Radio Tokyo, but had been cajoled into appearing for twenty minutes every day, telling GIs to 'be good' and openly calling the programme, *The Zero Hour* on which she appeared, 'another chapter of free propaganda'.

But Iva was not a natural radio star. She had been born Ikuko Toguri in Los Angeles in 1916, and would later anglicise her name, changing it to Iva. At the University of California at Los Angeles, she studied zoology, graduating in 1941, not long before America entered the war.

After graduating, she decided to travel to Japan, for reasons that have never been entirely clear. She has claimed that she was going to visit a sick aunt, but has also stated that she was going to study medicine. For some reason, she failed to obtain a passport before embarking on her journey and travelled on a Certificate of Identification issued by the US State Department. She set sail from San Pedro in California and arrived in July. Once there, she made efforts to obtain a passport so that she could return to her homeland as a permanent resident. Five months later, however, before a decision was made concerning her case, the Japanese bombed Pearl Harbor and the United States declared war on Japan.

Iva was now trapped in Japan with no hope of obtaining a passport or any means of getting back to America. Moreover, her Japanese was poor. She asked the Japanese authorities to intern her with other aliens – she was a United States citizen, after all, and refused to renounce her citizenship – but her requests were repeatedly denied.

She resigned herself to trying to earn a living and seeing out the war in Japan, giving piano lessons and trying to improve her Japanese by taking lessons at a Japanese language school. In 1942, she was given a job as a typist at a news agency before, in 1943, becoming a typist at Radio Tokyo.

The Japanese broadcast a number of radio programmes during the war that featured Allied prisoners of war reading the news, playing music and delivering messages from POWs in Japanese camps to their families back home and to troops still engaged in the war in the Pacific theatre. The objective was to demoralise and destabilise the troops and damage morale in the Allied war effort.

The Zero Hour was the first of these. It was dreamed up by Major Shigetsugu Tsuneishi who was a member of the Japanese Imperial Army's psychological warfare unit. He had already published a successful propaganda magazine entitled *Front* which copied the format of the popular American magazine *Life*.

Tsuneishi established an office at Radio Tokyo and brought in a captured Australian officer, Major Charles Cousens, who had been a widely respected radio news commentator in Sydney before the war. Cousens was given the choice of broadcasting for the Japanese or being executed. He chose to broadcast and was joined a short while later by an American, Captain Wallace 'Ted' Ince and a Philippine Army lieutenant, Normando Ildefonso Reyes, known as 'Norman'. Until their capture, Ince and Reyes had been in charge of Allied Voice of Freedom propaganda broadcasts at Corregidor in the Philippines. Ince produced for the Japanese a show called *From One American to Another* while 'Norman' broadcast his show, *Life in the East*.

The Zero Hour was the most effective of the propaganda broadcasts as well as the most damaging. By 1943 the Japanese had found a way to monitor medium-wave domestic radio broadcasts in the United States and learned from these about train crashes, natural disasters and major traffic accidents in America. They then forced the POWs to broadcast a news programme about these incidents to demoralise American soldiers. The first show was broadcast at 5.15 p.m. on 31 March 1943, consisting of fifteen minutes of jazz and news and popular music delivered by 'Norman' Reyes. The *New York Times* reported that 'The fellows like it very much because it cries over them and feels so sorry for them. It talks about the food that they miss by not being home and tells how the war workers are stealing their jobs and their girls.'

The programme was extended to forty or fifty minutes in length and Cousens read the messages from POWs, Ince read the US news and Reyes played records. However, even though the Japanese watched every move they made, the three men made attempts to undermine the propaganda message by reading items in jokey or inappropriate tones.

The Japanese considered the programme to be a success and decided in November 1943 to extend it further, to seventy-five minutes. They also decided to soften the message with the addition of a female voice. Cousens suggested the station typist, Iva Toguri D'Aquino, who had befriended the POWs and was unashamedly pro-American in her views. For the POWs, she would make a better announcer than someone they would be unable to trust. Perhaps they would also be able to involve her in their subversive approach to the broadcasts. She launched herself on the airwaves on 13 November as 'Orphan Ann', the name coming from the abbreviation 'Ann' for Announcer in her scripts and from her description of the Allied troops in the Pacific as 'Orphans of the Pacific'.

The new show, broadcast from 6-7.15 p.m. seven days a week, started with *Strike Up the Band*, played by Arthur Fiedler and the Boston Pops Orchestra. There were then five or ten minutes of twenty-five word messages from POWs, read by Cousens. Then Iva would do a twenty minute 'Orphan Ann' segment, the only part of the show that was not out-and-out propaganda. Tokyo Rose broadcasts usually opened with 'Rose, Rose I Love You', recorded in 1940 by Yao Lee, one of China's greatest singing stars. Iva would play three or four records and read from a script written by Cousens. Then, it was the turn of Ince to read five or ten minutes of 'American Home Front News', followed by pop music and jazz from Reyes and Ince again, reading 'Ted's News Highlights Tonight'. The man known as 'the Japanese Lord Haw-Haw', Nisei Charles Yoshii sometimes delivered a commentary on the news and Ince would sign off for the evening. On Sundays, Ruth Hayakawa would stand in for Iva.

By December 1944 Iva was writing her own material and earning around 150 yen per month, around $7. Although she was not a seasoned radio performer, her broadcasts were extremely popular, loved for the American popular music she played.

In December 1944, *The Zero Hour* was shortened to sixty minutes, but was the main programme among a whole range of similar propaganda broadcasts including such as *Three Missing Men, Saturday Jamboree* and *From One American To Another.*

It continued to broadcast until about 12 August 1945. Three days previously the Americans had dropped their second atom bomb on the city of Nagasaki and three days later Emperor Hirohito announced Japan's unconditional surrender. The Emperor's words were the last heard on Radio Tokyo. It was shut down immediately after he finished his speech.

The Americans' response to Tokyo Rose was Tokyo Mose. A twenty-six-year-old American journalist, Walter Kaner, broadcast to the occupying American troops six afternoons a week, between two and three in the afternoon, after the Japanese surrender. His theme tune, Moshi, Moshi Ano-ne, sung to the tune of London Bridge Is Falling Down, became popular with Japanese children and was known as 'the Japanese occupation theme song'. Kaner entertained the troops with the music of Benny

Goodman and Cab Calloway and irreverent comments about military life in the occupying army. He would come out with audience-pleasing lines such as, 'The lack of material prevents many junior officers from having personal jeeps. It is an indictment of current conditions to report that some lieutenants are sorely inconvenienced and must double-up on dinner engagements.'

Meanwhile, the Americans launched a nationwide search for Tokyo Rose, eager to charge her with war crimes. Two American journalists joined the search. Henry Brundidge and Clark Lee announced a reward of $250 for information as to her whereabouts. Iva, by this time married to a Japanese-Portuguese man, Felipe D'Aquino, was in hiding, but desperate to get back to her family in the United States. She came forward to claim the money. However, when she signed a contract to give the two men an interview, identifying herself as Tokyo Rose, she was arrested. She never did see the cash. From then on, although there had been a number of Tokyo Roses, she became the person associated with the name. Initially, however, the authorities concluded that the evidence they had accumulated did not merit prosecution and Iva was released from custody. However, when she again requested an American passport, veterans' groups and commentators, such as the famous broadcaster, Walter Winchell, became irate. They demanded her arrest and trial as a traitor.

The FBI had a vast amount of material relating to her case – Japanese documents, recordings of her broadcasts, interviews with her listeners, the troops who had served in the Pacific. These were turned over to the Justice Department. A grand jury was convened in San Francisco and she was indicted. She was arrested in Yokohama and brought to the United States. On arrival at San Francisco on 25 September 1948, she was arrested and charged with treason. Her case came to court on 5 July 1949, the day after her thirty-third birthday.

Although he did later admit to being prejudiced against Iva, Judge Michael Roche was careful with the testimony of the witnesses, disallowing much of it. A number of them had been flown in to testify against her purely for the daily allowance of $10 and an opportunity to visit the United States.

Iva was the seventh American citizen to be convicted of treason during the Second World War, joining the ranks of such as Mildred Gillars who had broadcast as 'Axis Sally' from Berlin and Martin James

Monti, a United States Army Air Force pilot, who had defected to the Waffen SS in 1944.

She served just six years and two months of her ten-year sentence before being released early for good behaviour from the Federal Reformatory for Women at Alderson, West Virginia, on 28 January 1956. After fifteen years she was finally able to return to her family who were now living in Chicago. She did not give up pleading her innocence of any crime, however, even though she was still under threat of deportation. She tried to obtain a Presidential pardon, appealing in 1954 and 1968. Slowly, the media began to come round and support her, describing the injustices she had suffered. Some campaigners argued that she should not only be pardoned, but should in fact be honoured for her bravery in helping the Allied cause from behind enemy lines.

On 19 January 1977, in his last hour as President of the United States, Gerald Ford finally signed the grant of executive clemency that cleared her of any guilt.

In Chicago, Iva worked in the family shop until she was in her eighties. Her husband, Felipe D'Aquino had become an undesirable alien when he had testified for her at her trial in 1949 and, as such, was barred from entering the United States. She, for her part was not sure that she would be allowed back into the country if she travelled to Japan to visit him. Under such circumstances, although she still loved him, the marriage was dissolved in 1980.

Iva Toguri D'Aquino, Tokyo Rose, the only American to be pardoned for the crime of treason, died, aged ninety, in December 2006.

PART FIVE

MAFIA MEN

EDWARD J. O'HARE

When the squadron was airborne, Butch O'Hare checked his controls and saw from his fuel gauge that someone on his ground crew back on the aircraft carrier had neglected to top up his fuel tank. His heart sank as he realised he would not have enough fuel to complete the mission and return to the ship. He radioed the information to his flight leader and, as he had feared, was ordered to leave the formation and return to the aircraft carrier.

On his way back, however, he spied some shapes on the distant horizon. It was a squadron of Japanese Zeroes flying towards the American fleet and making ready to attack. Butch understood at once the seriousness of the situation. The fleet was practically defenceless, with all of its fighters off on the mission he had been forced to abort. There was only one thing he could do. Without a moment's hesitation, he flew into the middle of the Japanese planes and began a desperate and courageous fight to destroy as many as he could. He fired at them until he ran out of ammunition and then dived at them, trying to clip a wing or a tail-plane and bring them down, trying anything to prevent them getting to the ships. Eventually, the Japanese had had enough of this madman and flew away. Butch and his plane limped back to base.

In those days, every American fighter carried a camera that recorded any action in which it was involved, with the aim of learning as much as possible from the enemy manoeuvres and tactics. When Butch O'Hare's film was developed and viewed, his colleagues were astonished. They saw just how brave he had been, how far he had gone in order to protect the American fleet. Butch was transformed overnight into a national, all-American hero and was given the Congressional Medal of Honour. Moreover, Chicago's main airport, O'Hare, would forever bear his name.

It is possible that Butch O'Hare would never have been a hero, probably would not even have been allowed entry to the Air Force if it had not been for his father, Edward J. O'Hare. He is thought to have made a deal that got Butch into the Air Force training school at Annapolis, no easy feat in those days, requiring the recommendation of a congressional representative. What was the subject of the deal, what could 'Easy Eddie' O'Hare offer in exchange for a secure future for his son? None other than the greatest gangster of them all; the hoodlum whose control of Chicago in the 1920s resulted in a blood-letting never before seen in gangland and who, with his immaculate suits and fedora hat, defined the classic image of the American mobster – Scarface, himself, Alphonse Gabriel Capone.

Eddie O'Hare's first real flush of success came from an unlikely source, the mechanical running rabbit, the small speedy bait that entices greyhounds to run at great speed around a greyhound racing track. O'Hare, a lawyer, represented the mechanical rabbit's inventor, Owen P. Smith, who also happened to be high commissioner of the Greyhound Racing Association. In 1930, that rabbit bought E. J. O'Hare a comfortably large house with a swimming pool and a skating rink in an upmarket Chicago suburb.

E. J., as his family called him, had come far. He was born in 1893 to first generation Irish-Americans, Patrick Joseph O'Hare and his wife, Cecilia Ellen Malloy. Nineteen years later he married a St. Louis woman of German origin, Selma Anna Lauth. Three children followed in the next twelve years, Butch in 1914, Patricia in 1919 and Marilyn in 1924.

The year before the birth of his third child, E. J. had

passed the Missouri bar exam and got a job with a law firm in St. Louis. By 1925, he was making good money and had branched out to run greyhound racing tracks in Chicago, Boston and Miami. He also developed a fascination with flying, befriending the great aviator, Charles Lindbergh, with whom he flew sometimes on the mail plane Lindbergh flew for the Robertson Aircraft Co. E. J. also began to take on commercial flying work and, whenever possible, took Butch up with him, allowing the boy to take the controls now and then.

O'Hare divorced Selma in 1927, moving to Chicago while she remained in St. Louis. It was there that he met Al Capone. Capone had made fortunes from Prohibition, controlling the manufacture and distribution of booze in Chicago. He earned additional income from the customary mob rackets of extortion, gambling and prostitution and, effectively, controlled the city.

In those days, if you were anybody, an entre-preneur or businessman trying to succeed in a city, you had to choose a gang with which to be affiliated. Nothing moved in any American city without the say-so of some mobster or other and, of course, they expected their cut of whatever you were making. So, it was a necessary evil. With Capone's gang the dominant force in late 1920s Chicago, E. J. had little option, as a new entrepreneur in town, but to hook up with Scarface and his boys.

E. J.'s mob ties did not end there, however, and even entered his personal life. He fell for a secretary, Ursula Granata, who happened to be the sister of a State Representative with mob ties. They were engaged for seven years as O'Hare, a good Catholic boy wanted to be married in church and as a divorcee, was not entitled to do so. He even made a request to the Pope for Papal dispensation for the wedding.

When he arrived in Chicago, O'Hare was already a wealthy man, but his involvement with Capone's affairs added hugely to his fortune. He was personally responsible for keeping Capone out of jail and, in that, he was very successful. Capone showed his appreciation by paying E. J. very well for his skills. So well, in fact, that O'Hare was able to own a house that took up an entire Chicago city block. He had servants and every convenience a rich lawyer could desire, including a fence around the whole building, just in case.

In 1930, however, all that changed. Whether he did it because he wanted the favour of getting his son into Annapolis or simply because he was tired of dealing with mob business, we do not know. It may even have been for purely selfish reasons. Perhaps he realised that there was a danger that he would go to jail one day. Whatever the reason, he asked a *St. Louis Journal* journalist, John Rogers, to set up a meeting with the IRS (the Internal Revenue Service). Rogers contacted an IRS government inspector, Frank J. Wilson, a man who would go on to be Chief of the US Secret Service from 1937 to 1946. Eliott Ness and his 'Untouchables', a team of agents who were selected because they were thought to be incorruptible, had been raiding Capone's distilleries and warehouses, destroying his bootlegging business and crippling his earning capacity. Meanwhile, the IRS were working on Capone's finances with the objective of convicting him of tax evasion and locking him up.

E. J. and Wilson had lunch and E. J. agreed to work undercover for the Revenue. As Wilson said in a 1947 interview: 'On the inside of the gang I had one of the best undercover men I have ever known: Eddie O'Hare.' The key to the arrest and conviction of Capone was a bookkeeper who knew everything about Capone's affairs, down to the last detail. It was O'Hare who led Frank Wilson to him and the bookkeeper would be the key witness in Capone's 1931 trial.

O'Hare additionally helped Wilson and his team crack the code that Capone's bookkeepers used in their ledgers at Scarface's illegal gambling dens throughout the 1920s.

Then, on the opening day of the trial, when he learned that the jury selected for the trial had been fixed by Capone's men, O'Hare informed Judge Wilkerson who famously ordered the jury to be swapped with a jury hearing another trial in another part of the building.

Al Capone's goose was well and truly cooked and he was found guilty of five of the twenty-two charges brought against him. That was enough, however, to get him sent to Alcatraz for eleven years. In prison, the syphilis from which he suffered, started to seriously affect his health and his mind deteriorated until he was released, a shadow of the man he once was. He died a few years later.

A few days before Capone's release, on Wednesday 8 November, however, Eddie O'Hare left his office at Sportsman's Park in the Chicago suburb of Cicero. Unusually, he was carrying a .32-calibre semi-automatic pistol. He climbed into his black 1939 Lincoln Zephyr coupé and drove away from the greyhound track. At the intersection of Ogden and Rockwell, a dark coloured sedan drove up alongside his car. Two men stuck shotguns out of the car's side windows and opened fire on E. J.'s car. He was killed instantly by the volleys and his Lincoln crashed into a lamppost at the side of the road. The car containing the killers sped off in an easterly direction on Ogden, getting lost in the afternoon traffic.

Several months after O'Hare's killing, Ursula Granata, his seven-year fiancée, married Frank Nitti, Al Capone's second-in-command.

When they found O'Hare, in his pocket was a poem that read:

The clock of life is wound but once
And no man has the power
To tell just when the hands will stop
At late or early hour
Now is the only time you own
Live, love, toil with a will
Place no faith in time
For the clock may soon be still

For 'Easy Eddie' the clock was finally still.

ANTONINO GIUFFRÈ

'It's very simple,' Antonino Giuffrè once said, describing the relationship of Cosa Nostra to politics. 'We are the fish and politics is the water.'

Antonino Giuffrè , known as 'Manuzza', the Hand, because his right hand was withered by polio when he was young, was one of the most important state witnesses to emerge from the Mafia, exposing the organisation's political links and implicating important officials of Italy's leading political parties – allegedly including Prime Minister Silvio Berlusconi, himself – in dealings with Mafia bosses.

Giuffrè, born in 1945, in the town of Caccamo in the province of Palermo, was trained as a teacher of agricultural sciences. However, like countless other men of the area, he also moved in Mafia circles, rising rapidly through the ranks to become the head of the *mandamento* – a district of three neighbouring Mafia families – of Caccamo.

He knew everything there was to know about the Mafia. He had looked after the *capo di capi*, supreme Mafia boss, Michele 'the Pope' Greco, when he was on the run for four years in the 1980s and took refuge not far from Caccamo. Then, when Mafia boss, Salvatore 'Toto' Riina was captured in 1993, he became the right-hand man of Bernardo Provenzano who took over from Riina and who, himself, was on the run for a remarkable four decades.

After Riina's arrest, Giuffrè was invited to join the directorate that ran the Sicilian Mafia. Other members, apart from Provenzano, were Salvatore Lo Piccolo from Palermo, Benedetto Spera from Belmonte Mezzagno, Salvatore Rinella from Trabia, Giuseppe Balsano from Monreale, Matteo Messina Denaro from Castelvetrano, Vincenzo Virga from Trapani and Andrea Manciaracina from Mazara del Vallo. This group only met infrequently, when it was necessary to make an important decison about Mafia business.

Provenzano who, according to one Mafia insider had the brain of a chicken, but could 'shoot like an angel', ran the organisation very differently from Riina and the men who had gone before him. Whereas Riina's method was to confront problems head on and, usually, with violence – assassinations or bomb attacks – Provenzano, known as 'Binnu u

Tratturi' (Sicilian for 'Bennie the Tractor') because of his capacity for mowing people down, adopted a different approach. He approached Mafia affairs with a great deal more subtlety, favouring the gradual infiltration of public institutions and then beating the authorities from the inside. For the thoughtfulness and care of this approach, he was also known as 'the Accountant'.

Pentito (informer) Balduccio Di Maggio was the first to bring Giuffrè to the attention of the authorities. Until then, he had been totally anonymous and prosecutors and investigators had never heard of him. In common with many of the new generation of Mafiosi, Di Maggio had become disillusioned with the domination of the Corleonesi, even though he had risen within the organisation by committing countless murders for Riina and for the Mafia of San Giuseppe Jato. Following Di Maggio's tip-off, the police acted immediately and raided Giuffrè's house in Caccamo that same day. He got away, however, only just managing to escape through the back door. Like many other Mafia bosses of the time, he went on the run. From then on, like all the other fugitives, he communicated through hand-written notes delivered by runners – telephones could be traced. And he lived in basic houses with no electricity so that there was little chance of listening devices or cameras being installed.

The difference of opinion between the imprisoned old bosses and the new way of Provenzano had begun to create a schism in Cosa Nostra. On the one hand, there were the hardliners, Toto Riina and Leoluca Bagarella, locked up, and another faction on the outside, led by Provenzano, Salvatore Lo Piccolo and Antonino Giuffrè.

Giuffrè was the first to feel the effects of the split. An anonymous phone call to police headquarters, probably made by someone loyal to the imprisoned bosses, alerted them to his location and he was arrested on 16 April 2002. It was a serious message to Provenzano that the incarcerated men meant business. They also wanted something done about the treatment meted out to convicted Mafiosi and the harsh prison regime under which they were being kept.

Conditions in prison were, indeed, tough. Article 41-bis had been introduced in 1975 and modified in 1992 after the assassination of the judge, Givanni Falcone by a Mafia bomb. It allows the Minister of Justice or Minister of the Interior to suspend certain prison regulations for the duration of that prisoner's incarceration. It is used only for the most serious crimes – drug trafficking, murder, kidnapping, terrorism and Mafia involvement. Under the article, the Mafia bosses in prison are forbidden the use of the telephone: are banned from association or correspondence with all other prisoners; are not allowed meetings with third parties; are allowed visits from family members only once a month and even then are separated by thick glass and can only communicate by intercom; are not allowed to receive sums of money over a stipulated amount; are forbidden from receiving parcels; are banned from sporting, cultural and recreational activities and are denied the vote in elections for prisoner representatives. It cut the bosses off from any opportunity to run Mafia affairs from behind bars, as had happened in the past.

Riina and Bagarella made it known that they wanted hits to be made on Marcello Dell'Utri and former Defence Minister, Cesare Previti, both close allies of Silvio Berlusconi. These would send a strong message to Berlusconi, but would be less likely to cause the kind of outrage the killings of Falcone and Boresllino had engendered, with the resultant clampdown on Mafia activities.

Political parties were vital to the Mafia's interests and, in the 1980s, the Christian Democrats had taken care of Mafia interests in Rome. However, in the early 1990s, Christian Democrat influence was on the wane and its relationship with the Mafia was also failing. This was brought into sharp focus when the Christian Democrats' man in Sicily, Salvo Lima, was shot dead by a motorbike gunman, on the road to Palermo. The Mafia looked around for a new *entrée* to the Italian political world and for a while even considered founding its own political party. However, it finally lighted upon Forza Italia, the political party founded by Marcello Dell'Utri, right-hand man to Berlusconi. As Giuffrè was later to tell the authorities: 'A new era opened with a new political force on the horizon which provided the guarantees that the Christian Democrats were no longer able to deliver. To be clear, that party was Forza Italia.'

Giuffrè began talking to the authorities even before becoming a *pentito*. It soon became evident that he was the most important supergrass since Thomas Buscetta, twenty years earlier. According to him, Dell'Utri had been the conduit to Berlusconi, now Prime Minister, and his task was to work on legislative efforts to take the pressure off the Mafia. In exchange, the Mafia would provide electoral support and deliver Italian voters. Giuffrè recounted how Provenzano told him in 1992 that, thanks to undertakings given by Forza Italia, the Mafia's judicial problems would be all over in ten years' time.

Giuffrè also fingered Berlusconi, himself, claiming that while still a property developer in the mid 1970s, the media tycoon had contact with Mafia boss, Stefano Bontade. He claimed that the two met at Berlusconi's villa in Arcore. Bontade was ostensibly there to meet former Mafioso, Vittorio Mangano, who was Berlusconi's stable manager, Giuffrè said, but he was actually meeting the future Prime Minister. Berlusconi had taken Mangano on because he was afraid of kidnapping and thought that Mangano would help to ensure that he need never worry about it. Giuffrè named other unsavoury Mafiosi who, he said, had contact with Berlusconi – Palermo Mafia bosses, Filippo Graviano and Giuseppe Graviano, the man responsible for the disgraceful murder of anti-Mafia priest, Guiseppe 'Pino' Puglisi in Brancaccio. Naturally, Silvio Berlusconi and Marcello Dell'Utri dismiss these accusations as 'monstrous slurs'.

However, the alleged Forza Italia pact with the Mafia ended in 2002. There had been no changes in the way Mafia men were treated, no abandonment of Article bis-41 and no halt to the seizure of land owned by convicted Mafiosi.

Giuffrè has been a witness for the prosecution in some of Italy's most notorious trials. He was the man who described eighty-three-year-old, seven-times

Italian Prime Minister, Giulio Andreotti's involvement with the Mafia during a long political career in which he served in no fewer than thirty governments. The Mafia had sought protection from investigation and prosecution by magistrates. Andreotti was charged with being connected to the Mafia, mainly on the testimony of Tommaso Buscetta. He had already been acquitted of being involved in the murder of a journalist who had been killed in 1979 and he was acquitted of this charge, too, but only because it had all happened too long ago.

In the trial Giuffrè had described Andreotti's links with Mafia boss, Nino Salvo and how Salvo had asked him to intercede on behalf of Cosa Nostra with the authorities. He told how Salvatore Lima, a minister in Andreotti's governments was the go-between for Andreotti and the Mafia. In a damning sentence he said: 'Thanks to the good offices of Andreotti, Cosa Nostra enjoyed a period of impunity.'

Giuffrè was also an important witness in the Roberto Calvi murder trial, in which he claimed that Mafia bosses had the head of the Banco Ambrosiano killed because he had mishandled Mafia money. He even named the hitman who had hung Calvi from Blackfriars Bridge in London, making it look like suicide – Giuseppe Calò. 'Cosa Nostra's problems get resolved in one way,' Giuffrè said. 'By elimination.'

He also told of a plot to murder Giuseppe Lumia, President of the Anti-Mafia Commission. Approved at the highest level, by Provenzano, for some reason it was never carried out. He talked about the 1992 killings of prosecutors, Giovanni Falcone and Paolo Borsellino and helped police understand more about the 1993 bombings of the Uffizi Gallery in Florence and the Basilica of St. John the Lateran in Rome.

Giuffrè gave his evidence in these trials from a secret location, his back turned to the camera or from behind a screen. He played with a ballpoint pen and his voice echoed around the court from poor speakers. He explained the reporting structure of the organisation and sometimes sent a shiver through the court. On one occasion he described a visit to Nardo Greco's ice factory in Bagheria. 'I noticed a strong smell…' he said. 'They told me the corpse of Piddu Panno was there, wrapped up in a sack.' Panno was a Sicilian Mafioso who had been strangled in the Mafia war of the 1980s, Giuffrè explained.

He described a Mafia 'call centre' where the organisation had set up telephones at which sat a dozen armed men. The calls coming in would be alerting the men to potential targets for murder.

Antonino Giuffrè was responsible for around forty

murders and is serving several life sentences for those. However, when asked why he had decided to turn his back on the Mafia and inform on numerous of his former associates and the organisation to which he had given his life, he replied that he had been inspired to do it by the Pope's canonisation of Padre Pio, the Italian Roman Catholic Capuchin priest who became famous for his stigmata. That may have been a confession too far.

ABE 'KID TWIST' RELES

'The Canary Can Sing, But He Can't Fly' sneered the headlines when Abe 'Kid Twist' Reles' crumpled body was found outside the Half Moon Hotel on Coney Island on 12 November 1941. The most feared of all the Murder Inc. hitmen and Brooklyn's Public Enemy Number One from 1931 to 1940 had plummeted to his death from the window of room 623 just hours before he was due to testify against Murder Inc.'s killer-in-chief, Albert 'Mad Hatter' Anastasia.

There is a myth that all Mafiosi are Italians, usually of Sicilian origin. Of course, most were and still are, but there is also a strong Jewish streak running through Cosa Nostra. Men like Lepke Buchalter, Bugsy Siegel and Artie Tannenbaum were Jewish and occupy legendary positions in the Mob pantheon. The most feared of all was possibly Abraham Reles, later known as 'Kid Twist', who was born in 1906, of

Austrian immigrant parents, in the Brownsville district of Brooklyn. As with most of the 'wiseguys' who drifted into the world of racketeering, Kid Twist grew up in abject poverty, surrounded by slum housing with no sanitation, existing on the principle of survival from one day to the next. Needless to say, he soon began to move in criminal circles, inspired by stories of the rich Jewish gangsters of the time.

Reles was, like so many gangsters, a little guy. But he was strong and, above all, callously violent. There are two theories as to why he enjoyed the nickname 'Kid Twist'. One has it that he was named after an earlier gangster, Max 'Kid Twist' Zerbach. Another says that it simply came from the fact that Kid Twist was the name of his favourite candy.

Abe Reles is said have had iced water flowing through his veins, rather than blood. He was a psychopath and one of the most cold-blooded killers who ever lived. He once killed a worker in a car wash for failing to get a mark off the fender of his car. On another occasion, a parking lot attendant died because he was too slow getting Reles's car for him. His arms were long, in spite of his stature and his fingers were broad and flat at the ends, hands with which to strangle a man.

In 1934, when Reles was on trial for assault, the

judge described him as 'one of the most vicious characters we have had in years. I am convinced he will either be sentenced to prison for life or be put out of the way by some good detective with a couple of bullets.' Reles is reported to have sneered at the judge and whispered to his attorney: 'I will take on any cop in the city with pistols, fists or anything else. A cop counts to fifteen when he puts his finger on the trigger before he shoots.'

His favourite method of dispatch was the ice pick, delivered behind his victim's ear and deep into the brain. He was an expert with it; so good, in fact, that his victims were often mistakenly believed to have died of a cerebral haemorrhage.

He was still a teenager when he began to work for the Shapiro brothers, the gang that controlled bootlegging (he was a bootlegger who never touched alcohol), extortion, illegal gambling and prostitution in New York City's Lower East Side. Reles worked with another teenager, Martin 'Bugsy' Goldstein, committing petty crimes. When he ended up in a juvenile institution and the Shapiros made no effort to get him out, he never forgave them. They would live to regret their carelessness.

When he got out, Reles went into the slot machine racket with a couple of friends, displeasing the

Shapiros, who took the view that Reles and his pals were elbowing into their territory. However, one of Reles's partners, George Defeo had connections to the powerful gangster, Meyer Lansky who was, himself, keen to expand his empire into Brooklyn's poorer areas. So, they brokered a deal with Lansky and everyone was happy, except the Shapiros, of course. But Reles was on his way.

One night, Reles, Goldstein and Defeo were ambushed by the Shapiros in East New York. Reles and Goldstein were shot, but they managed to make their getaway. On another occasion, Meyer Shapiro kidnapped Reles' girlfriend, took her to a field and orally raped her. Reles and his associates planned revenge.

They hired a couple of accomplished hitman to help them out – Frank 'Dasher' Abbondando and Harry 'Happy' Maione, both Murder Inc. men. There were several abortive attempts, but eventually, they cornered Irving Shapiro at his house. Reles dragged him out into the street where he beat him and then shot him dead. A few months later, Reles bumped into the other brother, Meyer, and shot him in the face. It took them another three years and nineteen assassination attempts to catch up with the surviving Shapiro, William. He was eventually garotted in a bar by Reles and then taken to a hideout. They beat him until he was close to death and then stuffed him into a sack and drove out to the Canarsie area of Brooklyn where he was buried. In the middle of their digging, they were spotted by a passer-by and fled the scene. When the corpse was removed from the ground, dirt was discovered in his lungs. William Shapiro had been buried alive.

Reles became one of Lepke Buchalter's favourite Murder Inc. killers. Lepke had put the organisation together at the request of the five crime families to deal with people who represented a problem to them and over the years Murder Inc. killers are thought to have been responsible for up to 800 murders. Lepke once told a friend, 'Those kids in Brooklyn got it taped real good. That Reles and Pittsburgh Phil, and that Maione know how to cover up a job so nobody knows a thing.' They were well paid for it, too, at $12,000 a year, plus pension and benefits as well as whatever they found on the body of their targets.

In 1940, however, while the body count was stacking up around Abe Reles, the authorities had a lucky break. When a small-timer called Pretty Levine was picked up by the police, he started to tell them about a murder the Brooklyn crew had carried out. A man called Walter Sage had been skimming off the proceeds from the gang's slot machines. Sage was strangled, had an ice-pick stuck in his head, probably courtesy of Kid Twist, and was then lashed to a pinball machine – a nice bit of symbolism – which was thrown into a lake in the Catskill Mountains.

When Reles turned himself in, hearing the police were after him, he was convinced it would be just like the other half-dozen times he had been fingered for murder and that he would walk out again without any charges being made.

This time, he was arrested, however, on the orders of King County District Attorney, William O'Dwyer, and, to his horror, was charged with a number of murders. Reles was in no doubt that he was going to be blamed by his associates for everything and would almost certainly face the electric chair. So, he decided to save his skin by turning state's witness and telling everything he knew about the Mob and its activities. He phoned his wife from prison and asked her to inform the appropriate authorities of his decision. It was a decision that was to create seismic waves in gangsterland.

He was held in protective custody for a year, at one point in Harbour Hospital under the name of Albert Smith, when it was feared that he had tuberculosis. Then, prior to the trial, he was moved to room 623 of the Half Moon Hotel on Coney Island where he was guarded round the clock by six uniformed police officers. The Half Moon was the name of explorer

Henry Hudson's ship, which anchored off Gravesend Bay, Coney Island, in 1609, before setting out to find a short cut to Asia. Now and then Reles and the other state's witnesses, Allie Tannenbaum, Mickie Syckoff and Sholem Bernstein were taken for exercise to Heckster State Park on Long Island.

Reles sang for two weeks. He seemed to have an amazing memory, recalling minute details of eighty-five separate killings in Brooklyn, who was involved, why they took place and what weapons were used.

Firstly, he provided information about the 1936 killing of a Brooklyn candy-store owner, forty-six-year-old Joseph Rosen. Rosen, a former garment industry worker, was shot so expertly that it could only have been the work of Murder Inc. His garment industry haulage company had been put out of business by a strike called by Lepke and he had become a pain in the neck.

That information, alone, sent Lepke Buchalter to the electric chair in Sing Sing three years later. In all, O'Dwyer was able to send a number of Murder Inc. operatives to the chair as a result of Reles's evidence – as well as Lepke, there were Harry 'Pittsburgh Phil' Strauss, Mendy Weiss, Harry 'Happy' Maione and Frank 'Dasher' Abbandando. Others, such as assassin, Charlie 'Bug' Workman, who is believed to have murdered Dutch Schultz, were sentenced to life. Reles also sent his loyal boyhood friend and partner, Martin 'Bugsy' Goldstein, to the chair. He and Goldstein had been arrested more than seventy times in their crime careers, but had served no more than fifty months in jail between them. Reles, in fact, had been arrested six times for murder, seven times for assault, twice for robbery and assault and a further six times for robbery or burglary. Yet, he had been convicted only once, for assault. He was arrested, on average, once every seventy-eight days.

At one point in his testimony, Reles provided a sickening description of a typical killing: 'Pep has an ice pick. Happer has meat cleaver. It is the kind you chop with, you know, butcher cleaver. Abby grabs Rudnick by the feet and drags him over to the car. Pep and Happy grab it by the head. They put it in the car. Somebody says: "It don't fit". Just as they push the body in it gives a little cough or something. With that, Pep starts with the ice pick and starts punching away at Whitey. Maione says, "Let me hit the bastard once for luck". And he hits him with the cleaver some place on the head.'

When New York prosecutor, Burton Turkus, asked Reles how he could be so nonchalant about the may-hem he caused, Reles replied that he was nervous the first time, less nervous the second and then he just got used to it.

Albert 'Mad Hatter' Anastasia was the next mobster O'Dwyer set his sights on. O'Dwyer was campaigning to be mayor of New York and these Mafia scalps were contributing greatly to his chances of success. The Mad Hatter's trial for the killing of union longshoreman, Pete Panto, was based solely on Reles's testimony and was set for 12 November 1941.

But, in the early hours of the morning of the trial, just hours before he was due to take the stand and send Anastasia to Death Row, Reles fell to his death from the open window of room 623.

The circumstances surrounding the fall were shrouded in mystery and conspiracy theories from the beginning. Of course, not far from everyone's thoughts was the fact that he was a 'stool pigeon' and as such was a target for the Mob. They say that Frank Costello, of the Lucciano crime family, a man destined to become one of the most powerful crime bosses of all, was behind the death, that he paid off the cops who were looking after him.

Others say that everyone got together to silence Reles – the police, the District Attorney and those in the Mob who were not in custody.

Another theory suggests that Reles was, in fact,

trying to escape. A couple of knotted sheets were found hanging from the window, but they were still a long way from the ground and safety. However, this did allow the police to say that he died during an escape attempt. An escape attempt from five floors up seemed a little strange to most people.

Some suggest that the whole thing was just a practical joke gone wrong.

Suicide seemed possible until someone pointed out that his body was found on the pavement some twenty feet out into the street away from the hotel. To do that, he would have had to have lowered himself to a flat roof on the third floor below his room and then jumped. This seems unlikely.

The Grand Jury's conclusion was that he 'met his death whilst trying to escape by means of a knotted sheet attached to a radiator in his room. We find that Reles did not meet with foul play and that he did die by suicide. It would be sheer speculation to attempt to disarm his motive for wanting to escape.'

But nobody believed them and Lucky Luciano said that Reles had been thrown out of the window by the police officers who were paid a contract price of $50,000.

They had finally silenced the canary; they threw him out of his cage.

JESSE STONEKING

It was shortly after one in the morning on a cloudless night in summer 1988. He was forty-two years old and was standing on the porch of his mother's house in North St. Louis County. As he always did, he checked out the vicinity before he climbed into his car, looking first one way and then the other. It looked clear, but as he pulled out into the street, a red Buick with a white top slid out from the kerb back down the street and followed him, its headlights off. He had lived his life with all his senses pricked, ready for such things and the Buick did not escape his attention. Just to ensure he was not mistaken, he played a little cat and mouse with it, slowing down and then speeding up. Whatever he did, the Buick did the same. Now there was no doubt.

Without indicating, he tugged on the wheel and swung abruptly onto a side street, but the Buick was still there. He tried a few more evasive manoeuvres, but it stuck to him like glue. He took a hand off the wheel and reached under his seat, hoping to feel the reassuring cold steel of his .45 – his 'guardian angel', he called it – but it was not there.

He pulled hard on the wheel and threw a sudden U-turn, sweeping back in the direction of the other car at speed. Slowing down, he saw them. One, the driver, was a killer he recognised. This would not be the first time he had tried to kill him. The other was a union racketeer. They were both faces he had known in another lifetime.

He put his foot down and gunned the Buick. They would not be picking up that $100,000 anytime soon.

One hundred thousand dollars was a lot of money, in anyone's book. Gang bosses had had less money on their heads than Jesse Stonehill and he knew it. But, after all, he had been responsible for the biggest shakedown ever in the history of the St. Louis underworld. By the time he had finished singing, thirty tough guys were looking at spending a long time behind bars and the St. Louis Mob was all but finished. He had humiliated the mobsters, shared their secrets with the Feds and now they were after him.

The trust he had betrayed had been great. After all, he had been a lieutenant of the mob on St. Louis' East

Side, second-in-command to Art Berne and, there-fore, the Chicago Mob's second most powerful man in Southern Illinois. St Louis Mafia don, Matthew 'Mike' Trupiano, for whom he had also worked, as an enforcer, was also less than pleased at Stoneking's betrayal, especially as he was one of the men arrested on Stoneking's testimony, alongside Berne.

A former choirboy, he had started out on a life of crime at fourteen, burgling some houses across the road from his childhood home. Forty dollars in small change they got, but his friend was picked up and ratted on Jesse. From then on, he would hate snitches and informants, little dreaming that he, himself, would become one.

By the age of twenty-one he was making a decent living from theft and from fencing stolen goods, but in 1970, all that changed when he was introduced to Arte Berne and a giant of a man called Don Ellington who would become Stoneking's partner. The big time beckoned.

Bizarrely, around this time, Stoneking, thief and fence, got a job as a police officer. He was no ordinary lawman, however. Now legally able to carry a gun, he could gain people's trust and could steal whatever he liked, no questions asked. But his law enforcement career was to be brief. After he arrested a drug dealer and beat him savagely back at the police station, it was revealed that the man was actually an undercover federal agent. Stoneking was asked for his badge and gun the following day.

He had stayed close to Berne and in 1973, having established a good reputation as a money-maker who feared nothing and no one, he was inducted into his Outfit. Within a few years, he had risen to become Berne's most trusted lieutenant, second-in-command, a man to be reckoned with. His sphere of influence included some important hoods such as Joey 'Mourning Doves' Aiuppa, head of the Chicago Mob and underboss, Jack Cerone.

One reason for Jesse Stoneking's success was his extraordinarily menacing presence. He was 'built more like a bull than a man', as one associate described him. Only five feet ten, but two hundred pounds of rock-hard muscle. His voice was loud and commanding and his eyes could be icy, when he wanted them to be. His face was emotionless and a head of jet-black hair hinted at his Native American blood. Above all, he had an ability to adapt quickly to whatever situation he found himself in, talking or fighting his way out as the situation required. Physical or verbal intimidation were his stock-in-trades.

The first contract he was given was for the

eradication of Patrick Hickey, a popular union official, state legislator and Democratic Party functionary. The half-dozen construction unions in the St. Louis area were controlled by the three organised crime operations that held sway in St. Louis – Berne's outfit, the Mafia and the Lebanese-Syrian gang. Berne had the Pipefitters Union Local 562 and he ruled it with a rod of iron, Jesse Stoneking at his side, just in case. Patrick Hickey would not play ball and he had to go. In 1976, Berne delegated the job to his two best men – Stoneking and Don Ellington.

The plan was for Stoneking to drive and Ellington to be the shooter. They followed Hickey's car to Lambert-St. Louis International Airport and when Ellington signalled, as Hickey pulled onto a sliproad, Stoneking accelerated, pulling up level with Hickey's car. Ellington lowered the car window and raised the cocked .38 he had in his hand. Suddenly, without firing, he shouted to Stoneking to get out of there. Stoneking braked hard and Hickey's car sped away from them. When Stoneking asked what happened, Ellington said that Hickey had seen him. Stoneking was furious. He had been exhilarated by the thought of the hit. Now he felt deflated.

Ellington rapidly became a problem. One time, when he asked Stoneking to find him a woman for a dinner date, Stoneking obliged, getting in touch with a part-time prostitute who was also a friend of Berne. Ellington had said that it was just dinner, no sex, but after dinner he went wild, savagely beating the woman, breaking her arm and disfiguring her face.

Stoneking was furious and was ready to kill Ellington immediately, no questions asked. He realised, however, that he would have to get Berne's approval for such an act. Ellington's relationship with the boss had been deteriorating for the last couple of years; so when the two met at a a meeting arranged by Stoneking, Ellington exploded, shouting at Berne: 'Go fuck yourself! Who needs you?' Berne icily told Stoneking to get Ellington out of there, adding chillingly: 'I don't wanna ever see him again.'

Eight days later, on the night of 22 October 1978, Stoneking obliged. Ellington was found dead, four bullets having blown his face and head apart, as he sat at the wheel of his Cadillac in a remote area of Jefferson County, south of St. Louis. The police said that he had known his killer and they knew exactly who had done it. Stoneking's stock rose still higher.

A year later, Stoneking, himself, came close to being hit. Mafia boss, Tony Giordano had become a good friend and Stoneking worked on the side for him. One of his jobs was looking after vending machines owned by Giordano and one night he got a call asking him to attend to a problem that had occurred with a cigarette machine located at the Kracker Box Tavern in East St. Louis.

Arriving at the bar, he was surprised to find that there was nothing wrong with the machine; it was working fine. Then a prostitute hanging out in the bar pulled him to one side and let him know that there were two hoods looking for him. He spotted them across the room and, never one to walk away from a fight, went over to see what their problem was. An argument broke out and one of the two men reached for his gun. Stoneking beat him to it and downed the man with two shots. He was dead before he hit the floor. The other man got two shots in, however, hitting Stoneking twice in the lower chest. Stoneking turned his gun on the man and emptied it into him.

Stoneking took himself off to hospital where the bullets were removed from his chest. Next day, still drowsy from the anaesthetic, he saw through a haze a woman enter his room. 'Jesse Stoneking, you're going to die,' she hissed, pulling a gun from her handbag. But, just as she was about to pull the trigger, Mark Stram, another member of the Berne outfit, came running in and disarmed her. She had been a friend of the two hoods in the bar. Stoneking was put under twenty-four hour guard by Berne and his trusty .45 lay in a drawer at the side of the bed.

He was a stonekiller, Jesse Stoneking, but he was not without compassion, it seems. When Mafia underboss, Joey Cammarata found a bomb in his pickup truck, he was certain it had been placed there by Tommy Callanan, a business agent for the Pipefitters Union. Callanan had, himself, been seriously injured when a bomb had ripped his car apart a few years previously and he had lost both his legs. Cammarata gave a contract for Callanan's death to Berne. Berne, in turn, passed it to Stoneking who did as he normally would. He watched the target for a few days to get an understanding of his movements before making the hit. But Stoneking was appalled. He was unable to bring himself to kill a man in a wheelchair. He went back to Berne and told him he was unable to get close enough to Callanan to kill him. Later, however, he said: 'I figured the guy had suffered enough...I ain't about to whack a guy in a wheelchair. Not for no one.'

Stoneking always needed to make money to be able to afford the expensive, gaudy jewellery he was partial to wearing, and the expensive cars that had become an obsession for him. He made around $2 million in a very short space of time but he had to, with one legitimate family of a wife and three kids, as well as the family he had fathered with his mistress – another three children. But he was never short – $200,000 in large denomination bills always lay stashed under the floorboards in the kitchen and he never left the house without a couple of thousand dollars stuffed into his wallet.

In 1978, he was involved in the biggest robbery of his career when he and three accomplices robbed a jewellery wholesaler in southwest Missouri as he transported boxes of jewellery from his car to his house. The haul was in excess of $2 million, and Stoneking's share was worth around $250,000. A large part of the loot belonged to the Kansas City Mafia who were, understandably, anxious to discover who had taken it. They never did and Stoneking used one of his diamonds to buy a shiny, brand-new Cadillac Eldorado.

He widened his horizons with a stolen car and chop-shop operation, a chop shop being a business that takes apart stolen cars and re-sells the parts. It was a decision that he would live to regret, for it would bring his world tumbling down. It transpired that his partner in the business was an FBI informant. Stoneking was arrested for involvement in an inter-state stolen car ring and for his chop shop operation and sentenced to three years in prison. Inevitably, he took his sentence like a man, claiming he could do it standing on his head. Anyway, Berne had promised to look after his family for him while he was away. It was only what Stoneking and other hoods did for their men when they had to do some hard time. But Berne let him down.

Stoneking found this betrayal hard to deal with. He had demonstrated unflinching loyalty to Berne and the outfit. He had put his life and his freedom on the line countless times for them. After a month of anguish in prison, he made a momentous decision. He would go straight. Not only that, but he would talk to the FBI. Strangely, at a party thrown for him before Christmas, just before he went into prison, Berne's wife, Loretta, who was an astrology aficionado, had predicted that Stoneking would go straight. Everyone had laughed about it and then had forgotten about it. He had not.

He made a deal with the agents who had arrested him, Tom Fox and Terry Bonheimer, and he became that thing he loathed above all others – a snitch.

For two years after his release, he worked for the FBI, wearing a wire whose discovery would have meant a sudden and probably very slow and painful death for him. Several times he was almost found out

– when a Mafioso playfully grabbed him by the shirt, touching the microphone, but not realising what it was. On another occasion, a mobster noticed the outline of the recording machine under his sock and Stoneking, thinking on his feet as usual, said he was developing his leg muscles and it was a weight.

It was tough maintaining credibility, however, without taking part in any illegal activity and risking arrest. Fox and Bonheimer had emphasised to him that in that event, they would not be able to help him.

As the two years came to an end, Stoneking was increasingly aware that he would have to somehow find the money to fund his life afterwards. He borrowed thousands of dollars from mob associates and even broke into Berne's house. Although he was unable to crack the safe in which he knew Berne always stashed $200,000, he got away with thousands of dollars' worth of jewellery.

In October, 1984, the two years came to an end. Telling everyone he was having a couple of weeks' holiday in Florida, he left St. Louis to enter the witness protection programme. He was issued with a new identity, credit cards, driving licence and other documentation. But he could not adapt. He felt hemmed in and constricted by the discipline that was designed to keep him alive. After just two weeks he walked out and returned to St. Louis, to find that his wife had had enough of the life and had, herself, entered witness protection. He never saw her again.

Nonetheless, it soon began raining indictments and the arrests began. It was not hard to work out who had snitched and life became very difficult for Stoneking. The trials were endless and tough. His former friends stared cold and hard at him from the dock, cocked thumbs pointed at him, as if to say his days were numbered. Finally, in July 1986, it was all over and he took off.

First, he went to Paducah, Kentucky, too close to St. Louis, argued Fox and Bonheimer, but he was past caring. It became too dangerous, however, when two men parked a pickup truck across the street from the house where he and his second family lived and took an interest in their movements. He moved on to a town in southern Illinois. There, he was betrayed once again and became a local attraction, stories about him appearing in newspapers and people gawping when he left the house.

By this time, Jesse Stoneking was broke, both financially and emotionally. One day, he met with an FBI agent, handed him an envelope and drove off. It said he was going to kill himself that night, but he didn't carry out the threat.

However, on 19 January 2003, a large man calling himself Jesse Lee McBride shot himself with a .38 revolver while seated at the wheel of his blue Ford Crown Victoria on the outskirts of Surprise, Arizona. He died an hour later at a nearby hospital. The local media largely ignored the story and only later did it emerge that his true identity was Jesse Eugene Stoneking, the 'Stonekiller'.

SAMMY 'THE BULL' GRAVANO

Joe Colucci was listening to a Beatles tune playing on the car radio. He was pretty drunk after a night's drinking and dancing in the neighbourhood clubs. He had a bite to eat in a diner around four in the morning and was now seated in the car with Tommy Spero and Sammy Gravano. He didn't feel much when Gravano put the barrel of his gun against the back of his head and pulled the trigger. Neither did Gravano. He pulled the trigger, but did not hear the gunshot. Colucci's head did not even seem to move. It was as if he had fired a blank and there wasn't even any blood. Gravano felt as if he was dreaming.

He pulled the trigger again and this time, the noise deafened him. He saw the flash as Colucci's head jerked back. Blood poured from the wound and Colucci was well and truly dead. It was 1970 and

Sammy Gravano had carried out the first of the nineteen hits he would be involved in.

Sammy's father, Gerry, was a Sicilian who had arrived in New York illegally after jumping ship in Canada. He married another Sicilian, Kay, and had five children of which Salvatore, known as Sammy, was the last. They lived in Brooklyn's Bensonhurst area where Gerry was a house-painter and Kay a talented seamstress. When Gerry contracted lead poisoning, they opened a dress factory.

Sammy was discovered to be dyslexic and a slow learner early on in his school career and at the age of ten was held back a grade, which was a humiliating experience for the young boy. He was already displaying a violent side to his temperament, beating up anyone who tried to make a fool of him. His dislike of authority was also beginning to show. But he was a tough little guy and once beat up two much older kids who had stolen a bike from him. One onlooker said that he was like a little bull and from that day on he was known as Sammy 'The Bull'.

He was eventually expelled from that school after breaking a school official's jaw and began to spend more time with the street gang he had hooked up with. Meanwhile, he looked on enviously at the gangsters hanging around street corners in their smart suits, enjoying the company of beautiful women. He went to high school but did not last long, beating up a fellow pupil on his second day. Just before his sixteenth birthday, his education came to an end and he ran full-time with his gang, the Rampers. Once, when he and another Ramper stole a car to carry out a robbery, they were shot at by the car's owner. One bullet hit Sammy's partner and another ripped a chunk out of Sammy's head just above the right ear. He was lucky to survive.

When he reached the age of twenty-three, in 1968, Sammy got his first introduction to serious crime when he met Thomas 'Shorty' Spero, a member of the Colombo crime family, who invited him to work with him. Shortly after, he met Shorty's *capo*, none other than the notorious Carmine 'the Snake' Persico, who would become head of the family several years later.

Sammy's first jobs for the Family were robberies and he experienced some bad luck when a witness to a robbery at a clothing store identified him from a mug shot. Luckily for Sammy, the witness was 'persuaded' not to identify Gravano in court. On another occasion, a bank guard developed a loss of memory that may have been connected to the $10,000 he was paid by Persico. Gravano had to pay it back at $300 a week, plus interest, of course. That was not a problem, however, as he was now earning around $2,000 a week from loansharking and from a club he had opened, even after he had paid off police and made his weekly donation to Family coffers.

After the Colucci hit, Gravano's star was on the rise and Persico was reported to be very pleased with him. He married seventeen-year-old Debra Scibetta in 1971 but marriage did not help him to mend his crooked ways. That same year, he created a scam whereby he would pretend to be a cop who would burst in when a drug dealer, called Michael Hardy, was doing a deal to buy dope. He would handcuff the men selling the stuff and he and Hardy would walk off with the money, as well as the drugs. Meanwhile, he was also making good money fencing stolen goods.

Sammy was transferred from the Colombo Family to the Gambinos after tensions between him and the Speros. He was sure he was being ripped off by Tommy Spero's father, Ralph. He now became part of a team headed up by Salvatore 'Toddo' Aurello, a *capo* whose career stretched back to the days when Albert 'Mad Hatter' Anastasia was head of the Family. Aurello became an influential figure to Sammy.

However, he was still unsure about the gangster life and at one point tried to go straight, working nine or ten hours a day in construction. He and Debra still had no money and were sleeping on the floor of his sister's apartment, but he planned to start his own firm. A phone call changed that, however. He, Louis Milito and 'Alley Boy' Cuomo' were being sought for the 1969 murder of the Dunn brothers. They were innocent and so, decided to turn themselves in. To pay their legal expenses, Sammy quit his construction job and joined Cuomo on a robbery spree lasting eighteen months. It paid off when they were acquitted one week into the trial.

Gravano had earned his spurs and was now proposed for full membership of the Gambino Family. He sat next to Paul Castellano, head of the Family, and underwent the ritual of pricking the index finger, burning the image of the saint, taking the vow of *omerta*, and kissing other members on the cheeks.

When he opened an after-hours drinking club, called The Bus Stop in Bensonhurst, a group of bikers walked in and told him to get out, that they were taking over. A fight broke out in which Gravano broke his ankle, but the bikers ran off. Observing the Mob protocol of not undertaking a hit without the permission of your boss, he went to Castellano and gained permission to murder the leader of the bikers. Still in his cast, Gravano, accompanied by Louis

Milito, killed the man and injured one of his associates. When Castellano heard that Gravano had carried out the hit himself, in a plaster cast, he is reported to have exclaimed: 'He's got the balls of a fucking elephant!'

He became more involved in the construction industry after helping Paul Castellano out with some building work at his mansion, the White House. Castellano used his influence to help a plumbing and drywall company Sammy started with his brother-in-law, Edward Garafola, and Sammy became part of Castellano's inner circle. By now, he also owned a disco in Brooklyn from which he was making $4,000 a week, alone. The money was finally starting to roll in and he used it to splash out on a thirty-acre farm in New Jersey.

In 1980, a power struggle in Philadelphia resulted in 'Little Nicky' Scarfo becoming top dog while 'Johnny Keys' Simone lost out. Castellano sent Gravano to eradicate Simone on Scarfo's behalf. When he trapped Simone and drove him in a van to a wooded area, Simone showed tremendous dignity which impressed Gravano, insisting that, as he had promised his wife, he would die with his shoes off and that he also wanted to be killed by a made man. Sammy obliged with a bullet in the back of Simone's head.

The year 1982 saw a man called Frank Fiala offer Sammy $1 million for his club, a deal that Sammy eagerly accepted, given that he figured it was only worth $200,000. However, Fiala made the huge mistake of acting as if he owned the place even before the deal went through. One night Sammy and Garafola walked into Sammy's office to find Fiala sitting behind Sammy's desk. He had already begun construction work to rearrange the office. When Sammy protested, Fiala pulled a Uzi from under the desk and pointed it at the two men, calling them 'greaseballs' and telling them he could do what he wanted.

The following night, as Fiala left the club, Gravano and his team were waiting for him. Garafalo shouted out to him and Sammy said: 'Hey Frank, how ya doing?' At that moment, Louis Milito ran up behind Fiala and shot him in the head. As Milito stood over Fiala's body and shot him once in each eye, Gravano strolled over and spat on him.

In September 1985, Gravano was approached to take part in the killing of Paul Castellano. Castellano was unpopular. He was never the street boss that the Colombo soldiers yearned for. He ran his Family like a business and did not care if the people below him starved. John Gotti hankered after the top slot and sought support from the main men in the Family as well as from the other families.

Gravano made sure that his close ally, Frank DeCicco supported Gotti's action before going along with it. That night, at Sparks Steak House, he was not in the team that killed Castellano, but was involved in the meticulous planning and drove past the scene with Gotti immediately afterwards, confirming that Castellano was, indeed, dead. In the aftermath, he was promoted to *capo*.

When Frank DeCicco was blown up by a car bomb a short while later, Gotti promoted Gravano again, to joint underboss with Angelo Ruggiero. Gotti was now in prison, but still running things. He ordered Gravano to hit Robert DiBernardo a mobster who ran a pornography operation and dabbled in the labour unions. When Gravano hesitated because he did not fully understand why Gotti wanted rid of DiBernardo, Gotti became angry. However, Gravano soon obliged, calling a meeting with DiBernardo and having one of his men put a couple of bullets in the back of his head. It transpired that Ruggiero owed DiBernardo $250,000 and this had seemed like a good way of getting rid of such an irksome debt.

But Gravano did well out of that killing, assuming control of DiBernardo's management of the local branch of the Teamsters' Union.

By now, Sammy was a big player in the legitimate construction business, kicking back some $2 million a year to John Gotti, but Gotti was still suspicious of him. Nonetheless, Sammy became *consigliere* of the Family around 1987. He had worked for it. Prior to Gotti becoming head of the Family, he had been involved in eight murders in fourteen years. Since Gotti's arrival, he was involved in eleven in six years.

For example, Mike DeBatt, a member of Gravano's crew, who had been close to him, became addicted to crack cocaine and his wife went to Sammy to plead for help. Sammy did the only thing he could; he had DeBatt murdered.

In 1988, he was involved in three murders. Louis Milito, his boyhood friend was first, after he had complained about someone else being promoted. A few months later, Francesco Oliverri was the second killing of the year. He had killed a member of the Family in a fight. Gravano sat in a stolen getaway car while the man to whom he gave the hit, Robert Bisaccia, shot Oliverri in the head in his car outside his house. The third was Wilfred 'Willie Boy' Johnson, an FBI informant.

In 1989 he took out Thomas Spinelli, who had recently testified before a Grand Jury. Gravano arranged his murder in a Brooklyn factory.

In August, 1990, he had a demolition contractor called Eddie Garafola – not his brother-in-law of the same name – gunned down in front of his home in Brooklyn and in October that year, he oversaw the death of his former business partner, Louis DeBono. He was found dead in his car in the World Trade Center car park.

The authorities began to close in on John Gotti and Gotti worried that Gravano would also be reeled in. He made Sammy official underboss of the Family and ordered him to go on the run. He went to Florida and then Alantic City, while the government officially declared him a fugitive. But Gotti insisted on a meeting with him back at his club which, Gravano reminded him, was under constant police surveillance. Nevertheless, Gotti insisted and Sammy returned to New York.

Inevitably, the police raided the club and Gravano, Gotti and Frank Locascio were arrested. Thomas Gambino was picked up elsewhere. When they got to court, the police played taped evidence and Gravano heard himself being described by his associates as an out-of-control killer. His relationship with Gotti deteriorated so badly that Gravano contacted the FBI and told them he wanted to cooperate.

When the news broke, Gotti's men peppered the

neighbourhoods with posters of Sammy's head on the body of a rat. Meanwhile, he was at the United States Marine base at Quantico, Virginia, singing his heart out. He signed a witness deal and prepared his testimony. At the trial, he was in the dock for nine days and he achieved his objective – the destruction of John Gotti who received multiple terms of life imprisonment.

Gravano's dismantling of the Family continued. He helped send seven Gambino *capos* to jail, as well as a number of high-ranking members of the Colombo, Genovese and DeCavalcante Families.

Sammy himself got five years, plus three years of supervised release. Not bad for a man responsible for the deaths of nineteen people.

He was released into the Witness Protection Programme, but left it early and moved to Arizona where he started up his own construction business. But, just to prove that you can't keep a bad man down, in 2002, he was convicted of being the leader of an ecstasy trafficking organisation.

He is currently serving nineteen years in the United States Penitentiary Administrative Maximum Facility in Florence, Colorado.

JOEY 'BIG JOEY'
MASSINO

When Joey Massino was convicted in New York, in 2004, his charge sheet was a roll-call of Mafia crimes of the past 100 years – murder, racketeering, arson, extortion, loan-sharking, illegal gambling, conspiracy and money laundering. This head of the Bonanno Crime Family had certainly come a long way.

Although Joey later became a restaurateur, his catering career had humble beginnings – a mobile food-wagon in the Queens area of New York, selling coffee and pastries to workers in the docks. He began his Mafia career as a protégé of Philip 'Rusty' Rastelli and his brothers, in the 1960s. Rastelli was a nasty, violent individual who, a few years later, would rise to the top of the heap in the Bonanno Family. With the Rastellis, he got into running numbers, hijacking trucks and fencing stolen goods.

In 1975, Paul Castellano, who would in the future become head of the Family, ordered Massino to carry out a hit on Vito Borelli. Borelli was dating Castellano's daughter and had made the fatal mistake of insulting Castellano in front of her by comparing him to a man called Frank Perdue, a businessman with a cooked chicken brand who used to advertise it personally on television. The fact that Perdue, himself, resembled a plucked chicken, did not endear Borelli to Big Paul. So, Massino, accompanied by John Gotti, another future Family head – the Gambinos in his case – killed the unfortunate Borelli at a Manhattan cookie business owned by Bonanno soldier, Anthony Rabito. Other men involved were Dominick 'Sonny Black' Napolitano, Rabito and Angelo Ruggiero, Roy DeMeo and Frank DeCicco. Massino's brother-in-law, Salvatore Vitale, was asked to drive the body to a garage where they were waiting. Borelli had been shot in the face and body and he was wearing only his underpants. Vitale noticed that one of the men was holding a knife and has speculated that the man with the knife was Roy DeMeo whose speciality was cutting up bodies like a Perdue chicken.

Borelli's murder provided a boost to Massino's career and in 1976 he became a made man of the Bonanno Family, reporting to Philip 'Lucky Phil'

Giaccone. Best of all, he was still a complete unknown to the Federal authorities.

In June of that year, the body of Joseph 'Doo Doo' Pastore was discovered in a dumpster, round the corner from Massino's restaurant in Maspeth. He had been killed with two shots to the head. There was a connection to Massino because Pastore was a truck hijacker who supplied Joey with stolen goods that Massino fenced for him. It did not take police long to make the connection and he and Richard Dormer, Pastore's half-brother were taken to the morgue to make an identification of the body. It was no coincidence that, just before the murder, Massino had asked his brother-in-law, Salvatore Vitale, to borrow $9,000 from Pastore for him. It looked like he would never have to re-pay that particular debt.

Massino was in court in 1977 on a charge of hijacking a truck, but was acquitted, while his co-defendant, Raymond Wean went to jail for three years.

In 1979 Rusty Rastelli took over at the top of the Family following the killing of Carmine Galante in his favourite restaurant, Joe and Mary's Italian-American Restaurant at 205 Knickerbocker Avenue in Bushwick, Brooklyn. The sixty-nine-year-old Galante died with his trademark cigar in his mouth, blasted in the face and chest at point-blank range with a shotgun.

Although Massino was not one of the shooters, he is reported to have been seen outside the restaurant on the day of the shooting. Whatever his involvement, Rastelli's promotion was good for Massino – he was promoted to the rank of *caporegime*, just three years after becoming a made man.

In 1989, when Massino heard that Alphonse Indelicato, Dominick Trinchera and Philip Giaconne were plotting to take over the Bonanno Family by purging Rastelli's men, he went to Family bosses, Carmine Persico and Paul Castellano, for advice. They told him that he had only one option; kill them or be killed himself.

Sonny Red Indelicato, Giaccone and Trinchera were lured to a meeting with their rival factions, accompanied by *capo*, Frank Lino. Gerlando 'George from Canada' Sciascia, Vito Rizzuto and Sonny Black Napolitano burst out of a closet in the room where the meeting was taking place and gunned down Trinchera, Indelicato and Giaccone. Lino escaped.

Napolitano would, himself, suffer at Joey Massino's hands in 1981 when he made the mistake of proposing a man called Donnie Brasco to become a made man in the Family ahead of Salvatore Vitale, Joey's brother-in-law. Vitale, Joey said, had been involved in killings for years, whereas Brasco had not been around for more than a few years and had not been part of any hits for the Family. Unfortunately for Napolitano, Brasco turned out to be Joe Pistone, an undercover FBI agent, a fact confirmed when he disappeared from view. Sonny Black Napolitano also disappeared from view in August of that year. He was taken to a meeting at the house of a Family associate. Frank Coppa, a Bonanno capo, greeted him and threw him down a flight of stairs into the basement of the house. He was shot dead and when Frank Lino handed Sonny's car keys over to a group of men in a waiting car, he noted that one of them was Joey Massino.

Another victim of the Donnie Brasco embarrassment in February of the following year, was the widely-feared street-soldier, Tony Mirra. Mirra had been the one who had introduced Brasco to the Family. Massino handed the contract for the killing to Mirra's cousin, Richard Cantarello. Mirra was lured to a parking garage in Lower Manhattan where another cousin, Joseph D'Amico, climbed into his burgundy Mercedes beside him and shot him in the temple. When the police found Mirra hours later, he had been shot twice behind his ear and once in the face.

When a number of the Bonanno hierarchy were arrested, Massino became a fugitive, indicted by a Federal Grand Jury in Manhattan along with five other men on a charge of conspiracy to murder Indelicato, Giaccone and Trinchera. On the run, his associates kept him in funds and many of his colleagues, including John Gotti made the trip to visit him.

Massino was now running the Family and, even though Rusty Rastelli had been released from a spell in prison, it was Joe calling the shots.

His next hit was Cesare Bonventre who had been Carmine Galante's – unsuccessful – bodyguard on the day he had been killed. Bonventre was invited to a meeting with Rastelli in Queens, but was picked up by Salvatore Vitale and Louie Attanasio and never made it to the meeting. They drove into a garage where Attanasio shot him twice in the head. Bonventre was a strong guy and he struggled, despite his wounds. They had to pull into a car park where Bonventre crawled out of the car. Attanasio jumped out and pumped another two bullets into him. Gabriel Infante was given the job of getting rid of the body, but it was found shortly after in April 1984, cut in two and stuffed into fifty-five gallon oil drums in a warehouse. It was the last mistake Infante made.

Things were becoming a little hot and Massino decided that the best thing would be to turn himself over to the police. He was given bail and released. In 1985 he was indicted for labour racketeering along with Rastelli, Carmine Rastelli, Nicky Marnagello and thirteen others. Then in October of the next year he was found guilty of violations of RICO Law, the Hobbs Act (robbery or extortion) and the Taft-Hartley Act (labour racketeering). In January 1987 he was sentenced to ten years.

As if that was not enough, April 1987 saw him in court again, on hijacking and murder charges. Joe Pistone/Donnie Brasco testified against him and tried to implicate him in a triple murder as well as the conspiracies to kill Pastore and Indelicato. He was acquitted of the hijacking charges due to a legal problem, but went to prison until 1993.

Rastelli had died in 1991 and, when Massino came out of prison, he seemed to be the one man who could fill his shoes. He made Salvatore Vitale his underboss and Anthony Spero, *Consigliere*. He gained a reputation for living according to the old rules, keeping Cosa Nostra and membership of it secret. He accused the government of being biased towards Italian-Americans. He was doing a good job. The Bonanno Family regained its seat on the Crime Commission and business was looking up. It did not last long, however. Spero was given life for racketeering and murder, and his replacement, Anthony 'TG' Graziano was indicted for murder, drug trafficking, extortion and illegal gambling.

Joey was, himself, indicted again in January 2003 and among the charges lurked seven murders: Alphonse 'Sonny Red' Indelicato, Philip 'Lucky Phil' Giaconne, Dominick 'Big Trin' Trinchera, Dominick 'Sonny Black' Napolitano, Tony Mirra, Cesar Nonaventre and Gabriel Infanti. Things began to go very bad when eight Bonanno men decided to give evidence for the prosecution, including Salvatore Vitale, his loyal associate of so many years. Massino had been best man at his wedding and was godfather to one of Vitale's sons.

In July 2004 he was found guilty on all counts and faced at least life or possibly execution. To the Mob world's horror, it was announced in February 2005, that Joey Massino had turned and was cooperating with the authorities, the first Mafia boss ever to do so.

As a result of his cooperation, he succeeded in escaping the death penalty, instead being sentenced to life. He also admitted ordering the killing of Bonanno *capo*, Gerlando Sciascia, waiving his right to appeal his conviction for the seven other murders.

Meanwhile the Mafia reeled.

HENRY HILL

'Henry was a rat as a kid. He'd sell his soul if he knew he'd get out of it.' Henry Hill's sister knows Henry Hill better than most and is under no illusions about her brother. After all, this is the man who, when he was about ten years old, used his younger brother, who suffered from spina bifida, to beg money from commuters on the New York subway.

Born in 1943 in Brooklyn, Henry Hill was the product of a mother who had emigrated from Sicily and an electrician father of Irish descent. Henry was the first boy after the couple had had four daughters and another couple of brothers followed him. They all lived in a small house close to a cab-stand run by a man called Paul Vario, a large, oily-haired character that everyone knew was a *capo* in the Lucchese crime family, one of New York's five crime families. Vario ran different types of businesses including a number of 'chop shop' operations which disassembled stolen cars and sold the parts.

Henry began running errands for Vario at the cab-stand, graduating eventually to working on his shoe-shine operation and then in the pizzeria that Vario owned on the same street as the cab-stand. Vario like him and Henry looked up to the mafioso as a father figure. He was in awe of the money that Vario had and the power it seemed to give him. On one occasion, the school Henry infrequently attended, told him they had sent a letter bringing Henry's absences to the attention of his parents. When he told Vario about it, the gangster had one of his men have a word with the postman. The letter was never delivered and Henry was impressed. For his part, Vario provided Henry with the approval that he never got at home from a father who became an increasingly violent drunk and who disapproved of the company Henry was keeping.

Nonetheless, Henry began to earn good money at an early age. Vario got him membership of the Bricklayers Union, entitling him to a weekly wage without doing any work. He was just fourteen and already earning almost as much as his father. This, of course, and the fact that Henry did nothing to hide the money he was bringing in, made their relationship even worse. Then, aged sixteen, he had his first run-in with the law when he was arrested for using a stolen credit card to buy tyres at a garage. His incarceration was brief, however; his mob friends spoke to the appropriate person and he was released shortly after he was picked up. They celebrated his arrest with a party, as if he had come of age. Henry became even more enamoured of the wiseguy way of life.

He could never, however, become a real wiseguy, a member of the Mafia. Although his mother was Italian, his father's Irish origins barred Henry from being any more than an associate member. Another mob associate whose Irish roots also prevented him from becoming a 'made' member, was Jimmy 'the Gent' Burke. Henry hooked up with Burke and became involved in crime of a far more serious nature – loan-sharking, running numbers and, especially, hijacking goods from lorries, mainly at Kennedy airport.

In 1960 his family wondered if perhaps Henry had seen the error of his ways when he unexpectedly enlisted in the United States Army. He was stationed at Fort Bragg in North Carolina but it soon became evident that old habits die hard. He began to hustle just as hard while in the service as he had in his civilian life. He sold food from the kitchens in which he worked as an army cook, he was loan-sharking salary advances to other soldiers and selling tax-free cigarettes. He spent two months locked up for fighting and stealing a sheriff's car and, eventually, they had had enough of him. He was discharged and returned to his old life in New York.

In 1965 Henry got married to Karen, and they had two children. Not that the kids saw much of their father. Henry would be gone for days, sometimes weeks, making deals and earning money out on the city streets. He was far from faithful to his wife and their relationship was fiery from the start – 'love-hate' as a member of his family described it. He treated his personal life like any other self-respecting gangster – Friday night was for the girlfriend, Saturday night for the wife.

Henry and Burke got into serious trouble in Tampa, Florida in 1972 when they beat to a pulp a gambler who owed a union official friend of theirs a large amount of money for a gambling debt. Unfortunately for them, the victim's sister worked at the FBI as a typist and she let it be known in the office who had beaten up her brother. The two men were arrested and sentenced to ten years. In prison, however, Henry realised the benefits of being associated with the Mafia. Even the prison guards treated them with respect and they enjoyed privileges that other prisoners could only dream of.

It was during this time that Henry first became involved with narcotics, selling them in order to be able to provide his wife with money to bring up his two children. He made some contacts that he was certain would come in very useful when he had done his time.

He was released after four and a quarter years, partly through the help of Paul Vario who falsely told the authorities he could provide Henry with a job. Henry became involved in the infamous Lufthansa heist at Kennedy Airport in 1978. Although he did not take part – the first he knew was when he switched on the radio one morning – Henry was the person who tipped 'Jimmy the Gent' Burke off about the millions of dollars of cash and jewellery that was going to be stored in a cargo terminal at the airport for a short while. Burke and his gang got away with $6 million in what was, until then, the biggest robbery in American criminal history. The robbery would lead to an unparalleled amount of bloodletting, however, in which Burke, paranoid that he was going to be exposed as the leader of the crew that carried out the heist, killed thirteen of his gang members.

Henry started to use the drugs contacts he had made in prison, in spite of the specific rule of the Mafia that no member or associate should ever deal in drugs. What the rule was sometimes said to mean, however, was that no Mafia member should ever get caught dealing in drugs. The logic was sound, however. The sentences imposed for drug trafficking were so long that arrested traffickers were more often willing to become informants in order to cut their sentences.

He began dealing in large quantities of cocaine in an interstate drug-trafficking operation that involved a Pittsburgh drug dealer, Paul Mazzei and the money flooded in. Things were so good in fact, that he cut Jimmy Burke and another gangster, Tommy DiSimone, in on the action which involved wholesaling marijuana, cocaine, heroin and Quaaludes. Henry stupidly began sampling his own product – never a good idea – and became sloppy. He also became paranoid when Burke delivered DiSimone into the hands of the Gambino crime family. He had committed the sin of killing two made members without permission. DiSimone was reported missing and never seen alive again.

With Mazzei, Henry also set up a match-fixing scheme in college basketball and the resulting scandal, involving Boston College centre Rick Kuhn and his team-mates, outraged American sports fans. Henry also claimed that he had a referee in his control who officiated at matches at Madison Square Garden during the 1970s. The referee had been compromised by a large debt he had accrued betting on horse races.

Before long Henry's sloppiness began to get him into trouble and he was arrested, as was everyone else in his drug-distribution chain. He was bailed but was then rearrested as a material witness in the Lufthansa job. He had reached a low point. Strung out on drugs and alcohol, he was certain that his life and those of his wife and children, were in grave danger. He knew too much about a lot of things, especially the Lufthansa caper and Burke would not want him disclosing his part in the robbery to the authorities. To reinforce the danger he faced, federal investigators played Henry a tape in which Burke tells Vario that they needed to have Hill 'whacked'.

His options were drying up fast.

Henry Hill became an informant and his testimony helped to nail many of his former associates. It would lead to fifty convictions, among them Jimmy Burke who was sentenced to twenty years in prison for fixing college basketball games. He was later sentenced to life for the murder of con-man, Richard Eaton. Burke died of cancer in prison in 1996, aged sixty-four.

Henry's former mentor and surrogate father, Paul Vario, was sentenced to four years for fixing Henry up with a bogus job to get him out of prison. He also got ten years for extortion of airfreight companies at Kennedy airport. He died in a Texas prison in 1988 of respiratory failure.

Henry Hill and his wife and two children entered

the Witness Protection Programme. They changed their names and moved, firstly to Omaha, Nebraska and then to Independence, Kentucky. Eventually, they wound up in Redmond in Washington State, living off the $1,500 he was given each month for rent and expenses. But Henry never took to life in the programme. His drinking and drug-taking got worse and he got into the dangerous habit of telling people, when very drunk, that he was Henry Hill, the Mafia informer. He was arrested on numerous occasions for drink-driving and he fought continuously with Karen, his wife.

In Seattle in 1987, he was arrested yet again on drug-related charges. He was lucky, managing to charm the judge into letting him off with probation. It was around this time, however, that he met and fell in love with a woman who was looking after the horses on the farm on which he was living. Unfortunately, she happened also to have a drug habit. Henry finally left Karen and started a new life with her. By this time, the authorities had given up on him and he was expelled from the Witness Protection Programme.

Henry was said to have finally kicked his demons by the end of the 1990s and was free of his addictions to booze and drugs. In 2005, however, he was arrested in North Platte, Nebraska, after leaving his luggage at the local airport. It was found to contain drug equipment – glass tubes with cocaine and metamphetamine residue on them.

He wrote a bestselling book about his life – *Wiseguy* – which made him half a million dollars when the movie rights were sold. Eventually made into the classic gangster movie *Goodfellows*, with Ray Liotta memorably playing him, he became even more famous. He opened a restaurant, Wiseguys in West Haven, Connecticut in 2007 and marketed a gravy sauce, Sunday Gravy, on the internet. He says that he learned his culinary skills from his mother when he was a child and plans to publish a book of recipes, mostly drawn from that time.

Henry Hill appears on chat shows and hangs out with film stars. He is getting married this year and he no longer needs to look over his shoulder. Everyone who would want to kill him for what he did is out of the picture, either in jail or dead. Henry, however, goes from strength to strength. As one cop said of him – 'Henry will never change and the one thing you must always remember when you sit with Henry or deal with Henry is that he is what is portrayed in the movie, a goodfellow who's thinking in the back of his mind what's good for him . . . not necessarily what's good for you.'

JOE VALACHI

There are several theories as to the origins of the word *omertà*. Some say it can be traced back to the Spanish word, *hombredad*, meaning manliness, through the Sicilian word *omu*, for man. Others trace its origins to the Latin *humilitas*, meaning humility, which evolved into *umirtà* and then *omertà* in a number of southern Italian dialects. Regardless of its origins, however, it means one thing – a code of silence that prevents men from speaking, even when their very own lives or freedom are at risk. Someone who has been wronged is forbidden by *omertà* from appealing to the legally appointed authority to redress that wrong – everyone has to look out for his own interests and prove his manliness by avenging himself or finding someone who will do it for him. The worst offence of all, however, is to become a *cascittuni*, an informant. No matter the reason, however, to violate the code of *omertà* normally results in one thing and one thing only – violent death.

In this age of *The Sopranos* and *The Godfather*, it is hard to imagine that once very little was known about organised crime as run by the Mafia. When asked about the Mafia during a trial, Joe Colombo, head of the Colombo Crime Family from 1964 to 1971, replied, 'Mafia? What's the Mafia? There is no Mafia.' Two events blew the lid off the entire organisation, however, and brought it straight into the public's very living room through the medium of television.

The first was the Appalachin Conference. On 14 November 1957 the mob held a conference at the Appalachin, New York, home of gangster, Joseph Barbara, attended by dons from New York as well as from families in other American cities. The State Police got wind of it and raided the house. The mobsters took off, running into the woods that surrounded the house, throwing their guns into the bushes as they did so. It was a humiliating moment for them – dozens of hoods were arrested and it demonstrated the extent to which crime in the United States was organised.

The second was the admission, in October 1963, by Mafia foot-soldier, Joseph 'Joe Cargo' Valachi that the Mafia did, in fact, exist. Valachi, a driver in Vito Genovese's Family, appeared before the McClellan Congressional Committee on organised crime and violated his oath of *omertà* in the full glare of television cameras and radio microphones.

The authorities, of course, already knew the Mafia existed. Official recognition occurred in 1890. A grand jury investigating the murder of a police chief, reported: 'The range of our research has developed the existence of the secret organization styled "Mafia".'

In the early 1900s there were media reports of an organisation known as the 'Black Hand'. They engaged in extortion and had emerged from Calabrian immigrants who were members of the Calabrian Mafia, otherwise known as the '*ndrangheta*.

Then in 1918, mafioso, Tony Notaro, had testified about the structure and organisation of the Mafia during a murder trial. A year later, the first book on the Mafia's activities in the United States, *The Barrel Mystery*, by William J. Flynn was on the shelves of bookshops.

The Justice Department had files on a notorious Mafioso, Nicolo 'Culicchia' Gentile, also known as 'Zu Cola', who had arrived in America in 1907 and had spent the next thirty years as a nationwide trouble-shooter for the Mafia. He may even have been a serving member of Lucky Luciano's Crime Commission. Gentile was involved in a drug-trafficking investigation when he fled to Sicily in 1939. In the 1950s, a Justice Department investigation team interviewed him there and he told the team his life story, including names and dates, but the information was filed away and never acted upon.

In 1940, Murder Inc's Abe 'Kid Twist' Reles stuck his head above the Mafia parapet and informed on former associates. Reles explained how the national crime syndicate was formed in the early 1930s, providing dates and names. Once again, none of the law enforcement agencies made a concerted effort to follow up on his assertions. In the meantime, he paid with his life by 'falling' from a window while in police custody.

There had been several investigations – the Chicago Crime Commission in 1922, the Wickershaw Commission in 1929 and the Kefauver Committee in 1950. Each found suggestions, but not conclusive proof that such a body as the Mafia actually existed.

It took Joe Valachi to finally confirm that it did.

Joseph Michael Valachi had been in the Mafia for decades, almost from the moment that it became the dominant criminal force in the United States. He was born in 1904, in East Harlem, to parents Marie and Dominick who had emigrated from Naples to New York. They had merely exchanged poverty in one continent for poverty in another. Of seventeen children to whom Marie gave birth, only six survived and they had it rough. Joe's younger brother, Johnny was found dead in the road and it was never proved whether he had been the victim of a hit-and-run accident, or had been beaten to death by the police. Anthony, his older brother, was committed to the State Hospital for the Criminally Insane at Danemora. Insanity ran in the family – two of his three sisters and his grandmother suffered the same fate as Anthony.

Aged just seven, Joe had his first brush with the law when he threw a rock at a teacher and was sent to a reform school. By fifteen, he had left school behind and was working alongside his father at a New York City garbage dump.

The Minute Men were a gang of teenage burglars and hooligans who took their name from the speed with which they worked. Joe joined them when he was eighteen and in 1923, experienced his second brush with the law when he was shot in the arm by a police officer while fleeing from a robbery. He was arrested and sentenced to nine months in Ossining Prison in Upper New York State. Ossining was better known as Sing Sing, the most notorious prison in America.

On his release, Joe took up where he left off, but this time forming his own gang. He was unlucky yet again, however, when he was shot by a passing patrolman while breaking into a Bronx warehouse filled with fur coats. This time he was wounded in the head, but escaped and recovered. In 1925, however, he paid another visit to Sing Sing – for three years this time – after a car used in a robbery was traced back to him.

Before entering prison, Joe had been blamed by some gangsters for driving a car in an incident in which the neighbourhood was shot up. They tried to punish him for this in prison and he was seriously wounded in an attack by another prisoner, Pete LaTampa. He received thirty-eight stitches and recovered once again. During this stint, he managed to complete his seventh grade education and learned to read and write, but almost more importantly, he was given an education in the ways of the underworld by an old-timer called Alessandro Bollero with whom he became friends. Bollero had been a leading mobster since the early years of the 20th century and had been locked up for the 1918 murder of Vincenzo Terranova, brother of vicious Mafioso, Ciro Terranova, known as 'the Artichoke King'. Ciro made a fortune by threatening vegetable sellers into buying his artichokes.

When Valachi emerged from Sing Sing in 1928, he resolved to iron out his problems with Terranova and was helped in this by a friend, Dominick 'The Gap' Petrilli. He then returned to business as usual. Before long, however, he had come to the attention of the

Mob and was invited to join a gang headed up by Gaetano Reina who controlled most of New York's ice distribution. There was still no electric refrigeration and the ice business was a lucrative one.

It was a difficult time in Mafia history. Giuseppe 'Joe the Boss' Masseria and Salvatore Maranzano were slugging it out to be the *capo di tutti capi*, boss of bosses, in a struggle that came to be known as the Castellamarese War, and which lasted almost two years. Meanwhile in the wings waited Charles 'Lucky' Luciano, who would pick up the pieces and become the most important gangster, and one of the most influential Americans of the twentieth century.

Valachi whose gang was allied to the Castellamarese boss, Maranzano, received orders for his first hit in November 1930. The target was Steven Ferrigino, a Masseria man. Accompanying him on the mission were a Chicago gunman, known only as 'Buster' and another member of his gang, Nick Capuzzi. They were meticulous in their planning. Valachi rented an apartment overlooking the entrance to Ferrigino's house. They then watched the Masseria man for weeks. In the late afternoon of 5 November, Ferrigino and an associate, Alfred Mineo, were gunned down as they walked towards Ferrigino's front door.

Valachi had impressed his new bosses and was

rewarded when, a month later, he was driven to a large, colonial-style house in upstate New York. He was led into a room at which forty men sat at a long table. At the head of the table sat Salvatore Maranzano. Valachi would later recall that the immaculately dressed Maranzano looked more like a banker than a racketeer.

All present held hands round the table as Maranzano intoned: 'This represents that you live by the gun and the knife', referring to the two weapons in the centre of the table. Valachi was then given a piece of paper that was lit by Maranzano with a match. He repeated after the boss as it burned, 'This is the way I will burn if I betray the secrets of this Cosa Nostra…The Cosa Nostra comes before everything – our blood, our family, our religion, our country…To betray the secret of Cosa Nostra means death without trial.' If they only knew.

He was assigned a boss – a *gombah* or godfather, Joseph Bonnano, who would later in life become an important Mafia leader.

Valachi's job was to be on hand as a shooter. 'Spotters' would call at any time of the day to let him know the whereabouts of members of the Masseria mob. He then had to go after them. Initially, he had little success, but on 3 February 1931 that changed.

Working again with Buster, the target was another Masseria lieutenant, Joseph Catania, who also happened to be a nephew of the man Valachi hated more than most – Ciro Terranova. Buster shot Catania six times in the street after he had kissed his wife goodbye while Valachi organised the getaway car.

Valachi landed himself a job as driver to Maranzano. Masseria had been shot in a restaurant on Coney Island and it finally looked as if Maranzano had it all sewn up. On the evening of 9 September 1931, he announced to Valachi and other close members of his team that he wanted Lucky Luciano and Vito Genovese eliminated. He saw them as a threat to his control and by removing them, he felt he would consolidate his position. The hit, to be carried out by a killer called Vincent 'Mad Dog' Coll, had been arranged for next day when Maranzano had invited the two men to a meeting. Unfortunately for Maranzano, however, Luciano, the consummate gangster, was one step ahead of him. At ten to three that same afternoon, four assassins strolled into Maranzano's office and shot and stabbed him to death.

That day, Valachi and 'The Gap' Petrilli were entertaining a couple of young ladies in Brooklyn. Valachi was in no doubt that 'The Gap' had saved his life by ensuring that he was not around Maranzano's office.

Valachi was even more grateful when he learned that three other members of Maranzano's team had been gunned down that afternoon. He went into hiding.

When it all blew over, Valachi joined up with Vito Genovese's family which was controlled by the Mob's new kingpin, Lucky Luciano, ruling Cosa Nostra from a suite at the Waldorf-Astoria Hotel. Joe answered to Anthony 'Tony Bender' Strollo, a close friend of Genovese.

Valachi now went into business, grossing $2,500 a week from slot machines. He also got married, in September 1932. Two months later, he received his first contract from Tony Bender. The victim was Michael Reggione, whose brothers Genovese had killed ten years earlier. Genovese was worried that Reggione might now want revenge for his brothers' deaths. As usual, Joe was meticulous in his preparation, making the acquaintance of the target at a coffee shop he used. He recruited two friends and lured Reggione to a card game in an old unoccupied tenement building. As they entered the building, Joe turned away and Reggione was shot three times in the head.

The new Mayor of New York, Fiorello LaGuardia, announced a clamp-down on slot machines and Valachi's business folded. He and his partner, Girolamo 'Bobby Doyle' Santucci, went in for the numbers racket next and they started earning good money. Arrested in early 1932, a quick bribe got them off with a suspended sentence.

By the end of the 1930s, Joe not only had a son, Donald, and a twenty-two-year-old mistress called Laura, he was also the owner of a restaurant, Paradise, and was a partner in a garment-manufacturing business. He also bought his first racehorse. Things were going well and got better during the war as the clothing business prospered due to lucrative military contracts.

Lucky Luciano was now behind bars on pimping charges and would be completely out of the picture on his release in 1946 when he was deported to Italy. Vito Genovese had fled murder charges and hid out for the duration of the war in Naples, returning in 1945. The new boss was Frank Costello.

As the war raged on, the numbers and loan-sharking businesses began to falter, so Joe went into selling black market goods and made big money. He sold enough stolen ration stamps to buy another restaurant, with his partner, Frank Luciano, as well as another racehorse. When he discovered, however, that Luciano had been funding a gambling habit with the restaurant's takings he went into a rage and almost beat Luciano to death.

In 1952 Joe was issued with another contract. The

victim was a soldier in the Gagliano family, Eugenio Giannini, who had become an informer for the Mob's least favourite government agency, the Narcotics Bureau. Joe subcontracted the job to three East Harlem hoods, the brothers, Joe and Pat Pagano, and his nephew, Fiore Siano. Giannini was shot in the head and left for dead outside a delicatessen on West 234th Street. Twelve years later, in front of the McLellan Committee, Valachi would solve what had, until then, been just another unsolved gangland hit.

In June of the next year, Valachi brutally murdered a man called Steve Franse in his restaurant. This was a personal favour to Vito Genovese, whose wife had embarrassed him in their divorce hearing by disclosing information about her husband's business. While Genovese had been in Italy during the war, Franse had been given the job of chaperoning Mrs Genovese. He had failed to do so and paid the price with his life.

Valachi was by now under close scrutiny from the FBI, mostly because they believed he was dealing in drugs. His good friend, Petrilli, had served a prison sentence for drug-dealing and had then been deported. Back in the United States, Petrilli was reported to be setting up Cosa Nostra members with the Narcotics Bureau. Tony Bender approached Valachi with this disturbing news, but Joe did not want any part of the hit on Petrilli. However, after 'The Gap' had showed up in his restaurant, he let Bender know. A few days later, his old friend was gunned down in a bar in the Bronx. Joe was distraught. 'I wouldn't have done nothing to him,' he said. '…how could I forget he took me to Brooklyn and kept me out of the way when Maranzano got his?… Gee, I felt bad, it wasn't much of a Christmas.'

The Narcotics Bureau finally got Valachi in 1955 on charges associated with drugs and he was sentenced to five years in prison. He was released on appeal, but arrested the next year. Again he won on appeal and walked.

The year 1957 was not a good one for the Mafia. Frank Costello decided to spend more time with his family after being wounded by a would-be assassin. Frank Salice, Albert Anastasia's underboss was gunned down in a fruit shop and Anastasia himself was famously shot dead in the barbershop at the Park-Sheraton Hotel. Things had started to come apart at the seams for Valachi. He lost the licence to sell alcohol at his restaurant and discovered that his partner in the garment business had been embezzling. He got back into drug-dealing, opened a linen supply company and became a partner in a lucrative juke-box business.

But the FBI was homing in on him and when they

raided his home he was forced to go on the run. They picked him up on 19 November and he was charged and then released on $25,000 bail. He fled to Canada, however, to hide out with a man called Alfredo Agueci, a drug-dealing Buffalo mafioso.

Tony Bender ordered him back to New York, telling him that it had been fixed so that he would only be sentenced to five years and after another month moving from place to place in the Bronx, he realised it was pointless and handed himself in. Bender had misled him, however, and the judge actually sent him to prison for fifteen years and fined him $10,000. He was sent to Atlanta Federal Penitentiary.

In 1961, he faced another trial on drugs charges. This time, he claimed he had been set up by Bender, the Agueci brothers and another gangster by the name of Vincent Mauro. It made no difference, however. He got another twenty years to run concurrently with his existing sentence.

In prison, Valachi found himself becoming isolated from the other prisoners. Genovese was in the same prison and people were poisoning him with information that Joe Valachi was an informant. The fact that he had been allied to Tony Bender who Genovese had had eliminated by now, did not help. By June 1962 there had been three attempts on his life. One evening in the cell he shared with Vito Genovese and six other men, Genovese kissed him on the cheek. Joe feared it was the Mafia 'kiss of death'.

It was now rumoured that Genovese had offered $100,000 for the murder of Valachi and to get himself out of the way, Joe committed himself to solitary confinement, trying unsuccessfully while there, to contact a number of people, including the head of the Bureau of Narcotics. Released, he could not eat, for fear his food was poisoned. He was spiralling out of control and one night when he saw three men approaching him in the exercise yard, he cracked. He grabbed a piece of iron pipe that lay beside some building work that was being carried out and attacked a man that he believed to be the Genovese associate, Joe DiPalermo. The man was actually John Saupp, a man with no connection to the Mob, whatsoever. Saupp died from his injuries two days later.

Valachi had never shown the slightest bit of remorse for anything he had done until the killing of Saupp. It was a turning point in his life and on 13 June 1962, he informed the authorities he was willing to cooperate.

On 17 July he received a life sentence for the murder of Saupp and on the same day was flown to Westchester County Jail, close to New York City. He was held on an isolated ward in the prison hospital under the name of Joseph DiMarco. Then he spent a year in front of the McLellan Committee, talking about the thirty years of his Mafia life, from his first theft at the age of nine, when he stole a bar of Fairy Soap to his most recent drug-dealing activities. From what appeared to be a photographic memory, he named names and provided details of Mafia operations, businesses and murders. He confirmed that there were five crime families in New York and one in New Jersey. He described other families in Buffalo, Chicago, Detroit, Tampa, Boston and Providence, naming bosses and identifying senior men. He confirmed that there were at least 2,000 'made' men – family members – in New York, and identified 289 of the 383 gangsters that had been profiled by investigators. When asked by Senator Edmund Muskie if the Mafia was the same as Cosa Nostra, he told him he never used the term 'Mafia'. 'Senator,' he said, 'as long as I belong, they never express it as Mafia.'

William Hindley, the man in charge of the Justice Department's onslaught on organised crime said of Valachi's testimony: 'What Valachi did is beyond measure. Before he came along, we had no concrete evidence that anything like this existed . . . But Valachi named names. He revealed what the structure was and how it operates. In a word, he showed us the face of the enemy.'

Valachi's memoirs appeared in book form, ghost-written by Peter Maas, as *The Valachi Papers* in 1968 and Charles Bronson played Valachi in the film of the book.

On 11 April 1966, Joe Valachi tried to hang himself after trouble over his book and the removal from his cell of a small hot plate and grill. He was then transferred to a prison in Texas where he remained for the rest of his life in a cell near the prison hospital that had its own bathroom, rug, television, stove and several electric heaters. Joe was forever cold, even in the heat of the south.

On 3 April 1971 he died following a gall bladder attack. For years, he had corresponded with a woman from Buffalo and she claimed his body and buried him in an unmarked grave in a cemetery near Niagara Falls. She left it unmarked because she feared that it would be desecrated by the Mafia if they knew where it was. He had survived Vito Genevese by two years and two months.

PETER CHIODO

Who says being overweight is bad for your health? On 8 May 1991, forty-year-old Peter Chiodo, a *capo* in the Lucchese crime family had stopped at a Staten Island service station, close to the Verranzano Narrows Bridge, because he had a problem with his car. He had just lifted the bonnet and begun to have a look at the engine when a black saloon car pulled up beside him. Three shooters inside the car opened fire on him and he immediately pulled his gun and returned some shots. But, within moments, he slumped to the ground beside his car having received twelve bullet wounds to the arms, legs and body, five of the bullets passing right through and out the other side. But, after being rushed in a serious condition to St. Vincent's hospital, he survived, none of the bullets having damaged a vital organ. His huge bulk – his weight was anything between 450 and 500 pounds and he stood six feet five inches tall – had cushioned a number of the bullets. Not for nothing did they did call him 'Fat Pete'.

Mafia crime syndicate, the Lucchese Family controlled the window installation business in New York. Smaller than either the Gambinos or the Genovese families, with just 125 members, the Luccheses had been headed by Vittorio 'Little Vic' Amuso since 1986. Although described by friends as a 'regular guy' who enjoyed sport and working out, he was probably responsible for nine murders. He listed his occupations over the years as security guard, a window-installation company salesman and a trucking company executive. Not many window salesmen order their men to 'hit Jersey', however, meaning that they should kill the entire Lucchese Family in Jersey, thirty men. They had made the mistake of cutting him out of their profits after the imprisonment of Anthony 'Tony Ducks' Corallo who had been sentenced to 100 years for racketeering. The Jersey boys were summoned to a meeting, but suspecting the way the meeting might end – in their massacre – they decided not to RSVP and went into hiding.

It was Little Vic, on the run with his underboss, Anthony 'Gas Pipe' Casso, following an indictment for racketeering, murder, extortion, labour pay-offs and tax fraud, who ordered the hit on Fat Pete, and acting boss, Alphonse 'Little Al' D'Arco put together a team that included his son, Joseph. Fat Pete had made the mistake of pleading guilty to charges under the RICO Act – the Racketeer Influenced and Corrupt Organizations Act – the only one of fifteen accused to do so. Pleading guilty would get him a lighter sentence and would also save him a fortune on legal fees.

While he was recovering in hospital, Charles Rose, the Assistant United States Attorney, tried to persuade him to become a government witness. Even though he knew that it had been the Lucchese bosses who had ordered his death, he was still reluctant to turn on his former associates. His mind was focused somewhat, however, when two mafiosi turned up in his lawyer's office with a chilling message for Chiodo. 'Tell him his wife is next,' they said. Naturally, Chiodo began to waver.

He agreed to become a government witness and they got his wife out of the way, entering her into the Witness Protection Programme. But the Lucchese hoods did not let that stop them. They decided to go after other members of Chiodo's family. This was surprising as it was completely against the unwritten Mafia code. They firstly tried to kill Fat Pete's sister, Patricia Cappozalo, but only succeeded in seriously wounding her. She had been dropping off her children at school and was shot as she returned home afterwards. Having failed once, they succeeded with their next effort, murdering Chiodo's uncle, Frank Signorino, stuffing his body into rubbish bags and leaving it in the boot of a car where it was found later.

D'Arco was horrified by these actions as he realised that all it would achieve would be a reaction from the authorities and the strengthening of Fat Pete's resolve. He was even more disturbed when he was shown other plans by the fugitive Amuso and 'Gas Pipe' Casso. They presented him with a list of forty-nine people that Gas Pipe wanted killed. What made it worse was that a number of the names on the list were members of the Lucchese Family. When asked why, Casso replied simply that they were 'creeps'. 'When I come home,' he said, 'I'm going to have a party and invite all the creeps I want to kill. Then I'll kill them all.' They talked about bombing Gambino Family boss, John Gotti. These men were seriously losing it, D'Arco thought.

D'Arco's failure to kill Peter Chioda had huge implications for his future. Amuso was finally captured in Scranton, Pennsylvania following a feature on him on the television show, *America's Most Wanted*. On 18 September, his trial was underway for rigging bids on public works in New York. That day, D'Arco was attending a meeting at the Hotel Kimberly in mid-town Manhattan. He felt a strange atmosphere as he waited for the meeting to start. Everyone was exuding nervous energy and among the other attendees, men he had known and worked with for many years, was one with a distinct bulge under his shirt. Guns were banned at Family meetings, but D'Arco was certain that the bulge was a weapon. The Lucchese Family at that time was an edgy operation where the normal conventions and rules no longer applied.

The man with the bulge in his shirt went into the toilet in the suite where the meeting was being held. D'Arco watched him carefully when he emerged. The bulge had gone. That meant only one thing – someone else was going to pick up the weapon from the toilet and come after him. He had to somehow get out of that room and find his driver and his car. He made an excuse and slipped downstairs, but they were nowhere to be found. He quickly hailed a taxi and went home where he and his wife packed some clothes and fled. Before too long, he had turned himself in to the authorities and began eleven years of testifying for the government at organised crime trials around the country. His son, Joseph, fearing for his life, had already handed himself over to the authorities.

The FBI had raided D'Arco's apartment in Little Italy shortly after, finding the radio and the lights still on, but no sign of D'Arco or his wife. 'It looked like he left in a hell of a big hurry,' said one agent.

Meanwhile, Fat Pete began his career as a government witness in September 1991. He was brought into court in a wheelchair from his hospital bed, Federal agents on each side of him and the courtroom closely guarded. His right arm quivered repeatedly during the proceedings that had been moved temporarily from Brooklyn to make it easier for Chiodo to take part. He was testifying that he had taken part in a scheme to rig bids in the New York window installation industry and, in the process, he described his life in the Lucchese Family and told of four murders in which he had taken part. Chiodo's role in the four murders was to carry instructions from the top echelons of the Family to other Lucchese Family members who actually carried out the killings.

Fat Pete described his initiation into the Mafia, explaining the blood oath of secrecy that all Mafia recruits have to swear and that he took in an apartment above a funeral parlour in the New York district of Queens. The oath included the line, 'If I ever betray my sacred oath, may my soul burn in hell forever'.

He explained how he had been promoted to *capo* – captain – the following year with the duties of supervising union bribes and disputes for the Family. 'I handled some of the unions that were under their control,' he explained, and carried cash payments from Local 580 of the Ironworkers Union to the bosses of the Family. The money was paid to the union by window-installation companies who had to do so in order to secure contracts.

Chiodo described one bid-rigging meeting he attended in 1989. It was a meeting with other crime Families and an official of Local 580, fearing that there would be some 'heavyweights' there, had asked Chiodo to attend as a representative of the Lucchese Family. Among those present, Chiodo identified some of the defendants in the case as being there – Peter Gotti, brother of 'Dapper Don', John, head of the Gambino Family and Venero Mangano, *consigliere*, or second-in-command, of the Genovese Family.

Defense lawyer, Frederick P. Hafetz, asked Chiodo if he believed Vittorio Amuso and Anthony Casso, not on trial, were responsible for his attempted murder. Fat Pete replied that he was certain they were. He added that Amuso wanted to kill him because of an argument about money. He went on to testify that eight of the nine defendants on trial were members or associates of Mafia Families, naming Benedetto Aloi and Mangano, in particular, as high-ranking Mafia men.

The prosecution, naturally, focused on Chiodo's own criminal career, quizzing him about his involvement in extortion, theft, armed hijacking and, of course, murder – his direct involvement in four and an additional four conspiracies to commit murder. Fat Pete responded that he had been 'totally immoral' in the past, but had changed.

'Would your conscience bother you about committing perjury today, sir?' Hafetz asked, more than a hint of sarcasm reportedly in his voice. 'That would bother your conscience?'

'Yes, it would, 'Fat Pete replied.

Asked then if he had used his massive girth to threaten and intimidate people, Fat Pete said that, on occasion, he had. He then acknowledged, in response to questioning, that he could conceivably go to prison for the rest of his life, if he were prosecuted for all his crimes, but explained that his cooperation agreement stipulated that if he cooperated and pleaded guilty to racketeering, he would receive a maximum of twenty years prison time. He was also aware that the prosecutors, in gratitude for his help, could ask the judge for a lesser sentence and possibly, no sentence whatsoever. He could walk out, scot-free. Hafetz asked him if he realised that it would be very much in his interest, in these circumstances, to lie about the defendants in this case. He agreed. 'Yeah. I guess so.'

There was laughter in the courtroom when Chiodo discussed his own financial arrangements. When it was put to him that he had used shell corporations – businesses without significant assets or operations, often used in the criminal economy to hide money – he conceded that he had hidden hundreds of thousands of illegally earned dollars, in this way. He said, however, that he had used so many companies that even he was confused as to where the money was.

The trial ended with three of the defendants convicted of extortion, but five others, including Peter Gotti, were acquitted of all charges.

Not long after, for the third time in a year, Chiodo testified for the prosecution in an organised crime trial – that of Vittorio Amuso, who was charged with heading the Lucchese family as well as nine murders.

Chiodo told how in 1989, in Amuso's presence, Anthony Casso had ordered him to kill a union official, John 'Sonny' Morrissey, who they suspected of cooperating with the police. He quoted Casso as telling him that 'Sonny Morrissey has to be taken care of and clipped.' In a soft voice, devoid of emotion, Chiodo explained how he had lured Morrissey to a construction site in Jefferson Township in New Jersey which was situated in a secluded, heavily wooded area. He had told him that Little Vic Amuso wanted a word with him and when they arrived, had led him into a small building that housed the site's office. Inside two gunmen were waiting. Chiodo said he stepped outside and heard four gunshots. He and the two men wrapped the body in a piece of carpet and buried it and he let Casso know that his orders had been carried out. Of the four murders he helped arrange, Chiodo said that one had been ordered by Amuso and the other three by Casso. In one of them, he had helped to kill a gambler as a favour to Spyredon 'Spiros' Velentzas, an associate of the Lucchese Family.

When Charles Rose asked Fat Pete if he saw any other Lucchese member in the courtroom, he pointed at Amuso, saying, 'He was the boss.'

Peter Chiodo was in court again in July 1997. This time it was the head of the Powerful Genovese Family, the eccentric Vincent 'Chin' Gigante, who was in the dock. It was the biggest organised crime trial since they had put John Gotti away five years previously.

Gigante had for years portrayed himself as feeble-minded and mentally ill, incapable of running an organised crime operation. He would turn up at meetings in his bathrobe and wandered the streets of New York similarly dressed, talking to himself. As Chiodo spilled the beans about characters with names like Benny Eggs, Allie Shades, Big Louie and Tommy Irish, Gigante, also in a wheelchair, talked to himself incessantly, did not put on earphones when tapes were played of secretly recorded conversations and ignored the transcripts that lay in front of him.

Chiodo testified once again about bid-rigging – the artificial hiking of bids for work replacing windows in New York's public housing projects. Prosecutors claimed that all five Mafia Families were involved in this lucrative business from 1978 to 1989.

Fat Pete, however, did not link Gigante to the scheme, placing the blame for it on another Genovese mobster, Peter Savino. However, he also admitted that Savino could not have operated such a scheme without the approval of the Genovese hierarchy. Savino had already turned government witness and he also testified against Gigante. What Chiodo did say about Gigante, however, was that when he joined the Mafia, he was told that Gigante was the boss.

The prosecution believed that Gigante's 'illness' was no more than a ruse to keep him out of prison and Chiodo again made a courtroom laugh with one particular incident. He told how, when he and Gigante had been brought into a courtroom in 1990, Gigante had suddenly begun to talk in a loud voice as if he thought he was at a wedding. 'Where's the bride?' he asked, looking round.

Despite his lawyers' claims that he had been legally insane for thirty years, Vincent Gigante was convicted for racketeering and conspiracy and sentenced to twelve years in a federal prison. On 7 April 2003 he pleaded guilty to obstruction of justice, acknowledging that his 'insanity' was a pretence in order to delay his racketeering trial. He did this to avoid another set of charges that would have resulted in a lengthy trial and a further three years were added to his sentence. He died in December 2005.

Peter Chiodo served no time in prison for all his crimes. Instead, he entered the Witness Protection Programme, although hiding a six feet five, 500 pound man may have challenged the programme, somewhat.

PART SIX

INFORMERS

FREDDIE
'STAKEKNIFE'
SCAPPATICCI

It could all have been so different for Alfredo 'Freddie' Scappaticci. In 1962 there was a knock on the door of his parents' house in the Markets area of South Belfast. It was Manchester United football legend, Johnny Carey, who wanted to sign sixteen-year-old Scappaticci for his club. Unfortunately, however, Scappaticci's father was not in favour of the idea, thinking his son too young for such a move. This was confirmed when the boy spent three weeks training with Forest and returned homesick. Instead of a potentially glamorous life of fast cars and packed stadiums, he became a bricklayer and a few years later, a prisoner in the notorious Long Kesh prison, also known as the Maze when, in 1970, he was interned without trial for riotous assembly as part of Operation Demetrius. It was there that his apprenticeship as an IRA hard man really began.

The Scappaticcis had emigrated to Ireland in the 1920s and Freddie was born in 1944. The family sold ice cream and were liked by all. Under the surface, however, the old hostilities still brewed and Protestant hatred for Catholics was not prevented by the fact that the Scappaticcis were Italian Catholics. The young Scappaticci got into scrapes and brawls as the troubles escalated throughout the 1960s, the British government eventually sending in troops in 1969 in an attempt to restore order. Scappaticci, or Scap as he liked to be called, took part in the stone-throwing and rioting that followed and in 1970, he received the ultimate accolade when he was severely beaten by a Protestant police patrol. It was good for his credibility.

The British policy of internment antagonised the Catholic population and politicised many who had, until that point, been moderate in their views. The wrong people were rounded up while the leaders of the paramilitary organisations simply went into hiding. In Long Kesh Scappaticci was imprisoned alongside, and made the acquaintance of men such as, Gerry Adams, Ivor Bell and Alex Maskey, future leaders of the Republican movement. By the time he was released from Long Kesh in 1973 he was a hardened IRA man and, like many similar young Catholic men, ready to use whatever type of violence was necessary to achieve his political aims. He was good at it, too, an excellent marksman who had no qualms about killing.

As the situation in Ireland deteriorated, the IRA increased its power base, its finances and its membership. But, the power was not always a good thing. Scappaticci objected to the behaviour of the IRA leadership who, he claimed, sent young men on missions fraught with danger while they sat at home or safely in the pub. A lot of money was being earned from extortion of local Catholic businesses and much of it was flowing into the pockets of the movement's leaders instead of being used to further its objectives. In fact, he suggested, they were behaving more like gangsters than freedom fighters.

Scap was also sceptical of the view promulgated by the leadership that the Protestant gangs were controlled by the British and that, therefore, the British were the real enemy. He came to believe that they spread this in order to tie the British down to a long campaign in Northern Ireland that would justify to Catholics the existence of the IRA for decades to come.

His outspokenness inevitably got him into trouble

with his own people and in 1978 he was beaten up after a disagreement one night about future policy. It was a serious warning that if he did not toe the line, worse would follow.

Around this time, the British forces, knowing of his disillusionment with the movement he had supported for years and for which he had gone to prison, decided to approach him to ask if he would spy for them.

The British had developed a new strategy under the leadership in Northern Ireland of General Sir Frank Kitson, a veteran of the Mau Mau uprising in Kenya, as well as insurgencies in Malaya and elsewhere. It was his opinion that there was little to be gained from sending troops out into the streets of Belfast in armoured vehicles just to be targets for IRA snipers. In Kenya, Kitson had adopted the tactic of infiltrating the enemy ranks – he had recruited locals and used sabotage, subterfuge and duplicity. They were called Low Intensity Operations and they worked.

Scappaticci was first involved in espionage in 1978, working as an agent for the RUC (Royal Ulster Constabulary) Special Branch. Then, two years later a new operation was set up – the Force Research Unit (FRU) – and Scap was assigned to it. Somewhat ironically, the unit's crest was a man with a net, and its motto was 'Fishers of Men'. The FRU's objective was to centralise army intelligence under the Intelligence Corps and to handle agents working undercover within paramilitary groups. Sometimes, these agents were involved in operations in which bombs were planted or assassinations were carried out. Some of them even occupied high ranks in the PIRA (Provisional Irish Republican Army) hierarchy.

There was one agent who was more important than any other in this set-up. His code-name was 'Stakeknife' and he was a part of the PIRA's internal Security Unit – responsible for counter-intelligence, interrogation of suspects and the court martial of IRA informers – known as 'touts' – and the vetting of potential recruits in the organisation's Northern Command. It was known as the 'Nutting Squad', 'nut' being Irish slang for head. After a British spy or informer had been tortured and interrogated, he was 'nutted' – a couple of bullets were fired into his head. Scappaticci rose to the very top of the Nutting Squad and he was in a position to access information about the very core of IRA operations – forthcoming operations, locations of weapons caches, travel and security arrangements and bombing and assassination targets. His information went as far as the ears of Prime Minister Margaret Thatcher.

He disclosed to his handlers the identities of the

IRA men who kidnapped Ben Dunne Jr., a wealthy Irish supermarket owner, in 1981. He blew the whistle on an operation to kidnap the Canadian multi-millionaire businessman, Galen Weston, at his mansion just outside Dublin in 1983 and he tipped off the FRU about the kidnapping of supermarket executive, Don Tidey, who was kidnapped at his home in Rathfarnham, Dublin, on 25 November and rescued on 16 December 1983. Three died in the last of these actions – a trainee Garda Siochana, Gary Sheehan and an Irish Army soldier, Private Patrick Kelly.

Of course, Scappaticci was in an ideal position, at the top of the Nutting Squad to easily divert any suspicions away from himself towards someone else. During this time, around sixty-three informers were killed and it is estimated that Scappaticci may have killed or been involved in the killing of as many as forty of them. Men like Stakeknife were instructed by the intelligence services to believe in serving 'the greater good'. Better to kill thirty people than 3,000 and the IRA believed that if you were a killer you could not be working for the British. Scappaticci used that belief to his own advantage.

Amongst the dozens of men the Nutting Squad executed were twenty-four-year-old Seamus Morgan, shot in the head and dumped on a roadside in 1982;

John Corcoran, a forty-five-year-old father of eight, who asked his killer to 'Go easy!' before being shot in the head and Paddy Flood who was horrifically tortured for two months before being dumped on a roadside. Flood turned out to have been innocent of the accusations they threw at him.

In fact, Stakeknife was so important to British intelligence services that they went to extraordinary lengths to protect him, even as far as allowing murder to be committed.

In 1986, for instance, an IRA volunteer, Frank Hegarty, was executed as a tout by the IRA. Scappaticci had been involved – as part of his duties with the Internal Security Unit – in the interrogation and eventual execution of Hegarty who had been implicated in the discovery of a large Libyan arms find. Hegarty, however, was, it is claimed, another FRU agent and Scappaticci and other undercover agents, had facilitated his rise through the organisation. Therefore, when it came to it, Hegarty was sacrificed in order to safeguard Stakeknife's position.

Another instance involved Francisco Notarantonio, father of Victor, a boyhood pal of Scap, who had been interned in Long Kesh with him. Francisco was a Republican to his very core. When the Queen paid a visit to the Province, Francisco was arrested and locked up for the duration of her visit, to prevent him doing anything to harm her. However, his last involvment with the IRA was said to have been in the 1940s when he was interned. In 1987, therefore, long retired from the IRA, he took to driving a taxi to make a living. It was around that time that the UDA (Ulster Defence Association) came into possession of a description of someone working at the highest level in the IRA. That description fitted Scappaticci and, ignorant of the importance of Stakeknife to the FRU, the UDA duly dispatched a hit squad to assassinate him. However, when the intelligence services learned what was about to happen, they used another British agent, Brian Nelson, the UDA intelligence chief, to persuade them to send the gunmen after another IRA man who also had an Italian name – Francisco Notarantonio. They caught up with him at home and he was gunned down in his bedroom in front of his family. Two UDA leaders were killed in reprisal attacks shortly after by the PIRA, the names of those men allegedly passed to the PIRA by the FRU using Stakenife as their conduit. In this way, they hoped to bolster Stakeknife's credibility and prevent anyone from thinking he might be an informer.

Notarantonio's execution sowed the seeds of

Stakeknife's downfall, however. On 11 May 2003, he was accused in the British and Irish media of being the high level double agent in the Provisional Irish Republican Army known as 'Stakeknife' after Notarantonio's family had successfully pressed for a police investigation into his death. Scap, by then living in West Belfast's Riverdale area, said that due to his wife's illness, he had not been a member of the IRA since 1990. Naturally, he also denied any links with the British intelligence services.

Sir John Stevens, the Metropolitan Police Commissioner had been appointed to investigate collusion between the British Army, the RUC and loyalist paramilitaries in two murders – Protestant student, Brian Adam Lambert in 1987 and solicitor, Pat Finucane who was shot fourteen times in front of his wife, Geraldine and his children, by two masked men in his North Belfast home in 1989. In April 2004 Stevens indicated that he wanted to interview Scappaticci who had already been named by a number of media outlets as 'Stakeknife' on 11 May 2003. A cassette recording, allegedly of Scappaticci detailing the Nutting Squad murders in which he was involved, was handed over to the Police Service of Northern Ireland that year and was then passed on to Lord Stevens a year later.

Scappaticci has since then denied any involvement with the intelligence forces. In March 2004 he requested a judicial review after failing in an attempt to get Security Minister, Jane Kennedy, to confirm that he was not 'Stakeknife', nor had he been an agent for the British security services. However, that request was abandoned for undisclosed reasons in April 2004.

Republicans say they believe him and many others believe that Stakeknife was, in fact, a construct of the British Army – a policy rather than a person. It served to destabilise Sinn Féin and damage the peace process. It also distracted attention from the allegations of collusion.

Nevertheless, in Riverdale, West Belfast, Freddie Scappaticci, ever mindful of the paranoid nature of the world he lives in and conscious of the passions of the men who used to be his colleagues and friends, lives in fear with his wife and six children.

DAVID SHAYLER

On Sunday, 12 May 1991, twenty-five-year-old David Shayler was absently scanning the job ads section of *The Observer* when one ad in particular caught his eye. 'Godot isn't coming', the ad said, referring to Samuel Beckett's play *Waiting For Godot*. The advert went on to ask if the reader had an interest in current affairs, had common sense and could write.

Shayler had been looking for a job in the media and presumed this was one. He had already gained some journalistic experience, firstly as editor of the Dundee University student newspaper, *Annasach*, in 1984 and then, after leaving university, when he had worked as a journalist for six months. Following that, he had even attempted to start his own student newspaper, once again in Scotland. *The Paper*, started in partnership with Matt Garranty, ended in bankruptcy for Garranty.

He applied for the job and was surprised to learn

that it was an ad for MI5 who were recruiting people. He got the job and started working in F Branch, the section of MI5 dealing with counter-subversion. In this department he helped to monitor left-wing groups and activists, even including the vetting of Labour Party politicians before the 1992 election.

In August 1992, he was transferred to T Branch, the department responsible for investigating Irish terrorism. One of the cases on which he worked was that of Sean McNulty who was an associate of the Provisional IRA's Phelim Hamill, coordinator of the PIRA's campaign in Britain.

His next port of call was in G9 Branch which dealt with Middle East terrorism. He headed the Libyan desk as G9A/5. Here he first heard from his opposite numbers in MI6, David Watson and Richard Bartlett, of an MI6 plot to assassinate the Libyan leader, Colonel Muammar Gaddafi without the knowledge of the British Government, or the authority of Malcolm Rifkind, Foreign Secretary – necessary for permission to kill – using Osama Bin Laden's Al-Qaeda terror network.

Watson was handling a Libyan agent, known by the codename, 'Tunworth', who was providing him with information from within his cell. Shayler learned that MI6 handed over £100,000 to the plotters for an assassination attempt on Gaddafi in early 1996 in the Libyan coastal city of Sirte. An operation by the Islamic Fighting Group was actually foiled in March of that year when a bomb was placed under the wrong car. Gaddafi survived, but three civilians died in the blast.

Disllusioned with the service and reportedly disappointed at being passed over for promotion – a claim that he denies – Shayler resigned in October 1996. He initially had plans to write a book about his experiences at MI5. Instead of that, however, he approached the *Mail on Sunday* who offered him £39,000 for his story. On 24 August it exploded onto Sunday breakfast tables the length and breadth of the land, creating a scandal.

Shayler and his girlfriend, Annie Machon, also an employee of MI5, had taken off for Europe the day before the newspaper was published, travelling first to Utrecht in Holland before going on to France. There, they moved from hotel to hotel to avoid detection.

The article created a storm. Apart from the Gaddafi claims, it alleged that Peter Mandelson's phone had been bugged in the late 1970s; a file had been kept on the Home Secretary, Jack Straw, twenty years earlier, as a Communist sympathiser; the Foreign News Editor of *The Guardian* had been suspected of laundering money for the Libyans and had been bugged and kept under surveillance. He also claimed that British Intelligence was misinforming British journalists, planting untrue stories such as the one that said that Colonel Gaddafi's son was involved in a currency counterfeiting operation. He said that the intelligence services had prior knowledge of the 1994 bombing of the Israeli embassy in London and could even have prevented it, but chose not to.

In 1998 he further described in *The Spectator* that the security service again had information about the IRA's bombing of Bishopgate, but had again done nothing to prevent it.

More revelations were to follow the next Sunday. However, an injunction was taken out by the Government on Saturday 30 August, preventing publication. In the meantime, the police broke into the Pimlico flat shared by Shayler and Machon and searched it.

Annie Machon returned briefly to Britain in September and was arrested on arrival at Gatwick Airport, questioned for six hours and then released. Shayler remained in a farmhouse in rural France, as a loophole in the extradition agreement between Britain and France prevented his arrest and return to Britain. In July 1998 he tried to set up a website with the intention of publishing more facts about the

Gaddafi plot. This proved too much for the British intelligence services.

On 1 August 1998 Shayler was arrested by French police who presented him with an extradition warrant and locked him up in La Santé Prison for four months. Finally, on 18 November, the French courts declared that the British Government's extradition request was politically motivated and ruled against extradition. But in August 2000, Shayler decided to return to Britain voluntarily. He was arrested as soon as he set foot on British soil, and held on remand in Belmarsh Prison for three weeks.

On 21 September, three charges of breaching the Official Secrets Act were brought against him, as well as one of passing on information acquired from a telephone tap and two further charges of passing on information by virtue of his membership of the service.

Shayler represented himself at his trial and claimed that the Official Secrets Act was contrary to the Human Rights Act. It cannot be a crime to report a crime, he argued. However, the judge, Mr Justice Moses, declared the latter claim to be irrelevant. Shayler also claimed that he had no other means of pursuing his claims about the intelligence service.

During the trial, Public Interest Immunity Certificates signed by Home Secretary, David Blunkett and Foreign Secretary, Jack Straw, forbade newspapers from publishing the allegations about the Gaddafi murder plot. A row ensued between the Attorney general and the D-Notice Committee – the committee that makes the official request to media outlets not to publish something because it might affect national security. The committee objected to the prosecution's demands that the Official Secrets Act should be applied retrospectively in order to cover information already broadcast or published, as a result of what Shayler had disclosed. This was seen by members of the committee as an unprecedented attempt to censor the media while the trial was taking place.

Mr Justice Moses instructed the jury to return a guilty verdict, citing another case in which the House of Lords had determined that a defendant could not argue that the information he had revealed was in the public interest. After three hours the jury returned a verdict of guilty and Shayler was sentenced to six months. He served a mere seven weeks, in Ford Open Prison but, on his release on 23 December 2002, he was electronically tagged and placed under a curfew between the hours of 7 p.m. and 7 a.m. for a further seven weeks.

That was not the last we were to see of David Shayler, however. Still anxious to make his case, he put himself forward in the 2005 general election against Prime Minister Tony Blair in his Sedgefield constituency. But he withdrew before the election, transferring his support to Reg Keys, father of a British soldier who died in the Iraq War.

He next appeared supporting the 9/11 Truth Movement, a group of organisations and individuals who question the mainstream account of the 11 September 2001 attacks against the United States. Shayler has been reported as saying that there were no planes involved in 9/11, that they were holograms used to camouflage missiles that the United States had, itself, fired on the Twin Towers and the Pentagon. People within these organisations have disowned Shayler, stating that he is actually an agent of government disinformation, spreading ridiculous theories deliberately designed to discredit the entire movement and prevent legitimate questions being asked.

In July 2007 David Shayler was due to speak at the Glastonbury Symposium at the Glastonbury Rock Festival. When he stood up to speak, however, Shayler surprised his audience by unexpectedly announcing the news that he was the new Messiah. He had arrived at this conclusion, he said, as a result of taking drugs that induced altered states of consciousness. He said he had used mushrooms,

Ayahuasca, Ibogaine and marijuana to arrive at this conclusion. He claimed to be the reincarnation of a Jewish revolutionary, Astronges, who was executed by the Romans at the end of the last century BC. Interestingly, there are no historical references to Astronges. There is, however, a record of a man by the name of Athronges, to whom he is probably referring.

'I am the last incarnation of the Holy Ghost or the Yeshua or Jesus Spirit,' he has stated. 'I am God incarnated as spirit and man.'

Friends and family are reported to be desperately trying to stop him from taking any further hallucinogens.

ROBERT ROZIER

It was a Saturday night in April 1986. Robert Rozier stepped out of the floor-length gleaming white robes he always wore in the temple, removed his equally white turban and pulled on some everyday street clothes. He slipped a sharp, long-bladed knife inside his jacket and and stepped out into the warm spring evening. He was going hunting for 'white devils'.

Coconut Grove was a bustling restaurant and bar area that had been colonised by Miami's gay community. It was there that Rozier found himself. Looking for a likely victim, he followed groups of people as they milled around. He suddenly caught sight of a white man, stumbling along the street, as if he was drunk or stoned and decided to follow him. The man shambled through the area for a distance before stopping at a doorway. He pulled out a key and opened the door. Rozier, hovering nearby, rushed forward as the door opened, pushing the man inside.

He pulled out his knife and, without a second thought, thrust it deep into the man's heart. Another occupant of the apartment stepped into the hallway to see what the noise was and Rozier stabbed him as well, killing him.

He stood there, considering what to do next. Yahweh ben Yahweh had ordered them to bring back a piece of their bodies to prove they had carried out his orders and, for a moment, he considered cutting the dead men's heads off and taking them back with him as trophies. But, how would he get them through the busy streets on foot back to the temple? He wisely decided against it and made his way back.

Next day, he showed his leader the blood-stained knife and described what he had done the previous night. Yahweh ben Yahweh praised him and suggested that next time he might remember to bring back a body part.

Robert Rozier had found the Temple of Love in 1982, following a six-month spell in prison for a series of petty crimes. The six foot four inch man-mountain, who had once played football for the Saint Louis Cardinals and the Oakland Raiders, had plummeted to the depths after he was thrown off the football teams for drugs violations and by the time he found the temple, was virtually homeless. It seemed to offer him another chance at life and he grabbed it with both hands, changing his name to Neariah Israel. He worked hard in the factory they had established to make beer and wine and became the main enforcer for the temple's charismatic leader, Hulon Mitchell Jr, who went by the name of Yahweh ben Yahwe.

Hulon Mitchell had, himself, made a long journey to get to this point. Born in 1935, he was the first of the fifteen children of a Pentacostal minister who preached fire and brimstone in the town of Kingfisher, Oklahoma. Times were hard and Hulton Jr grew up in poverty, his mother and father having to find any work they could to scrape by and feed their large family.

Hulon Jr did his military service as an airman and also studied psychology at a university in Enid, Oklahoma. He married his teenage sweetheart and she gave birth to four children in four years. He was posted to bases in California and Texas and began to do well, being promoted through the ranks to instructor.

Around this time, however, he began to take an interest in black politics. The civil rights movement was beginning to make inroads on the plight of black people across America, but segregation still prevailed and they had to eat in their own restaurants and drink in their own bars. Mitchell became a civil rights leader in Enid, staging sit-ins and helping to break down the racial barriers in the town. But the speed of change was too slow for him and he began to look at other ways to achieve his goals – he became involved with the Nation of Islam, led by Malcolm X, as well as various spiritual movements. By this time his wife had tired of it and sued for divorce.

He moved to Atlanta, now known, as was the way of adherents to the Nation of Islam, as Mitchell X. He studied the Koran and took a Master's degree in Economics. He used only black businesses, sold copies of the Nation's newspaper, *Muhammad Speaks*, on street corners and home-schooled his children with the help of a new wife.

Changing his name again, to 'Minister Shah', he preached in his own church and started businesses – a restaurant, a bakery and a clothes shop. He fell foul of the Nation of Islam, however, when he was accused of embezzling $50,000 from church funds and, even worse, of molesting children in the congregation. Minister Shah disappeared.

Not long after, Mitchell reappeared in Atlanta, calling himself 'Father Michel', wearing a long white robe and, along with a colleague, 'Father Jone', promising health, happiness and winning lottery numbers, all for a small donation. The Black Muslims were still after him, however, and he hired bodyguards and upped the security in his house.

When 'Father Jone' was gunned down in May 1969, Mitchell stayed put; the money was too good. It was the mid-1970s, and he had moved into a large house, owned two El Dorado cars and was dressing in white satin tunics, carrying a sceptre and wearing a gold crown on his head. His congregation called him 'King'. Before too long, however, it all began to fall apart and, threatened with a suit for fraud, he fled, leaving his wife behind.

His next incarnation was in Orlando, Florida, as a street preacher called 'Brother Love'. He had soon built up a small following and gained himself another wife, Linda. He was studying all kinds of religions now and believed that the Bible contained coded messages. The result was a new religion based on the Black Hebrew movement. Africans, it claimed, were the 'true Jews' descended from the lost tribes of Israel while Christianity was a slave religion. He became Och Mosche Israel.

In 1978, he claimed to have a vision telling him to move to Miami, a city whose black neighbourhoods were poverty-ridden and ravaged by drugs. Here, he would adopt his last identity and create the movement that made him one of the most feared men in America.

In Miami, he worked hard and had soon built up a group of followers who would gather round and listen to his sermons telling them that they were the 'true Jews' and that black people were superior to whites. They began to go out and recruit people on the doorsteps and in the streets of the ghetto. Mitchell styled himself 'Yahweh ben Yahweh', 'God, son of God' and began to urge members of his growing band of followers to separate themselves not only from white society, but also from friends and family who were not members. His followers wore white robes, pooled their money, lived together and taught their children at home. They were encouraged to take Biblical names such as Solomon and Gideon.

In 1980 the 150 members bought a disused warehouse in Liberty City, Miami and thirty of them sold everything and moved in, christening it the Yahweh Temple of Love. It was sub-divided into a café, a grocery store, a laundry, a health centre and a bookshop selling Mitchell's writings. A group of ten young men, known as the Circle of Ten provided protection, armed with wooden staffs, known as the 'staffs of life'.

He preached hellfire sermons to pounding rock

music, demanding of his growing flock on one occasion: 'How many of you would die for Yahweh? Would you kill for Yahweh?' 'Yes!' they screamed back in unison.

Mitchell's behaviour became increasingly erratic and suspicious. There were stories of him creeping into the rooms of women followers at night and he was reported to conduct bizarre sex education classes. He reportedly had sex with girls as young as ten, including the young daughter of his wife, Linda, and in midwife classes he had women undress and inspect each others' genitalia. It is reported that he would tell one woman to lie on her back while another would blow into her vagina. He claimed that was the way to perform artificial respiration on an unborn baby.

His sex classes for men and boys featured videos of white women having sex with animals and he personally carried out agonising circumcisions on male followers.

Dissent was not allowed and the Circle of Ten became increasingly thuggish in the application of the word of Yahweh. Their first victim was a former Sunday school teacher called Ashton Green. Green had taken the name Elijah Israel on joining but had become disillusioned and left the temple. Foolishly, although he had been warned to stay away, he kept returning to visit friends. One Friday, the 13th, while he was visiting, he was grabbed by the Circle of Ten and dragged to a corner of the warehouse/temple and beaten to a bloody pulp. He was then taken by car to an isolated quarry where they rested his head on a piece of rock and hacked it off, probably while he was still alive. The blade they used was blunt and it took about twenty hacks before the head was separated completely from the body.

Mitchell was delighted, but for some dissident members it was the last straw. One man, Carlton Carey, went to the police, but when he returned home, several of the Circle of Ten were waiting for him. They shot him dead and shot his wife Mildred Banks in the chest before slitting her throat. She survived her horrific wounds, however, and when her attackers had left, she was able to get help and the police were called.

The authorities now moved in on the temple, police officers patrolling in plain clothes close to it. It was proving difficult to find evidence linking Mitchell and his men with the murders of Green and Carey until a piece of green carpet, similar to one that had been found beside Ashton Green's body was seen hanging from a wall. They went to see Mitchell. Seated between two large bodyguards, however, he barely allowed them to talk, lecturing them during their brief meeting on the oppression of the blacks. The interview yielded nothing.

Meanwhile, the Nation of Yahweh was expanding. Satellite churches appeared in forty-five American cities and new recruits kept arriving at the Miami Temple of Love.

One such was twenty-two-year-old Leonard Dupree, a karate black belt from New Orleans. He immediately attracted the attention of the temple guards and rumours spread that he had been sent to assassinate Mitchell. One afternoon, he became involved in a fight with another of Mitchell's followers. Seventy members stood watching but when someone screamed 'Kill him!' they began to surge forward ominously. One man hit Dupree on the head with a crowbar and the crowd began to beat him, ripping off his clothes and kicking his privates. Someone used a broom handle to poke out one of his eyes. The body was dumped and Mitchell was delighted.

To bring in money, Mitchell opened a food-distribution firm and made bottles of Yahweh Beer and Wine, none of which could be drunk by members, of course. They sold Yahweh key-rings, T-shirts and other merchandise on the street, working, sometimes, eighteen hours a day. He began to be hailed as a black role model, but his people were starving. Meals were cut back to save money and children became emaciated. The money he saved was invested in property. The Temple of Love had $8.5 million in the bank and was hailed as one of Miami's largest black-owned corporations.

Robert Rozier continued to cruise the streets of Miami, in search of white devils, usually in the company of another Death Angel. On one occasion, they found a man asleep in his car in the car park of a bar. They stabbed him to death and then cut off his ear. However, they dropped it and were unable to find it in the darkness. Never mind, at least there was another one they could cut off and take back to Mitchell. As ever, he lavished them with praise and gave them the following day off.

More and more dead men, usually helpless drifters or drunks began to turn up on the streets of Miami and Rozier was responsible for seven of them.

In 1986, the Nation of Yahweh bought an apartment block in Opa-locka, a small city northwest of Miami. They tried to evict the residents, but some refused to leave and when some Yahweh men were sent in to forcibly evict them, two residents were shot to death.

Rozier was identified by a witness as one of the

gunmen and on 31 October 1986, he was arrested and charged with murder. At first he refused to cooperate with investigators, giving his age as 404 and answering questions only with the words 'Praise Yahweh!' But, he eventually cracked and agreed to turn state's witness and testify against Mitchell, marking the beginning of the end for the Temple of Love. A federal Grand Jury put together a case against Mitchell, charging him and fifteen disciples with fourteen murders, extortion and racketeering.

A couple of weeks after the Miami Mayor had embarrassingly hosted a Yahweh ben Yahweh Day in the city, Mitchell was arrested in New Orleans. 'Obviously I was wrong,' said the Mayor, sheepishly when questioned about it.

When the case came to court in 1992, the dissenters had their day. A dozen former followers betrayed Mitchell. Robert Rozier, already sentenced to twenty-two years in prison, chillingly described the murders he committed for Yahweh. Mitchell himself took the stand, introducing himself as 'grand master of the celestial lodge, the architect of the universe.' He claimed his religion was about love, not death.

They could not pin the murders on him, however. There was no conclusive proof that he had ordered them. But, there was shock in the courtroom when seven of the accused were sentenced to fifteen or sixteen years each. Even greater moans of disappointment greeted Mitchell's eighteen-year sentence.

A ruling when the case came to appeal shows some of the true horror of what went on in the name of Yahweh. The judge described it as 'the most violent case ever tried in a federal court: the indictment charged the sixteen defendants on trial with fourteen murders by means such as beheading, stabbing, occasionally by pistol shots, plus severing of body parts such as ears to prove the worthiness of the killer. They were also charged with arson of a slumbering neighbourhood using molotov cocktails. The perpetrators were ordered to wait outside the innocent victims' homes wearing ski masks and brandishing machetes to deter the victims from fleeing the flames.'

Mitchell did his time and was freed after ten years, but was barred thereafter from contacting his congregation which had resurfaced in Canada. Only in the last few months of his life, when he was seriously ill, was this ban relaxed. He died of prostate cancer on 7 May 2007, the Yahweh ben Yahweh website stating 'The Nation of Yahweh officially announces the Ascension of our Founder and Savior, Yahweh ben Yahweh…'

Robert Rozier was freed in 1996 after serving ten years. He entered a Witness Protection Programme, under the name of Robert Ramses. In February 1999, however, he was arrested for bouncing a cheque for $66 in payment for the repair of his car. The police then discovered a succession of bounced cheques in his name, to the value of more than $2,000 and had little option but to charge him with a felony. Unfortunately for Rozier/Ramses, this took place in California where a three strikes and you're out policy operates. As this crime represented his third strike, he was sentenced to twenty-five years to life.

His new identity was now revealed for the world to see and there is little doubt his life is in danger. Speaking of the Nation of Islam, Assistant United States Attorney, Richard Scruggs said, 'He is probably their most hated enemy. He is their Judas, their number one.'

Rozier, for his part, said, 'This county has no idea of the Pandora's box they've opened.'

YVES 'APACHE' TRUDEAU

Canada is often viewed as a liberal country, pleasantly free of violent crime. During the last thirty years, however, the country has been terrorised by an explosion of biker gangs that have behaved more like the Mafia than the motorbike-obsessed groups we consider them to be. Extortion, drug-dealing and contract-killing are just some of the activities that have turned these hog-riding gangs into a national threat as well as a national disgrace with shootings, knifings and even bombings.

It began in 1977 when Sonny Barger, the most famous Hells Angel of all, decided to launch a chapter of his gang in Montreal, a city he thought promised rich pickings for the Hells Angels. Immediately, the Montreal Chapter strong-armed its way to dominance in Montreal, absorbing the home-grown Canadian biker gangs and turning them into a well-organised bunch of killers. Turf wars broke out across

Canada as rival gangs such as the Outlaws and the Bandidos resisted the Angels. By 1985 more than 100 people had died as a result of biker-gang violence.

Circumstances could not have been better for a psychopathic killer and that's exactly what Yves 'Apache' Trudeau was. Also known as 'The Mad Bumper', at a mere five feet six inches tall and weighing only 136 pounds, he did not resemble a typical member of a biker gang, but he would go on to become the Hells Angels' most prolific killer.

Born in the mid-1940s, he was a founding member of the Quebec Chapter of the Hells Angels in 1977. The Montreal Chapter grew so large that it became unmanageable and Trudeau and others formed the breakaway North Chapter, based in the city of Laval. This group became renowned for its violence and wild behaviour, especially its excessive drug use. Trudeau was no slouch when it came to drugs, himself. In one three-week period, he blew $60,000 on cocaine.

From September 1973 until July 1985, Trudeau was a killing machine and the assassin of choice for several people. Of the forty-three people he killed, twenty-nine were shot, ten were blown up, three were beaten to death and one was strangled. Two were innocent bystanders; one, William Weichold was mistaken for a member of rival gang, the Outlaws and was killed in 1978 and the other, Robert Morin was blown up in 1981 when he had the misfortune to borrow a friend's car in which Trudeau had placed a bomb. Some people were not quite innocent, but just happened to be in the wrong place at the wrong time. Lucille Vallières, for instance, who was shot in 1981 as she shared her porch with one of Trudeau's targets, a drug dealer by the name of Donat Lemieux. Rachelle Francoeur was shot and killed in 1984. Her mistake was being in the company of another intended target, a drug dealer called Phillip Galipeau.

For his record of ruthless killing, Trudeau earned one of the highest accolades that can be bestowed upon a Hells Angel – the 'Filthy Few' patch, depicting the words 'Filthy Few' with two Nazi-style lightning bolts beneath. It is awarded to those who murder or are prepared to murder for the Hells Angels.

Apache Trudeau's first murder took place in 1970. He shot to death Jean-Marie Rivières who stole a motorcycle from the Popeyes, the gang that Trudeau was in before it became a Hells Angel chapter. It was followed quickly by a number of further killings.

Donald McLean was a member of the Outlaws, a rival biker gang. Trudeau attached a bomb to his Harley Davidson. It blew up, killing McLean and his girlfriend, Carmen Piche.

He showed no mercy, even to the elderly. He battered grandmother, Jeanne Desjardins, to death in 1980 for trying to help her son André, an ex-Hells Angel. Then, for good measure, he killed André and his girlfriend, wrapped their bodies in sleeping bags, attached them to some concrete blocks and dumped them in the St. Lawrence River.

In 1983 he gunned down Michel Desormiers, brother-in-law of powerful crime boss, Frank Cotroni. Desormiers had been the driver in a hit carried out by the Angels and, presumably, knew too much. This was Trudeau's first proper hit, and it had to be sanctioned first by the heads of the Montreal Mafia.

He was several times recruited by notorious Montreal drug trafficker and leader of the West End Gang, Frank 'Dunie' Ryan. The West End Gang were at the time the city's most powerful and most ruthless criminal organisation and it did not pay to be in debt to it, the way Hugh Patrick McGurnaghan was. A career criminal with links to the Westenders, McGurnaghan owed a great deal of money and drugs to Dunie Ryan and his men. When it did not look as if McGurnaghan was going to deliver either cash or drugs, Dunie recruited Trudeau to teach him a lesson – a terminal one.

On 27 October 1981 McGurnaghan, a bookie called Joseph Frankel, and another man, William Obont, were driving down Melville Avenue in Montreal when a car bomb, placed by Apache Trudeau, blew up the gaudy yellow Mercedes Benz in which they were travelling. The explosion was powerful enough to shatter the windows of nearby buildings and the car was blown some 200 feet along the street. McGurnaghan was seriously injured, with his left leg blown off and a serious wound to an arm. He died in the ambulance on the way to hospital, due to loss of blood.

Trudeau did not balk at carrying out hits on fellow Hells Angels. With some other Angels, he killed a member of his own chapter, Charlie Hachez whose heavy drug habit had led to him owing Dunie Ryan close to $150,000. They lured the unfortunate Hachez to a meeting, killed him and dumped his body in the St. Lawrence River.

When Dunie Ryan was himself killed in 1984, and Allan 'The Weasel' Ross took over the leadership of the West End Gang, the first thing Ross wanted to do was to take revenge on Paul April and Robert Lelièvre, the men who had murdered his old boss. He called in Apache Trudeau.

Just twelve days after the death of Ryan, two Hells Angels turned up at the apartment that April and Lelièvre worked out of. They had a delivery for the men – a television, a VCR and a video of the documentary film, *Hells Angels Forever*. They made the delivery and left. A few minutes later, a massive explosion almost destroyed the entire apartment building. April, Lelièvre and two associates died in the blast and eight other people working or living in the building were injured, one woman losing an eye.

Trudeau was to be paid $200,000 for the hit and have all his drug debt wiped out – a considerable payday for him. It would not be that simple, however. Ross told him to collect it from the Montreal Chapter of the Hells Angels and another biker gang, the 13th Tribe of Halifax, who both owed him a lot of drug money. When Apache approached the Montreal Chapter, they refused to pay him the money, creating bad blood and resentment between Trudeau's North Chapter and the Montreal gang. It came as no surprise. Other Hells Angels had long considered the North Chapter to be out of control. They were suspected of ripping off their own in drug deals and were known to use a great deal of the drugs they were supposed to be selling.

Consequently, a meeting was called, ostensibly to take the heat out of the situation. The meeting at the clubhouse of the Sherbrooke Chapter turned into a massacre in which five members of the North Chapter were shot dead. Their bodies were put into sleeping bags and dumped in the Angels' graveyard of choice, the St. Lawrence River. The members who were allowed to live joined the Montreal Chapter.

Trudeau had, fortunately for him, missed the meeting. Wary of the fate of members who were perpetually stoned, he had decided to clean himself up, enrolling in a detoxification programme. He learned of the slaughter at the Sherbrooke clubhouse and was informed that he was no longer a Hells Angel and would have to have his Angel tattoos removed. Obediently, he had the tattoos blacked out.

Worse than that, when he was released from rehab, he discovered that they had stolen his motorbike as well as $46,000 that he had in the clubhouse used by the North Chapter. He was furious and insisted on the return of his bike and the cash. The Montreal boys replied that he could have it all back if he carried out a hit on two people for them.

He agreed and succeeded in killing one of his targets, strangling Jean-Marc Deniger in May 1985. He put the body in a car and telephoned the Journal de Montreal. It was always Angels policy to have a hit verified in the media. In spite of the fact that he had not completely fulfilled his task, the Montreal boys relented and Trudeau got his motorcycle back.

He learned shortly after that a $50,000 contract had been taken out on him.

He had been arrested on a theft charge and was due to be released, but a zealous officer, Sergeant Marcel Lacoste, let him see the report of an inquest during which the contract had been mentioned. He reminded Apache that he would soon be back on the streets and at the mercy of any number of would-be assassins. Trudeau considered his situation, but it did not take him too long to see that it was hopeless. He pleaded guilty to the charge and was moved to the fourth floor of the Parthenais prison, where he was being held. He took the only option remaining to him – he became a government witness.

The police had not a shred of evidence to implicate Trudeau in any of the forty-three murders he had committed. There was nothing but his confessions and they were given only on condition that the charges against him be reduced to manslaughter and not murder. He admitted to the forty-three killings and provided the authorities with details of forty others as well as fifteen attempted murders. He named ninety-five murderers, of whom thirty-four were already dead. As a result of his information, backed up by other high-profile Hells Angels informants, the Hells Angels in Quebec were decimated. After the police had swept up the people that Trudeau had fingered, only two of its five chapters remained in existence.

He received a mere seven years' imprisonment, not bad for forty-three murders. The government also set up a trust fund for him – he was to be paid $10,000 a year and in prison he lived a life of comparative luxury. He had a private bathroom and colour cable television. They gave him a weekly cigarette allowance of thirty-five dollars and every fortnight he was taken to visit his partner and their children.

Released in 1991, he lived in the town of Salaberry-de-Valleyfield, a city in southwestern Quebec, under the name of Denis Côté. It looked like Apache Trudeau's wild days were over.

But that was not the last the courts saw of him. In March 2004, a thin, unshaven Trudeau, wearing manacles, made an unexpected appearance in a courtroom in St. Jerome, Quebec, to face six charges of sexual assault against an adolescent boy, taking place between 2000 and 2004. He represented himself in court, but it did not help. He was sentenced to four years in prison.

As was widely noted at the time, prison probably did not represent the most pleasant of prospects to him. After all, to go into prison as an informant is one thing. To go in as an informer as well as a paedophile...

SEAN O'CALLAGHAN

Like many young men in the Republic of Ireland,
Sean O'Callaghan was moved in 1968 by the Civil
Rights Movement's agitation for reform in Northern
Ireland. He had been born in 1954 into a republican
family in Tralee, County Kerry, an area that had been
steeped in republican tradition for centuries and still
is. His father believed in a united Ireland and, in the
face of British political intransigence, that it could
only be achieved through force. Consequently, the
young Sean would sometimes stumble across guns
and explosives which had been hidden in the house.
There were clandestine meetings in either his house
or, sometimes, his grandmother's – the entire family,
aunts, uncles, cousins, were embroiled in the
republican cause. In the early 1940s, his father and
uncle were interned without trial.

By 1970, more than fifty years after the 1916
Uprising, Irish unity was on the political agenda once
again and O'Callaghan, fifteen years old, was
desperate to enlist and fight for the cause. The IRA

had split and the Provisional IRA had been created, a move which disappointed O'Callaghan, to the extent that he has described it as 'the greatest tragedy in modern Irish history'. He distrusted the overt militarism of the PIRA, felt that it was a little too close to fascism for his liking. However, he was passionate about the cause and joined the IRA. Anyway, with his family background, it was expected of him.

The young men who came to Tralee to train in the use of weapons and explosives, originated from the Catholic ghettos of Belfast or Derry and had joined up in order to protect the areas in which they lived against what they saw as the British and the Protestant threat. They were not political, but were anti-Protestant and had a fascination with the weaponry of revolt – the guns and the bombs. They were encouraged in their hatred of the British and the Unionist Protestants by the IRA leadership.

On 20 April 1972 O'Callaghan was preparing explosives for a training camp in a few days' time in a shed at his parents' house. Just after he stepped outside, there was an explosion and before he knew it, he was on remand in Limerick prison, charged with possessing explosives. In a special court without a jury, he got six months.

He was undeterred, however, and on his release, was back, helping to train new recruits. In June 1973, however, he was transferred to Donegal, to work in an IRA bomb factory. He was to learn how to make bombs and then train others so that similar factories could be established. Back in Kerry after his training, he worked on the staff of the IRA General Head-quarters, running a training camp. Then, he was moved into active service.

In May 1974, now a member of the Mid Ulster Brigade of the IRA, he and forty other men attacked a base used by the British army and the Ulster Defence Regiment in Clogher, County Tyrone. The gun battle lasted twenty minutes and resulted in the death of a UDR officer, Eva Martin.

He remained in Tyrone until August 1975, taking part in around seventy attacks against members of the security forces. In one, he was responsible for the murder in an Omagh public house, of Inspector Peter Flanagan of the Royal Ulster Constabulary Special Branch.

By this time, however, O'Callaghan was beginning to have doubts about the PIRA. He did not seem to hate the Protestants quite as much as many of his associates, who were driven by a vicious brand of Irish Nationalism to which he did not relate. They were fighting against the Protestants who, they believed had the better jobs, the better farms, the better houses, having stolen them from the Irish a couple of centuries ago. While they were happy to carry out an attack on a part-time UDR man or a police reservist, who was probably their neighbour, O'Callaghan saw his fight as being against the British and British imperialism and wanted to attack an army patrol or a barracks.

One night, in a flat in Moynaghan that was used as a base for the men of the IRA's East Tyrone Brigade, O'Callaghan heard something that was to change his life irrevocably. A news item came on the TV about the death of an RUC woman in an explosion. One of the men present said 'I hope she's pregnant and we got two for the price of one.'

O'Callaghan was disgusted, especially as this man was second-in-command of the Provisional IRA and would, later, become its chief of staff. He was also a man O'Callaghan had respected until that moment. He returned to Tralee and resigned from the IRA. He was twenty years old.

Making a complete break with the 'Troubles', he went to London and started an office and industrial cleaning business and married. Watching it all from a distance, however, he was amazed and horrified at what he had been involved in. He decided he wanted to do something about it and resolved to become that most hated of beings – an informer.

He moved back to Ireland with his wife and re-enlisted in the IRA. He then contacted a detective he knew could be trusted and began a working relationship that lasted six years. O'Callaghan claims to have been involved with every part of the IRA and its leaders during this time and was able to stop many IRA operations.

Amongst these was a plot to assassinate the Prince of Wales in retaliation for the deaths of IRA hunger strikers in 1981. It was to occur during the British general election of 1983 while the Prince was attending a charity concert featuring Duran Duran at the Dominion Theatre in Tottenham Court Road in London. O'Callaghan was to place a bomb containing twenty pounds of explosive in the toilet behind the royal box. It would be buried in the tiles many days in advance with a timer set to go off on the night, killing anyone in its vicinity.

Callaghan's handlers devised a plan to foil the attack and to remove suspicion from O'Callaghan and allow him to continue to provide valuable information. Scotland Yard called a news conference and named O'Callaghan as a member of an IRA bomb team tasked with the assassination of a prominent British politician before the general election. This allowed him to abandon the attack on Prince Charles and return to Ireland, not only free of suspicion, but with an even greater reputation.

In 1984 he participated in an operation that severely damaged the IRA. They had a shipment of around $2 million worth of arms, ammunition and explosives coming in from the United States on a trawler, the Valhalla. O'Callaghan had kept the Garda informed of the operation and when the weapons had been loaded onto another vessel, the Marita Ann, off the Irish coast, it was intercepted by an Irish Navy frigate. A senior IRA man was arrested on board and the remainder of the gang in America were also rounded up.

By 1985 O'Callaghan was responsible for the IRA in the South of Ireland, a member of the IRA's GHQ staff that ran the everyday business of the organisation. Finance, engineering, training – he was involved in it all. He was also involved in the planning of the IRA campaigns in England. He was in contact with men such as Martin McGuinness and Gerry Adams through the Sinn Fein national executive, of which he was also a member.

Divorced and remarried by 1985, he became a Sinn Fein local councillor on Tralee, but began to get the impression that he was coming under suspicion and decided to keep a low profile. He moved back to England and was there brought into contact with MI5 who asked him to move to Holland. There he engaged in debriefing sessions until September 1986 before returning to England.

In 1988 O'Callaghan walked into a police station in Tunbridge Wells, wearing only his trousers and confessed to a bewildered desk officer his involvement in the two 1974 murders of Eva Martin and Peter Flanagan. He was taken back to Northern Ireland by two RUC officers that evening.

O'Callaghan claims that he handed himself in because he wanted to give evidence against the IRA leadership and by so doing somehow stop the killing. He says however, that it soon became apparent that he was never going to be allowed to give that evidence. In an interview with the *Sunday Times* later, however, he said that he handed himself in while suffering from depression. It seems that he had a history of mental health problems – his father took him for a psychological examination at the age of fifteen and he is reported to have 'cracked up' in 1985. Furthermore, it is reported that he had been drinking heavily during his time in Tunbridge Wells. His partner was working and they were living on a smart, middle class housing estate, but he was lonely and turned to the bottle. MI5 had cut him off and he felt he had outlived his usefulness.

He is said to have walked into a pub in London that day where a friend from Tralee worked. When he asked him if he wanted a drink, the friend said he didn't want a drink from him. When O'Callaghan asked why, his friend replied, 'Because you're a spy.'

He pleaded guilty in May 1990 at Belfast Crown Court to two murders and sixty terrorist attacks and was sentenced to life imprisonment, plus another 539 years.

O'Callaghan is reported to have twice tried to kill himself while incarcerated in Crumlin Road jail, once trying to hang himself with his shoelaces which broke. He was on suicide watch and withdrawn, hardly leaving his cell. He attacked Michael Stone, the loyalist who had shot dead three people at Milltown Cemetery during the funerals of the three IRA men killed in Gibraltar.

He was eventually released after serving only a few years of his sentences and wrote an autobiography, *The Informer*. However, many within the Republican movement have poured scorn on the claims he makes in the book. They say that he has seriously over-stated his position in IRA ranks and that he had made 'increasingly outlandish accusations against individual republicans.' In one particular instance, O'Callaghan claims to have attended an IRA finance meeting alongside Pat Finucane, the Catholic Belfast solicitor killed in 1989 by Loyalist paramilitaries, and Gerry Adams. However, Adams has consistently denied that he has ever been a member of the IRA and the Stevens Enquiry found that Finucane was not an IRA member.

Sean O'Callaghan now lives and works in England as a security consultant, occasional adviser to the Ulster Unionist party and appears on television as a media pundit whenever the IRA is in the news.